GARDENS IN BABYLON

SOCIETY OF BIBLICAL LITERATURE

DISSERTATION SERIES
David L. Petersen, Old Testament Editor
Pheme Perkins, New Testament Editor

Number 141

GARDENS IN BABYLON
Narrative and Faith in the Greek Legends of Daniel

by
Marti J. Steussy

Marti J. Steussy

GARDENS IN BABYLON
Narrative and Faith
in the Greek Legends of Daniel

Scholars Press
Atlanta, Georgia

BS
1795.2
.S74
1993

GARDENS IN BABYLON
Narrative and Faith
in the Greek Legends of Daniel

Marti J. Steussy

Ph.D., 1992
Vanderbilt University

Advisor:
James L. Crenshaw

© 1993
The Society of Biblical Literature

Library of Congress Cataloging in Publication Data
Steussy, Marti J., 1955–
    Gardens in Babylon: narrative and faith in the Greek legends of
Daniel/ Marti J. Steussy.
        p. cm. — (Dissertation series; no. 141)
    Includes bibliographical references and index.
    ISBN 1–55540–870–2 (cloth: alk. paper). ISBN 1–55540–871–0
(pbk.: alk. paper)
    1. Bible. O.T. Apocrypha. History of Susanna—Criticism,
interpretation, etc. 2. Bible. O.T. Apocrypha. Bel and the
Dragon—Criticism, interpretation, etc. 3. Narration in the Bible.
I. Title   II. Series: Dissertation series (Society of Biblical
Literature); no. 141.
BS1795.2.S74   1993
229'.606—dc20   93–12923
                                                       CIP

Printed in the United States of America
on acid-free paper

TABLE OF CONTENTS

LIST OF TABLES

LIST OF FIGURES

ACKNOWLEDGMENTS

While today's scholars "stand on the backs of giants," they also stand on the backs of the families and co-workers who must abide with them through all the efforts and anxieties of research and writing. With warm appreciation, I acknowledge the support received from my committee, especially Dr. James Crenshaw. Help and encouragement also came from my colleagues at Christian Theological Seminary, particularly reference librarian Dick Doolen.

My task was made easier by the new era of electronic tools. I thank the creators and supporters of the Nota Bene multilingual word processor[1] for making the composition and layout of this document far less laborious than they might otherwise have been.

But most of all, I am grateful to my family--my husband Nic, who has supported me unflaggingly, and my children David and Cally, who cannot remember a time when their mother wasn't working on her Ph.D. (Computer calculations for figure 1 were done by the children at five cents per verse.) I thank you, loved ones, and I fervently hope that this work contains something valuable enough to justify the sacrifices you have made for me.

Marti Steussy
Indianapolis
November 10, 1991

---

[1] Versions 3.1 (original dissertation) and 4.0 (current text), published by Dragonfly Software, 285 W. Broadway, Suite 600, New York, NY 10013.

Chapter 1

INTRODUCTION

Many traits characterize humanity. To taxonomists of the Enlightenment, knowledge seemed our most striking trait, and thus we became *Homo sapiens*. But as the key roles of hand and technology in brain and culture development have become evident, some have proposed that we are most essentially *Homo faber*, the tool-makers. Still others, noting the juvenile traits which persist through human life, and the roles of experimentation and exploration in culture, have termed the species *Homo ludens*, humankind which plays. Recently, as the fundamental role of story-telling in acculturation and culture-creation has become evident, we have become aware of the human being as *Homo narrans*, the storyteller.

Narrative's ubiquity suggests that it plays a more than casual role in human culture. Social and psychological research shows ever more clearly that indeed, sacred and secular stories define our worlds. They provide patterns and reinforcement for our perceptual and decision-making schemata.[1] Experience in turn colors our telling and interpretation of stories, as we try to coordinate them with other literature and our own lives.[2] Religion in particular seems rooted in story's power to form consciousness.

---

[1] For the distinction between sacred story/myth, legend, and folktale, see William Bascom, "The Forms of Folklore: Prose Narratives," *Journal of American Folklore* 78 (1965): 3-20; reprinted in *Sacred Narrative*, ed. Alan Dundes (Berkeley: University of California Press, 1984), 5-29. For a good discussion of schemata, see Daniel Goleman, *Vital Lies, Simple Truths: The Psychology of Self-Deception* (New York: Simon & Schuster, 1986).

[2] For introduction to these issues see *Reader-Response Criticism: From Formalism to Post-Structuralism*, ed. Jane P. Tompkins (Baltimore: Johns Hopkins University Press, 1980) and *The Reader in the Text: Essays on Audience and Interpretation*, ed. Susan R. Suleiman and Inge Crosman (Princeton: University Press, 1980).

The Semitic version of Daniel, transmitted to us by the Masoretic scholars, contains six stories and four dream-visions. Christian tradents preserved the book in two Greek versions, the "Old Greek" and "Theodotion," different enough to suggest different Semitic *Vorlagen*. These Greek versions include minor and major additions to the basic chapters, and two additional chapters: "Susanna" and "Bel and the Dragon."

These Greek Daniel legends offer an interesting opportunity to explore narrative's intersection with faith:

(1) Given that these stories circulated (and still do) as religious literature, what kind of faith do they encode, and how does it inhere in the narratives' structure and wording?

(2) Is the "same" story (e.g., "Bel and the Dragon") told in different words (e.g. the OG and TH) really the same story? How do different versions differ in impact?

(3) How do connections with other texts affect the stories' meanings?

(4) How do the literary/theological features of these stories relate to the concerns of their times and places?

I shall begin my inquiry by reflecting on the relationship of narrative and faith (chapter 2). What do we mean by faith, how does it inhere in narrative, and how can one go about studying it there? Next (chapter 3) comes a survey of the narrative material at hand—the Greek books of Daniel, and especially their two extra legends. What have earlier scholars had to say about their provenance and worldview? I then turn, in chapters 4 and 5, to detailed studies of "Bel and the Dragon" and "Susanna" (in both their versions), with special attention to encoded theological agendas.

Having dealt with the legends individually, I inquire into their relations with the rest of the canon (chapter 6). While connections to the book of Daniel must certainly be reckoned with, we shall find the stories more fundamentally driven by the problems and ambiguities of Jeremiah's advice to the exiles in Babylon: "Build houses and live in them; plant gardens and eat what they produce . . ."[3] With these results in hand, I ask in the final chapter (7) about connections between the stories and the concerns of the communities which told them—

---

[3] Jer 29:5 (LXX 36:5).

communities which were attempting to build gardens in the new Babylons of Hellenistic Egypt and, later, the Roman Empire. The study closes with some brief reflections on its implications for life and interpretation in the Babylons of our own day.

Chapter 2

NARRATIVE AND FAITH

Western culture, heavily influenced by its Jewish and Christian lineage, commonly defines "faith" in terms of "belief and trust in and loyalty to God."[1] Like most definitions, this raises a string of further questions. What sorts of beliefs? In God as opposed to what or whom else? Trust and loyalty expressed how? And how do the beliefs, values, and behaviors of faith relate to other aspects of culture? By the time the ramifications of these questions are taken into account, faith resembles not so much a creed as a worldview: "a comprehensive conception or apprehension of the world esp. from a specific standpoint"[2]—in this case, the standpoint of belief in a particular God. Such a faith's comprehensiveness does not ensure its absolute consistency: a working faith rarely displays the coherence of a systematic theology.[3] Yet coherence remains a concern, as religions' ongoing concern with theodicy demonstrates.

Judaism (which produced the Greek Daniel legends) and Christianity (which inherited them as "scripture") contend that the Bible (as variously defined) supplies source material for faith.[4] But how

---

[1] *Webster's New Collegiate Dictionary* (Springfield, Massachusetts: G. &. C. Merriam Company, 1974), s.v., definition 2 a (1).

[2] Ibid., s.v. "Weltanschaung."

[3] This is why we shall find ourselves making special use of those literary theorists who allow for contradiction and multivalence within a text.

[4] This is not to deny that modes of *using* biblical source material vary dramatically. Some groups attach authority to the biblical text *qua* text; others stress events to which the words refer. Some (especially Christians) think of faith as a matter of belief and thus look to their Bible for doctrinal teaching; others (especially Jews) stress action and look to Torah for behavioral guidance. Protestants turn directly to their Bible (at least in principle—*sola scriptura*), while other Christians, along with Jews, defer to interpretive traditions which explicitly control use of scripture. One

5

exactly are beliefs about—and loyalty to!—God encoded in or derived
from narrative? Let us first consider the general issues at stake in this
question, with special attention to light shed by literary-critical theory.
We shall then review specific strategies—some developed by biblical
scholars, some by literary critics—for discerning the "theology" of narrative texts.

The Issues at Stake

Upon what does one focus when studying a written work? M. H.
Abrams divides critical responses to this question into four general
categories.[5] Some critics emphasize the *mimetic* aspect of writing, its
claim to represent "reality." Others stress writing's *expressive* function,
exploring the relationship between the work and the person who has
produced it. Or one may investigate the work's effect on its audience,
its pragmatic or *affective* function. Finally, reacting against the extra-
literary stresses (on "reality," author, or readers) of the previous
approaches, some would attempt to focus on the literary work in and of
itself (*objective* approaches).

Mimetic, expressive, and affective approaches have long been
applied to Jewish and Christian scriptures. The mimetic orientation
evidences itself not merely in fascination with questions of historicity,
but more fundamentally in religious claims that the scriptures provide
access to an otherwise unavailable knowledge of reality. Apologists
often ground this claim in doctrines of inspiration which focus our attention on the authorial (expressive) process. Historical criticism also
focuses on the relation between text and writer, but accents the historical, cultural, and psychological contingencies at play. Some faith communities have responded by relocating inspiration in the interaction
between text and reader. Reader-response analysis may also be used by
observers outside the faith community, for instance in Marx's description of religion as the "opiate of the people." The relevance perceived

---

reason I define faith in terms of worldview is that the broader definition encompasses
these many understandings.

[5] This division is followed by Hazard Adams in the introduction to *Critical
Theory Since Plato* (San Diego: Harcourt Brace Jovanovich, Publishers, 1971), 1–7.

in these three approaches, by people who embrace the Bible as authoritative and people who do not, suggests that all three must be taken into consideration when investigating the relation of faith and scripture.

What about "objective" approaches? In light of modern challenges to scripture's historical claims, and the inaccessibility (in direct terms) of biblical writers and their original audiences, methods centering on the text in and of itself might seem best suited to our material. Objective approaches have indeed provided a helpful tonic to biblical scholarship and interpretation, by urging attention to the received text (not some hypothetical Ur–form), challenging the adequacy of paraphrase, and asking about the role of internal structure in literary works—in short, by focusing attention on the specific features of the texts we have.

But such approaches in their pure form address neither the historical interests of scholars nor the reality claims made by the religious community on behalf of scripture. They also fail to reckon with the inherently social and historical qualities of language and literature (aspects easily overlooked when studying modern works, but more difficult to ignore in connection with biblical writings). We shall bypass purely objectivist approaches in favor of their successors (structuralist and post–structuralist) which integrate questions of historical matrix, authorial plan, and reader response into the study of the particular text and its structure.

Mimetic, expressive, affective and objective types of analysis may be applied to any type of writing. Biblical writings, however, take predominantly narrative form. The overall structure is narrative, moving from creation to restoration in the Tanakh[6] and from creation to new creation in the Christian Bible. Narrative also forms the dominant subtype within this overall structure. Wesley Kort offers a classification of literary approaches to scripture which he grounds in its specifically narrative character. Drawing attention to four key components of narrative (character, plot, tone, and atmosphere), he suggests that each

---

[6] Gen 1:1 to 2 Chr 36:23. Within this span, of course, occur some texts looking even further than the time of Cyrus.

corresponds to a component of worldview (beliefs about humanity, causality, values, and the universe of possibilities).[7]

He groups methods of narrative criticism into four broad types, each tending to focus on a different one of the four elements. Structural approaches, highlighting stable entities and oppositions, often zero in on characters.[8] "Myth criticism" is Kort's umbrella term for theories which focus on "recurring, conventional, or traditional patterns of human behavior" (so most folklore analyses, for instance, would fall into this category).[9] Such approaches naturally enough tend to focus on plot. Composition critics, on the other hand, study the surface wording of texts, evincing a special sensitivity to tone, which in turn reveals the values embedded in the telling.[10] Critical hermeneutics, finally, tends to highlight narrative atmosphere, the relatively transparent but all-pervading set of assumptions which provides the setting for a story's action.[11] Each of these methodological types supplies useful insight into a text; none, by itself, covers the waterfront (in part because of the tendency of each to focus on only one element of narrative). Investigation of a text's faith-world calls for use of all of them.

Kort's four types of analysis each draw, in different ways, on developments stimulated by the teachings of linguist Ferdinand de Saussure.[12] Departing from linguists' then-current fascination with etymology (a historical or "diachronic" approach to language), Saussure insisted that languages need to be understood synchronically, in terms of the arbitrary, socially controlled conventions for meaning operative in a given society at a given time.

---

[7] Wesley Kort, *Story, Text and Scripture: Literary Interests in Biblical Narrative* (University Park: Pennsylvania State University Press, 1988), 15-16.

[8] Ibid., 29-35, 61-71.

[9] Ibid., 24-28, 52-61. Quote from p. 52.

[10] Ibid., 40-48, 84-96. Close reading, rhetorical criticism, and literary criticism are some of the terms used within the biblical studies field for this type of approach.

[11] Ibid., 35-40, 71-84.

[12] Saussure's work was published from course notes by his students and appears in English as *Course in General Linguistics*, trans. Wade Baskin (The Philosophical Library: 1959). Excerpts appear in *Contemporary Literary Criticism: Literary and Cultural Studies*, 2nd ed., ed. Robert Con Davis and Ronald Schleifer, (New York: Longman, 1989), 152-168. (Page references are to the excerpts in Davis

Inspired by Saussure's notion of the *langue* (rules and conventions) which guides specific linguistic utterances (*parole*), Eastern European critics known as the Russian Formalists embarked on an attempt to elucidate a comparable but higher-level *langue* for literary activity. Given their roots in linguistic theory, it is not surprising that they dealt with literature as a communicative act, in which an author, drawing on and playing against the existing genre patterns of the literary *langue*, produces a work which does not contain "meaning" in and of itself, but must be "concretized" by the hearers or readers, likewise in interaction with existing expectations. The uniqueness of literature, according to these theorists, is that unlike ordinary communication (where an utterance's referential meaning can usually be determined so smoothly that the message seems "transparent" and the coding process involved remains invisible), literature frustrates expectations and, in so doing, calls attention to its medium. Form becomes content.[13]

The Russian Formalists' work provides important insights into the interplay between genre expectations and the actual structure of a given work (compare Alter's chapter on the type-scene[14]). Reader-response critics have made especially strong use of such approaches. However, Formalist stress on the self-referentiality of literary language may hamper appreciation of work from cultures and eras in which literature makes strongly referential claims, or which value traditional patterning above novelty.[15]

Another of Saussure's distinctions, between horizontal or *syntagmatic* linguistic relationships (e.g., the relationship between a sentence's subject and its verb), and vertical or *paradigmatic* ones (the relationships between synonyms or antonyms), also sparked a search for narrative analogues.[16] Vladimir Propp's name dominates the history of work on

---

and Schleifer.) While I use Kort's categories to organize the discussion below, examples and connections cited are my own.

[13] For a succinct sketch of the major Russian formalists, see Edgar V. McKnight, *The Bible and the Reader: An Introduction to Literary Criticism* (Philadelphia: Fortress, 1985), 15–48.

[14] Robert Alter, "Biblical Type-Scenes and the Uses of Convention," chap. in *The Art of Biblical Narrative* (New York: Basic Books, Inc., 1981), 47–62.

[15] One may likewise ask whether the Russian Formalists misjudged the complexity of "ordinary communication." Most parents develop the ability to communicate one message to children while simultaneously sending a quite different message to other adults.

narrative syntax, while Claude Lévi-Strauss developed the study of paradigmatic relationships in narrative.

When Propp began his work in the early twentieth century, folklorists were heavily engaged in cataloging stories by motif in an attempt to discern their phylogeny.[17] Propp approached the issue of classification from a new direction, focusing not on content motifs (such as dragon–fights or wise maidens) but on functional patterns (such as defying an interdiction or meeting a helper). His landmark study of Russian fairy tales uncovered a remarkable similarity in basic structure—a "grammar" for fairy tales, as it were. Folklorists have since developed Proppian–type templates for a variety of tale types, and many of his methods have found their way into biblical form criticism.[18] Knowledge of the relevant template contributes importantly to the study of a reader's interaction with a story, since it alerts us to expectations which guide interpretation. Such plot–oriented approaches fall into Kort's category of "myth criticism."

It remained for the French anthropologist Claude Lévi-Strauss to undertake serious investigation of the paradigmatic structure of myths

---

[16] Roman Jakobsen, drawing parallels between these types and the symptoms involved in various kinds of aphasia, has argued for two fundamental modes of mental process, the metonymic (syntagmatic) and metaphoric (paradigmatic). See his essay, "The Metaphoric and Metonymic Poles," reprinted in *Critical Theory Since Plato*, ed. Hazard Adams (San Diego: Harcourt Brace Jovanovich, 1971), 1113-1116.

[17] This project, the folkloric equivalent of etymological studies, culminated in Antti Aarne's *Verzeichnis der Märchentypen*, Folklore Fellows Communications no. 3 (Helsinki: Academia Scientarum Fennice: 1911), the most recent edition of which is *Types of the Folktale: A Classification and Bibliography*, trans. and enlarged by Stith Thompson, 2nd rev., Folklore Fellows Communications no. 184 (Helsinki, Academia Scientarum Fennice, 1961).

[18] Propp's work, first published as *Morfologija skazki* (Leningrad: Academia, 1928) is available in a corrected English edition as *Morphology of the Folktale*, 2nd ed., ed. Louis A. Wagner (Austin: University of Texas Press, 1968). For a careful assessment of Propp's views and their application to biblical studies, including experimental analyses of the stories in Dan. 1-6, see Pamela J. Milne, *Vladimir Propp and the Study of Structure in Hebrew Biblical Narrative*, Bible and Literature Series (Sheffield: Almond, 1988). In chapter 3 I shall have more to say about the application of folklore analysis to Greek Daniel legends.

and folktales.[19] Comparing multiple variants of the same myth, Lévi-Strauss isolated fundamental contrasts (such as life/death, male/female, insider/outsider) and contended that these stories set up transformative relations which function, by means of a deep "mythic logic," to resolve those oppositions.

This mode of analysis highlights the social/psychological functions a story may perform, and may illuminate relationships between stories which are variants of a single pattern. ("Pattern" here refers to the deep structure of oppositions, not the surface sequences investigated by Propp.) This belongs to the category of approaches designated by Kort as "structuralist." A number of studies have applied this branch of structuralism to biblical narrative, including one by Michael P. Carroll which relates Esther, Judith, and Susanna as transformations of the same basic set of oppositions.[20]

All these post-Saussurean approaches use *other texts*, in some way, to illuminate dynamics involved in a given sample. These other texts help us discern the *langue*, as it were, of the *parole* represented by one particular text.[21] Such tactics help us work around the problematic fact that when working with ancient texts, we have access to the teller only through the tale, and to the audience only through this and other tales. The Proppian and Lévi-Straussian methods emphasize similarities between different individual narratives, seeing them as exemplars of a common pattern or process (thus scholars using these approaches may stress the ways in which biblical narratives express cultural norms), while the Formalists tend to celebrate contrasts, emphasizing the uniqueness of each work's configuration (leading to comments on the genius of a given biblical writer, or the distinctiveness of the faith community in its pagan environment).

---

[19] Lévi-Strauss's approach is well illustrated in his classic essay, "The Structural Study of Myth," in *Structural Anthropology* (New York: Basic Books, Inc., 1963), 206-231; reprinted in *Contemporary Literary Criticism: Modernism Through Post-Structuralism*, ed. Robert Con Davis (New York: Longman, 1986), 307-22.

[20] Michael P. Carroll, "Myth, Methodology and Transformation in the Old Testament: The Stories of Esther, Judith, and Susanna," *SR* 12 (1983): 301-312. Other well-known biblical structuralists are Robert Polzin, David Jobling, and Daniel Patte.

[21] Recall that *langue* is Saussure's term for the collection of conventions governing speech; *parole* designates a particular utterance (Saussure, 153 and 155).

This emphasis on contrast associates the Formalists' work with Kort's remaining two types of approach, composition criticism and critical hermeneutics. Composition criticism elucidates specific strategies used in a text to guide the reader and shape evaluative responses (for instance, showing how point of view functions to align our sympathies with certain characters).[22] Critical hermeneutics attends less to the internal dynamics of the text and more to its interplay with other texts, including that of the reader's own mind.

While Kort's discussion of critical hermeneutics draws primarily on the work of theologian Paul Ricoeur, the same issues are being intensively investigated by French literary critics, particularly Roland Barthes and Julia Kristeva. These critics continue to explore the question raised by the Russian Formalists: if (as linguistics and anthropology suggest) language is an immensely conservative vehicle of culture, shaping our perception of reality and organization of experience, how is it that literature (composed, after all, in the medium of language) can challenge and overturn that reality?[23]

Like the Formalists, these French critics respond that literature subverts language's ordinarily unquestioned (but arbitrary and highly ideological!) claim of reference to "reality" by highlighting the function of language itself. But they associate the multivocal quality of literary texts with the very structure of human reality, as illuminated by Lacanian psychoanalysis. That is, texts, which are *not* logical, coherent wholes, reflect their makers, who are *not* the consistent, unified, individuals of Cartesian thought. Texts become part of the human person's struggle to exist between the painful security of (internalized) Law and the deadly pleasure of Desire:[24]

> "Art". . .weaves into language (or other "signifying materials") the complex relations of a subject caught between "nature" and [punct. *sic*] culture," between the immemorial ideological and scientific *tradition*, henceforth

---

[22] Composition criticism surfaces both in particular studies of texts (such as Phyllis Trible's essays in *God and the Rhetoric of Sexuality* and *Texts of Terror*, OBT (Philadelphia: Fortress, 1978 and 1984) and in books on narrative poetics, which attempt to elucidate the general repertoire of techniques used by writers in a given genre or body of literature. Among the best-known studies of biblical poetics are those by Alter, Berlin, and Sternberg, discussion of which begins on p. 18 below.

[23] Again, as with the Formalists, we find a tendency to contrast "literature" with "ordinary language," along with an expectation that literature will function to overturn rather than reinforce the status quo.

[24] Kristeva, *Desire in Language: A Semiotic Approach to Literature and Art*, ed. Leon S. Roudiez (New York: Columbia University Press, 1980), ix–x.

available, and the *present*, between *desire* and the *law*, the body, language, and "metalanguage."[25]

This offers a whole new horizon for exploring relationships between literature and "reality" (a "reality" which must henceforth wear quotation marks, since we always experience it in interpreted and non-absolute fashion).

At this point we must pause to ask whether critical theories and methods developed in explicit conversation with self-consciously innovative works (by artists like Joyce, Mallarmé, Picasso, Kafka, and Lautréamont) are applicable to the LXX. A general response would be that yes, these theories are applicable to *any* texts, because when Kristeva's arguments are pursued to their conclusion, the contrast between literary and ordinary language collapses—*all* discourse contains the seeds of revolution.

Let us look, however, more closely at Kristeva's definition of a "text." She sees a text as

> a trans-linguistic apparatus that redistributes the order of language by relating communicative speech, which aims to inform directly, to different kinds of anterior or synchronic utterances. The text is therefore a *productivity*, and this means: first, that its relationship to the language in which it is situated is redistributive (destructive-constructive), and hence can be better approached through logical categories rather than linguistic ones; and second, that it is a permutation of texts, an intertextuality: in the space of a given text, several utterances, taken from other texts, intersect and neutralize one another.[26]

While in principle all writing exhibits this dialogical character, Kristeva focuses especially on overtly polyphonous texts. In "Word, Dialogue, and Novel" she recalls Mikhail Bakhtin's distinction between an author's quotation of another's utterance which "accepts it as a whole, changing neither meaning nor tonality," and quotation which gives "a new meaning while retaining the meaning it already had."[27]

It is this second type of quotation which interests Kristeva. She herself traces its development to the novel's evolution between the thirteenth and fifteenth centuries, but Jewish writing of the Hellenistic era clearly employs extensive quotation and allusion (use of other utterances) *in a manner which often gives new meaning to the material*

---

25 Kristeva, "How Does One Speak to Literature?", in *Desire*, 97.
26 Kristeva, "The Bounded Text," in *Desire*, 36.
27 Kristeva, "Word, Dialogue, and Novel," in *Desire*, 73.

quoted.[28]   Such layering of language occurs in two ways in the Greek Daniel legends.   First, the material of the stories themselves seems to have been recast several times, acquiring new emphases without entirely losing the old ones.[29]   Second, texts from other parts of the Hebrew Bible resurface in the Greek Daniel legends. This abundance of internal and external "citation" makes the Greek Daniel legends prime arenas for the kind of interplay that Kristeva posits.

If "meaning" is truly as culturally dependent as this discussion indicates, we may well ask how it will be possible to evaluate the "truth" of our conjectures as to the functioning of texts in ancient contexts. To this, the only answer I know is that suggested by Thorkild Jacobsen in his introduction to a study of ancient Mesopotamian religion:

> Ultimately, the coherence of our data must be our guide. True meanings illuminate their contexts and these contexts support each other effortlessly. False meanings jar, stop, and lead no further. It is by attention to such arrests, by not forcing, but by being open to and seeking other possibilities, that one may eventually understand—recreate, as it were—the world of the ancients.[30]

True, Jacobsen's formulation rests on an assumption of unity and coherence that, according to Lacan, humanity never achieves. Nonetheless we seek it, we presume that ancient people did as well, and it provides our only anchor in the quest to understand their narratives and them.

Specific Strategies

The foregoing discussion suggests the need for a multifaceted approach to narrative: a model that will attend to plot, character, composition and tone, mindful of the text's status as communication involving culture-specific conventions, and of the possibility that it may

---

[28] This is quite obvious in writings of the New Testament. For instance, Matthew concludes the tale of Jesus' family descent to Egypt with the comment, "This was to fulfill what had been spoken by the Lord through the prophet, 'Out of Egypt I have called my son'" (Matt 2:15). This puts a decidedly new spin on the words of Hos 11:1.

[29] While older historical scholarship tended to see such multivocality as evidence of confusion, newer studies often celebrate it as a source of meaning. Cf. Daniel Boyarin's discussion in "Textual Heterogeneity in the Torah and the Dialectic of the Mekilta," chap. in *Intertextuality and the Reading of Midrash*, Indiana Studies in Biblical Literature (Bloomington: Indiana University, 1990), 39–56.

[30] Thorkild Jacobsen, *The Treasures of Darkness* (New Haven: Yale University Press, 1976), 19.

embody a conversation rather than a simple monologic message. To achieve such a many-sided analysis, I shall employ an eclectic approach, organized according to a central narratological scheme but supplemented by input from various writers in the fields of biblical studies and literary criticism. Here I shall indicate the general shape of the model and discuss the types of supplementary input to be employed; explication of fine points will come in conjunction with actual study of texts in chapters 4 through 6.

As an overall framework I have chosen the model presented by Mieke Bal in *Narratology*.[31] The first advantage of this choice is its convenient level of generality: Bal speaks specifically of narrative texts (rather than of literature in general) but does not limit herself to the narrative text as found in modern avant-garde novels. It is recent enough (the Dutch edition was published in 1980) to be informed by all of the varieties of structuralism discussed in the earlier part of this chapter; it also "aims at an integration of different types of theories, at showing the necessity of a rational critical discourse within whatever view of literature one may hold."[32] It is designed to be used as we shall use it, in conjunction with other theoretical sources and period-specific information.[33]

Bal separates narrative into three layers. The most abstract layer (farthest from the actual words of the text) is the *fabula*, the "series of logically and chronologically related events caused or experienced by actors." "Events, actors, time, and location together constitute the material of a fabula."[34] Isolation of this fabula layer proves particularly helpful in analyzing a tale's plot, but it also lays bare some of the paradigmatic relationships (equivalencies and oppositions) set up by a narrative.

Between the functional, formal level of fabula, and the concrete, detailed level of text, Bal distinguishes a middle level which she terms the *story*. A story particularizes its fabula in the following ways: (1) events are arranged in a certain sequence (not necessarily chronological), (2) some are summarized quickly, while others are related at

---

[31] Mieke Bal, *Narratology: Introduction to the Theory of Narrative* (Toronto: University of Toronto Press, 1985).

[32] Ibid., xi.

[33] "Hence, the need of more theory, beyond narratology: a theory that accounts for the functions and positions of texts of different backgrounds, genres, and historical periods" (ibid., x). Bal is a critic of great flexibility whose own analyses may incorporate feminist, psychoanalytic, or other varieties of criticism; these are allowed by but not inherent in the program outlined in *Narratology*.

[34] Ibid., 5, 7, 11-48.

something approximating the pace at which the events themselves would take place,[35] (3) the actors are given characteristic traits (they become "characters" rather than role–fillers), (4) locations are correspondingly characterized as specific places, (5) symbolic, allusive, and other relationships may be developed in addition to the functional ones of the fabula, and (6) a particular point of view is adopted.[36] Bal appeals to the example of "Tom Thumb" in justifying her distinction between story and text.

> Everyone in Europe is familiar with the story of Tom Thumb. However, not everyone has read that story in the same text. There are different texts. Some texts are considered to be literary while others are not; some can be read aloud to children, others are too difficult. Evidently, narrative texts differ from one another even if the related story is the same.[37]

A clue that "the related story is the same" may be found (according to Bal) in the fact that readers sympathize with Tom and applaud the destruction of the giant's own children, even when the story is presented in an entirely different medium such as film.

Once the fabula and story levels have been analyzed, the level of *text* presents us mainly with issues regarding narratorial style: who tells the story? With what non–narrative additions (including description)? How do the different levels of narration (narrator's words, characters' words, stories–within–the–story, etc.) relate to each other?[38]

Bal's distinctions between "story" and "text," and in particular the concept of "the same story," are the most problematic elements of this narratology. The distinction between "story" and "text" is troublesome because story aspects (especially characterization, pacing, and focalization) are realized by manipulation of words at the text level. Where does one draw the line between a teller's style and actual change in story content? Marion Zimmer Bradley's *Mists of Avalon* retells the Arthurian legend from female characters' viewpoints, yet we recognize it as "the same story" presented in Malory's *Le Morte Darthur*. The story (in Bal's technical sense) appears in yet another permutation in White's

---

[35] Many writers refer to this as "tempo." Theoretically the narrative may take even more time to describe events than required by their happening, but this happens relatively infrequently.

[36] Bal, 7. Story forms the subject of chapter 2 of this book. I list the aspects of story in a different order than Bal does.

[37] Ibid., 5.

[38] Ibid., 8, 119–150.

Sword in the Stone.[39]   The "sameness" of these stories needs to be described in terms of degrees of *similarity* in a multidimensional space (involving separate axes for fabula, characterization, localization, and so forth) rather than simply as identity or non–identity. However, with this reservation noted, Bal's tri–level scheme remains useful for analysis, and I shall follow her in singling out the "story" level for separate discussion.[40]

While Bal's narratology proves very helpful in examining plot, paradigmatic structures, and some aspects of atmosphere, it provides less guidance for the study of composition and intertextual interactions (in part because of its generality). What methodological help can we find for studying culture–specific aspects of narrative, including specific conventions and linguistic techniques?

Substantial help can come from historical–critical studies (too quickly dismissed as "excavative" by some literarily oriented scholars). Although the *goals* of historical critics may be quite different from those of literary critics—asking, for instance, "did these things really happen?" rather than "why is the story told this way?", or "how many sources do we have?" rather than "how do the variations interact?"—their *observations* on vocabulary, allusion, plot similarities, and so forth are often quite keen.

Form and redaction criticism offer particularly rich insights for literary application (and historically appear to have paved the way for introduction of literary interests into biblical studies). Form critics provide crucial literary information as they elucidate the historical genres which, while they may not absolutely control the development of a given story, nonetheless provide the web of expectations against which the text plays. Form–critical attention to *Sitz im Leben* also helps elucidate the communicative context.

Already in the days of Hermann Gunkel, form critics were in conversation with folklore studies, and this partnership has dominated genre study of the Daniel legends (note that "legend" is itself a tech-

---

[39] Marion Zimmer Bradley, *Mists of Avalon* (New York: Alfred A. Knopf, Inc., 1983); Sir Thomas Malory, *Le Morte Darthur*, published in English as *The Acts of King Arthur and His Noble Knights* by John Steinbeck (New York: Farrar, Straus and Giroux, 1976); T. H. White, *The Once and Future King* (New York: Putnam, 1958).

[40] Bal herself justifies the distinction by its heuristic value, and not by any ontological claim. In particular, she specifies that it helps to describe the experience of readers, rather than that of writers (48).

nical term from the folklore field).[41] Despite internal controversy among folklorists about their field's proper relation to ancient written texts,[42] both content-oriented and formal (Proppian) approaches have been fruitfully applied to the Daniel stories. In addition to culture-specific genre studies, folklore study on occasion offers very fruitful cross-cultural observations.[43]

Redaction criticism, with its careful attention to an editor's work and its purposes, also shows a deep affinity with literary study. The Greek additions to Daniel offer a uniquely suitable subject for such criticism because, at least in the case of Susanna, the redaction critic has access to both an edited text (the "Theodotion" version) and its *Vorlage* (the OG). In Daniel proper, unfortunately, redaction-oriented interest in the Greek versions has usually been subordinated to text-critical agendas aimed ultimately at the Semitic text. However, a very fine redaction-oriented study has been done for Susanna by Helmut Engel, which points in the direction of my own conclusions.[44]

Recent decades have also seen the development of a specifically biblical discipline of composition criticism. Three books have been particularly influential: Robert Alter's *Art of Biblical Narrative*, Adele Berlin's *Poetics and Interpretation of Biblical Narrative*, and Meir

---

[41] Hermann Gunkel, *Das Märchen im Alten Testament*, Religionsgeschichtliche Volksbücher (Tübingen: Mohr, 1921), published in English as *The Folktale in the Old Testament* (Sheffield: Almond, 1987).

[42] Issues in the controversy are well expressed by Barrè Toelken's statement that "a clear delineation of genre or structure of a folk item is only one small part of understanding a folk performance. Without the whole live context and the comment of the performers, it is unlikely that we will ever get very close to understanding—or even seeing—the dynamics that underlie the traditional process." Toelken, *The Dynamics of Folklore* (Boston: Houghton Mifflin, 1979), 103. Heda Jason, to whose work we shall refer in the discussion of Susanna, takes up these questions in "Literary Documents of the Past and Their Relation to Folk Literature," in *Folklore and Oral Communication* (Zagreb: Zavod za istrazivanje folklora Instituta za filologiju i folkloristiku, 1981), 167-178. Specific folklore studies on the Daniel stories will be cited as our study progresses.

[43] E.g., Susan Niditch's use of cross-cultural information to elucidate the cultural functions of the Genesis sister/wife tales, in *Underdogs and Tricksters: A Prelude to Biblical Folklore*, New Voices in Biblical Studies (San Francisco: Harper & Row, 1987), 23-69. We shall also see cross-cultural observations at work, within the general matrix of the ancient Near East, in Lawrence Wills, *The Jew in the Court of a Foreign King: Ancient Jewish Court Legends*, HDR (Minneapolis: Fortress, 1990), esp. 39-74.

[44] Helmut Engel, *Die Susanna-Erzählung: Einleitung, Übersetzung und Kommentar zum Septuaginta-Text und zur Theodotion-Bearbeitung* (Freiburg: Universitätsverlag, 1985; Göttingen: Vandenhoeck & Ruprecht, 1985).

Sternberg's *Poetics of Biblical Narrative.*[45] (One should note, however, that observations and methods employed in these general discussions of biblical poetics had already been used by other authors in studies of specific biblical texts.[46])

Alter intends his book as "a guide to the intelligent reading of biblical narrative. . .to illuminate the distinctive principles of the Bible's narrative art."[47] Challenging those who would denigrate the Bible's storytelling as "primitive," or even disintegrate it entirely into a patchwork of "sources," Alter identifies and explores biblical narrative's characteristic compositional techniques. In so doing, Alter calls attention at least passingly to almost all the features which have engaged later writers.

Among the compositional techniques discussed by Alter are the following: (1) *Type-scenes* (typical scenes sharing clusters of motifs, such as the "meeting at the well"). Alter's discussion here has a strong Russian-formalist flavor as he explores the interplay between established literary conventions and their nuancing in a particular exemplum:

> Much of art lies in the shifting aperture between the shadowy foreimage in the anticipating mind of the observer and the realized revelatory image in the work itself.[48]

(2) *Dialogue.* Here Alter calls attention to the biblical preoccupation with speech, and in particular to its uses in characterization.[49]

(3) *Repetition.* Alter identifies a spectrum of levels on which repetition occurs, from reiteration of a word within a sentence to the level of the type-scene, and discusses the literary functions of such

---

[45] Robert Alter, *The Art of Biblical Narrative* (New York: Basic Books, 1981); Adele Berlin, *Poetics and Interpretation of Biblical Narrative*, Bible and Literature Series (Sheffield: Almond, 1983); Meir Sternberg, *The Poetics of Biblical Narrative: Ideological Literature and the Drama of Reading*, Indiana Literary Biblical Series (Bloomington: Indiana University Press, 1985).

[46] Three significant composition-critical studies appeared in 1978: James L. Crenshaw, *Samson: A Secret Betrayed, A Vow Ignored* (Atlanta: John Knox, 1978); David M. Gunn, *The Story of King David: Genre and Interpretation*, JSOTSup (Sheffield: University of Sheffield, 1978); and Trible, *Rhetoric*. Another early practitioner of this approach was J. P. Fokkelman, whose *King David (II Samuel 9–20 and I Kings 1–2)*, vol. 1 of *Narrative Art and Poetry in the Books of Samuel* (Assen: Van Gorcum), appeared in 1981.

[47] Alter, ix.

[48] Ibid., 47–62, quote from p. 62.

[49] Ibid., 63–88.

repetition in bringing various pieces of the text into dialogue with each other.[50]

(4) *Characterization.* After discussing various means of characterization, in ascending order of reliability, Alter observes that there is "an abiding mystery in character as the biblical writers conceive it. . . .This unpredictable and changing nature of character is one reason why biblical personages cannot have Homeric epithets."[51] Also, significantly, he calls attention to the reticence of biblical narrators and the importance of attending to what they do *not* say.

(5) *Literary uses of difference.* Here Alter makes the important claim that the presence of differing, even contradictory accounts and styles is not simply the untidy residue of a composite compositional process, but performs a positive function in conveying worldview:

> The biblical outlook is informed. . .by a sense of stubborn contradiction, of a profound and ineradicable untidiness in the nature of things, and it is toward the expression of such a sense of moral and historical reality that the composite artistry of the Bible is directed.[52]

(6) *Narratorial voice and knowledge.* Alter suggests that the interplay of narratorial and other perspectives in biblical storytelling

> . . .might usefully be regarded as a narrative experiment in the possibilities of moral, spiritual, and historical knowledge, undertaken through a process of studied contrasts between the variously limited knowledge of the human characters and the divine omniscience quietly but firmly represented by the narrator.[53]

Adele Berlin's book on *Poetics and Interpretation of Biblical Narrative,* published two years later, covers much the same ground, but with even closer attention to characterization and, in particular, the complex dynamics of point of view. Drawing on the works of non-biblical critics like Chatman, Uspensky, and Lanser,[54] Berlin calls attention to

---

[50] Ibid., 88–113.

[51] Ibid., 114–130, quote from 126. Alter's conclusion agrees, obviously, with Erich Auerbach's observations in his famous chapter on "Odysseus' Scar" in *Mimesis: The Representation of Reality in Western Literature* (Garden City: Doubleday, 1957), 3–23.

[52] Alter, 131–154, quote from 154.

[53] Ibid., 155–177, quote from 157.

[54] Seymour Chatman, *Story and Discourse: Narrative Structure in Fiction and Film* (Ithaca: Cornell University Press, 1978); Boris Uspensky, *A Poetics of Composition: The Structure of the Artistic Text and Typology of a Compositional Form* (Berkeley: University of California Press, 1973); Susan S. Lanser, *The Narrative Act: Point of View in Prose Fiction* (Princeton: Princeton University Press, 1981).

the multiple levels of point of view (ideological, spatial, temporal, and so forth) and the means used by biblical narrative to shift our viewpoint, sometimes within a scope as narrow as a single sentence.[55]

Point of view remains center stage in Meir Sternberg's *Poetics of Biblical Narrative*, third in our trio of books on biblical composition. Sternberg's vigorously argued text again deals with the topics of viewpoint (chaps. 3-5, 12-13), characterization (chaps. 9-10), and repetition (chap. 11), but with several new twists. First, he challenges Alter's classification of biblical narratives as "prose fiction."[56] Sternberg argues that the biblical narrators intended to write historiography, not fiction. If the narratives do not stand up to modern tests of historicity, that may make them erroneous historiography, but it does not erase their historiographical claims. If they employ a brand of narratorial omniscience that the modern mind associates with fiction, the explanation lies in ancient conventions of inspiration.[57]

Second, Sternberg makes the issue of narratorial viewpoint one of the central themes of his work, arguing that the biblical narrative is a highly ideological work attempting to "justify the ways of God to man" and that the reader's sympathies are manipulated throughout in whichever ways will be most conducive to that end.

Third and finally, Sternberg makes an exhaustive investigation of the ways in which limited or incomplete information forces the reader into active participation in the reading process (chs. 6-8). Again the discussion traces dynamics like those investigated by the Formalists in their discussions of narrative ambiguity and the concretization process.

All three of these books deal specifically with *Hebrew* narrative. Inasmuch as our Greek Daniel narratives were either translated from Semitic originals or written in close imitation of such translations, we may expect similarities of technique. Even the Synoptic gospels, composed in Greek, show a strikingly similar style.[58] We shall find Alter, Berlin, and Sternberg of great help in discerning the workings of our Greek narratives, but we shall also note, at points, departures into more characteristically Hellenistic style.

---

55 Berlin, esp. 43-82.

56 A designation used in the title of Alter's second chapter.

57 Sternberg, 23-34. I shall have more to say about Sternberg and narratorial omniscience in my studies of Susanna and Bel and the Dragon (chaps. 4 and 5).

58 Cf. Rudolf Bultmann's section on story technique in *History of the Synoptic Tradition* (New York: Harper and Row, 1963), 307-317.

At this point, Robert Funk's book *The Poetics of Biblical Narrative* deserves mention.[59] Funk's book deals specifically with Greek (New Testament) poetics and offers an admirably detailed set of criteria; unfortunately, the method concerns itself mostly with indices of narrative segmentation. In general, the features Funk observes in Greek narrative correspond to those discerned in Hebrew narrative by the three authors just discussed. I shall use Funk's method in segmenting the Daniel legends, but the results will not be noticeably different than if I had depended on suggestions by Alter or Berlin.

Finally, we need some method for discerning and interpreting the interplay of various textual voices in our Daniel stories—for studying *intertextuality*. Kristeva's work, already discussed, provides the theoretical underpinnings for this enterprise, while many of the practical tips come from Michael Riffaterre.

We have already cited (p. 13 above) Kristeva's definition of a "text" as an intertextuality, a permutation of texts, a place where multiple voices intersect. In Kristeva's thought, culture and society themselves comprise a "text" with which an individual text is inevitably in dialogue (note the stubborn historicity of this approach).[60] At this level, "intertextuality" is but another name for the cultural rootedness embedded in the nature of language itself, of which any decent interpretation must take account. Traditional historical–critical commentaries can be of significant help in untangling this variety of intertextuality.

Another obvious type of intertextual voice is that of a text directly cited by another. Such citation has been noted in Susanna, but its significance has not been elucidated. Why Jeremiah? How do the meanings of the words in the prophetic book compare to their implications in the Daniel legend? These are questions to which we must turn our attention if we really mean to understand the "web" of significance in Susanna.

---

[59] Robert Funk, *The Poetics of Biblical Narrative*, FFNT (Sonoma, California: Polebridge, 1988).

[60] Kristeva, "The Bounded Text," 37. Semioticists refer to this as the "sociolect": "language viewed not just as grammar and lexicon, but as the repository of society's myths. These are represented by themes, commonplace phrases, and descriptive systems (stereotyped networks of metonyms around any given lexical nucleus). Sociolect is opposed to 'idiolect,' an individual's specific semiotic activity, and in the case of literature, the lexicon and grammar specific to a text and whose rules and verbal equivalencies are valid only within its limits." (Michael Riffaterre, "Intertextual Representation: Mimesis as Interpretive Discourse," *Critical Inquiry* 11 [1984]: 160 n. 2.)

Yet another variety of intertextuality involves conversations *within* a given text.

> Any subtext, or, more broadly still, any unit of significance that can be identified as the narrative unfolds, any segment of the narrative that can be isolated without cognitive loss, may serve as an intertext to some further such unit, if the latter has features in common with the former. Such features make it possible or necessary for the reader to see the two units as different versions of the same episode or the same description, or two variants of the same structure. Components of the second will thus acquire a meaning other than what they convey in their context because they will be perceived as referring also or primarily to their homologues in the first.[61]

Repetition (of specific words, themes, or patterns) serves as the marker. Our theorists in biblical poetics give excellent guidance for the detection and interpretation of this variety of intertextuality.

Finally, the text under study may converse with literary texts outside itself, without directly citing them. Such conversations may involve literary *custom* (gathered from a variety of texts) or particular texts. In cases of custom, an awareness of genres, type–scenes, and verbal clichés will alert us to the "intertext" which guides reader expectation of our own text.[62]

The most difficult case involves invocation of specific intertexts *without* direct citation. The means of such invocation is seeming "ungrammaticality," a roughness or apparent lack of sense in the text at hand.

> In literary texts there are certain phrases or sentences that seem less acceptable than their context, a phenomenon linked to the intertext. As soon as the reader becomes aware of that intertext, the relative ungrammaticality is corrected or palliated.[63]

The hypogram (allusion) is encoded *in* the text at hand even if we do not have the key to it; the interaction is not a "felicitous surplus," but obligatory. We know that "our reading of the text cannot be complete

---

[61] Riffaterre, "The Intertextual Unconscious," *Critical Inquiry* 13 (1987): 380.

[62] Riffaterre refers to genre plays as "explicit" or "idiolectic" intertexts because the facts are observable entirely within the text. I am uncomfortable with this description since the "facts" in question involve reader knowledge "from comparing texts and recognizing what features they have in common," but I agree with his description of the dynamic involved. See Riffaterre, "The Poetic Functions of Intertextual Humor," *Romanic Review* 65 (1974): 278–293, quotes from pp. 287 and 280.

[63] Riffaterre, "Intertextual Scrambling," *Romanic Review* 68 (1977): 197.

or satisfactory without going through the intertext."[64] We may know the intertext and relate it immediately, we may experience a delayed discovery, we may even deduce the nature of the hypogram simply from the given text and our knowledge of the linguistic system, but the clue is there; it is an "icon of [authorial] intention."[65] Thus, awkwardnesses in our texts will need to be investigated as possible pointers toward intertextual references.

The combination of Bal's narratology, findings from form criticism and folklore studies, redaction criticism, biblical poetics, and intertextual theory, will allow us a well-rounded study of the Greek legends of Daniel: their plots, characters, tone, and atmosphere. Before launching into our application of these methods, we turn to a review of the studies which have already been made of these stories.

---

[64] Riffaterre, "Intertextual Representation: Mimesis as Interpretive Discourse," *Critical Inquiry* 11 (1984): 142.

[65] Riffaterre, "Scrambling," 200 n. 8, 206. Much of what biblical scholars "know" about Israelite culture results from precisely the deduction process described!

Chapter 3

LEGENDS OF DANIEL

We have mentioned three forms of the Book of Daniel: the MT (written in a combination of Hebrew and Aramaic), and two Greek versions[1] commonly referred to as the LXX (or OG) and TH. We noted further that the Greek versions contain two stories ("Susanna" and "Bel and the Dragon") not present in the MT.[2] What are the historical contexts of these Greek Daniel books, and what literary and theological meanings have modern interpreters found in them?

The Figure of Daniel

A wise and influential man named Danel (*dnil*) appears as early as the second millennium B.C.E. in Ugarit's *Aqhat* epic.[3] A name with

---

[1] Some limit the term "version" to a fresh translation, while referring to revised translations (such as TH appears to be) as "recensions." This study will use "version" in the sense of "translation," with allowance made for the fact that if Susanna and Bel and the Dragon were originally composed in Greek (which I doubt, but the point is not essential to our study) the "versions" may not be translations at all. "Recension" will refer to a translation revised with or without reference to a source language text. Context will supply what further specification is necessary.

[2] As mentioned in chapter 1, the Greek versions differ from MT and one another in other ways as well. Especially striking are the long poems present in both Greek versions of Daniel 3. In chapter 6 I shall give some consideration to overall differences between the Greek Daniel books.

[3] J. C. L. Gibson, *Canaanite Myths and Legends*, 2nd ed. (Edinburgh: T. & T. Clark, 1978), 103-22. Danel's name appears again on a fragmentary tablet, CTA 20, ibid., 135.

the same spelling[4] appears in the book of Ezekiel, which twice mentions "Noah, Daniel, and Job" as paragons of righteousness (Ezek 14:14,20), and also names Daniel as an exemplar of wisdom (Ezek 28:3). These associations with Noah, Job, and (in 28) Adam suit the idea of Daniel as a non–Israelite hero of yore.[5] An identification with Ugarit's Danel seems possible, especially given Ezekiel's tendency to draw on ancient traditions.[6]

The book of Daniel also contains motifs with close parallels at Ugarit (most notably, the Ancient of Days and One Coming on the Clouds), and we know that Hellenistic Jews sometimes attributed their books to pre–Israelite authors.[7] These observations, like the usage in Ezekiel, support an association between Daniel and ancient Canaanite tradition.

The book of Daniel explicitly presents Daniel as a Jew of good family[8] deported to Babylon by Nebuchadnezzar. Educated for court service, Daniel climbs to high rank, along with his friends Hananiah, Mishael, and Azariah (also known as Shedrach, Meshach, and Abed-nego). Yet for all this specificity in place and time, several lines of evidence suggest that the stories presented in the book of Daniel are not

---

[4] דנאל (*kethib*). The LXX reads Δανιηλ, in agreement with the *qere* (דָּנִיֵּאל). For a discussion of the connection between Ezekiel's Danel and Ugarit's, see Shalom Spiegel, "Noah, Daniel and Job," in *The Louis Ginsberg Jubilee Volume* (New York: American Academy for Jewish Research, 1945), 305–35.

[5] A similar indication comes from the fact that the Book of Jubilees gives Dan'il as Enoch's father–in–law. Michael Edward Stone, *Scriptures, Sects and Visions: A Profile of Judaism from Ezra to the Jewish Revolts* (Philadelphia: Fortress, 1980), 41.

[6] E.g., the Tyre oracle in ch. 28 appears to draw on an alternate version of the Eden story.

[7] For a concise statement and bibliography on the connections between Daniel 7 and Ugarit, see John E. Goldingay, *Daniel*, WBC (Dallas, Texas: Word Books, 1989), 151. For attribution to ancient authors, cf. the Apocalypse and Testament of Adam, the Books of Enoch, The Treatise of Shem, and the Testament of Job. Matthias Delcor follows Rowley in arguing that the book of Daniel establishes the precedent for pseudonymity in later works (Delcor, *Le livre de Daniel* [Paris: J. Gabalda, 1971], 13–14).

[8] Dan 1:3–6. Bel OG, by contrast, describes Daniel as a priest of the tribe of Levi; Josephus (*Ant.* 10 § 265) also refers to Daniel as a priest.

reliable historical reports.[9]   Instead, we appear to be dealing with a coalescence of legends.[10]   Above and beyond the historical issues of the book of Daniel, evidence that legends tended to accumulate around Daniel includes the following facts:

(1) The Greek versions of Daniel contain additional stories and a dramatically expanded version of chapter 3.

(2) Source-critical studies suggest that the stories in Daniel 1-6 and the Greek additions developed from earlier sources which in most cases did not refer to Daniel at all.[11]   One can easily imagine, for instance, that the Susanna story originally featured an anonymous "young man," although Daniel's name has now been inserted a few times (five in OG, six in TH).[12]

(3) Qumran's "Prayer of Nabonidus" parallels Daniel 4 in important ways but does not (in the known fragments) name the king's Jewish exorcist as Daniel.[13]

---

[9] For specific arguments and bibliography, see any recent critical commentary on Daniel.

[10] Legends might have gathered around the name because of its meaning, its ancient associations, the adventures of an actual courtier named Daniel, or the appearance of the name in Ezekiel, Ezra 8:2, or Nehemiah 10:6. Ezra-Nehemiah seem likely sources since these books also contain the names of Daniel's friends (Hananiah in Ezra 10:28, Neh. 3:8,30, 7:2, 10:23, 12:12,41; Mishael in Neh. 8:4; Azariah in Ezra 7:1,3, Neh 3:23,24, 7:7, 8:7, 10:3, and 12:33). 1 Chr. 3:1 mentions a son of David named Daniel, probably unrelated to our problem. (Citations, here and throughout, follow the verse numbering of original language texts in their standard editions.)

[11] For detailed source analysis of Daniel 1-6 and Bel and the Dragon, see Lawrence M. Wills, *The Jew in the Court of a Foreign King: Ancient Jewish Court Legends*, HDR (Minneapolis: Fortress, 1990), 75-152. I discuss Wills's work further below, beginning on p. 43.

[12] Charles James Ball, after citing a number of Jewish parallels to Susanna, points out that "the conception of Daniel as a judge cross-questioning the witnesses is conspicuous by its absence from the Talmudic and Midrashic stories about the wicked prophets and about Susanna." He concludes from this that Daniel was not part of the source tradition. Ball, "The Additions to Daniel," in *Apocrypha of the Speaker's Commentary*, ed. Henry Wace (London: John Murray, 1888), 2:328.

[13] J. T. Milik, "'Prière de Nabonide' et autres écrits d'un cycle de Daniel," *RB* 63 (1956): 407-11. Frank Moore Cross offers an improved suggestion for assembling the fragments, along with an English translation of the text, in "Fragments of the Prayer of Nabonidus," *IEJ* 34 (1984): 260-64.

(4)   Qumran's Cave 4 also yields three Aramaic fragments in which Daniel discourses on past and future history. These scenes do not occur in any known copies (in any language) of the book of Daniel.[14]

(5)   Josephus's *Antiquities* describes Daniel building and presiding over a royal burial tower in Ecbatana.[15]   Again, this occurs in no known form of the book of Daniel.

(6)   We know that such legend cycles built up around other similar figures in Hellenistic times.[16]

(7)   Daniel stories continue to emerge in post–biblical sources. At a minimum, this shows Daniel an attractive subject for storytelling. In some cases, the stories may reflect traditions as old as the biblical ones.

Dating the Greek Versions of Daniel

When Origen compiled his Hexapla in the early third century C.E., two different versions of the book of Daniel were in use by the church: the LXX version, attributed to the same translators as the rest of the accepted Greek Bible, and one attributed by Origen to Theodotion, a translator who worked (according to Epiphanius) in the late second century C.E.   By the time Jerome made his Vulgate translation (late fourth century C.E.), "Theodotion's" translation had completely displaced the earlier version in church usage.[17]

The LXX version, which we shall refer to as the OG (since the version which now appears in the LXX is Theodotion's), comes to us in a very limited number of manuscripts: (1) a Syriac translation of Origen's Hexapla (the Syro–Hexapla or SyrH); (2) a ninth–century manuscript known as Codex Chisianus or simply "88"; and (3) Papyrus 967, a second–century manuscript (thus, pre–hexaplaric) published in the 1960s and 70s.[18]   Citations from OG Daniel also appear in many early Christian writings.

---

[14]   Milik, 411–15.

[15]   Josephus *Ant.* 10 §264.

[16]   Wills, 39–74.

[17]   "The Septuagint version of Daniel the prophet is not read by the Churches of our Lord and Saviour," Jerome says in the opening sentence of his "Preface to Daniel," NPNF Series 2, 6:492.

[18]   Since it lacks Hebrew and transliteration columns for these books, the Syro–Hexapla is sometimes referred to (more correctly) as the Syro–Tetrapla. Field listed the OG portion of the manuscript from the Chigi library as 87, and its TH portion as 88.   Current usage generally follows Holmes and Parson in referring to the entire manuscript as 88.   Papyrus 967 also contains Ezekiel and part of Esther. Unfortunately, the codex was torn and the bottoms of the pages are missing throughout

The second version, attributed to Theodotion, appears in all other manuscripts and underlies all versions of the additions other than the Old Latin and the Syro–Hexapla mentioned above.[19] While we shall see that this textual tradition probably predates Epiphanius's Theodotion, for convenience we shall continue to refer to it as TH. Critical editions containing the two versions in parallel have been prepared by Alfred Rahlfs and Joseph Ziegler. We shall use Ziegler's more comprehensive and commonly cited edition as a base, with modifications in the OG (discussed in the opening sections of chapters 4 and 5) to accommodate the witness of the more recently published Papyrus 967.[20]

When were the OG and TH translations of Daniel made? Scholars usually date the Semitic text of Daniel to the mid–160's B.C.E. based on the shift from *vaticinium ex eventu* to genuine prophecy at about Dan 11:40 (the chapter correctly describes oppression under Antiochus Epiphanes up through desecration of the Temple and the Maccabean response, but errs when predicting the final events of Antiochus's life). While one may certainly conclude that a major edition of the book, including its apocalyptic chapters, must have been released at that point, we must also reckon with the fact that the OG seems to represent a text type *older* than that of the MT = TH.[21] The OG does contain the

---

Susanna and Bel and the Dragon. See Angelo Geissen, *Der Septuaginta-Text des Buches Daniel: Kap. 5-12, zusammen mit Susanna, Bel et Draco, sowie Esther Kap. 1,1a-2,15, nach dem Kölner Teil des Papyrus 967*, Papyrologische Texte und Abhandlungen no. 5 (Bonn: Rudolf Habelt, 1968); and W. Hamm, *Der Septuaginta-Text des Buches Daniel. . .nach dem Kölner Teil des Papyrus 967*, Papyrologische Texte und Abhandlungen, nos. 10 (Daniel 1-2) and 21 (Daniel 3-4) (Bonn: Rudolf Habelt, 1969). F. C. Burkitt argues that the Old Latin translation of Daniel also stems from the OG, in *The Old Latin and the Itala* (Cambridge: Cambridge University Press, 1896).

[19] Thus, the Vulgate, Arabic, Armenian, Sahidic, Bohairic, and Ethiopic follow TH. So does the Peshitta, although it expands on the story. Carey A. Moore, *Daniel, Esther, and Jeremiah: The Additions*, AB (New York: Doubleday, 1977), 34.

[20] Joseph Ziegler, ed., *Susanna, Daniel, Bel et Draco, Septuaginta*, Vetus Testamentum Graecum auctoritate Societatis Gottingensis editum, vol. XVI, part 2 (Göttingen: Vandenhoeck & Ruprecht, 1954); Alfred Rahlfs, *Septuaginta*, 2 vols. (Stuttgart: Deutsche Bibelgesellschaft, 1953; one-volume edition, 1979). Variations between the texts of these two editions are are minor, especially in the additions, but they number verses differently. My OG Susanna follows Helmut Engel's revision of Ziegler in *Die Susanna-Erzählung: Einleitung, Übersetzung und Kommentar zum Septuaginta-Text und zur Theodotion-Bearbeitung* (Freiburg: Universitätsverlag, 1985; Göttingen: Vandenhoeck & Ruprecht, 1985), 78-85. Henry Barclay Swete's *Old Testament in Greek*, vol. 3 (Cambridge: University Press, 1894) also contains both versions.

[21] For a thorough demonstration of this with respect to Daniel 2-6, see Wills, 75-152.

much-cited shift in chapter 11, so it cannot be dated earlier than 165 B.C.E., but if it also represents an older text type than the MT, then the Semitic book (in the text type we have) must have undergone significant editing *after* splitting from the text tradition from which the OG was translated—in other words, it must have undergone significant editing *after* the Maccabean crisis.

The greatest differences between OG and MT/TH occur in chapters 4-6. Papyrus 967 (mid-2nd century C.E.) places chapters 5 and 6 of Daniel *after* chapters 7 and 8, another indication that this section of the book was still in flux.[22] This runs contrary to the usual assumptions that the legendary core of Daniel (chs. 1-6, 2-6 or 2-7) stabilized in approximately its present form *before* the Antiochan crisis.[23] Later in our study (chapter 7) we shall attempt some reflection on the implications of the fact that it is the legendary rather than the apocalyptic part of Daniel which seems to have undergone the greatest post-Antiochan evolution.

To say that the OG appears to translate a more "primitive" form than the MT does not rule out post-Antiochan evolution for the Greek book. Daniel 9:26 OG adds seventy to the period of seven-and-sixty-two weeks, thus giving a more distinctly Antiochan date,[24] and its expanded version of 9:27 makes clear that many "weeks" will elapse between removal of the abomination and the final fulfillment. This redating of the end suggests a lapse of some decades since the Temple's rededication.

This gives us a *terminus a quo* of perhaps 135 B.C.E. for the OG. What evidence have we for the *terminus ad quem*?

---

[22] Geissen 12-13, 31. This puts the chapters in proper order with respect to the dates of the events they purport to record. One might explain this as a peculiarity of this particular copy; or our other, post-hexaplar sources may have rearranged the LXX's chapters to align them with the MT/TH standard.

[23] This view received classic expression in H. Louis Ginsberg's *Studies in Daniel*, Texts and Studies of the Jewish Theological Seminary of America, no. 14 (New York: Jewish Theological Seminary of America, 1948). Harold H. Rowley countered by arguing for "The Unity of the Book of Daniel," *The HUCA* 23 (1950-51): 233-73, reprinted in *The Servant of the Lord and Other Essays on the Old Testament* (London: Lutterworth, 1952), 237-68. Although the Greek evidence clearly implies that it was the legendary part of the book, not the apocalyptic part, which was last to take its present form, commentators continue to treat the apocalyptic chapters as younger—probably reflecting the critical tendency to think in terms of Ur-forms rather than final ones.

[24] Goldingay, xxvi, points out that the 139th (7 + 70 + 62) year of the Seleucid era would be about 172 B.C.E.

(1)   The Greek version of 1 Maccabees appears to cite the OG of Daniel in several places, meaning that the OG must have been available by the time 1 Maccabees was translated (ca. 100 B.C.E.).[25]

(2)   Several commentators believe that the OG of Daniel comes from the same translator as the LXX of Chronicles, Ezra, and Nehemiah.[26]   The Jewish historian Eupolemus, who wrote around 150 B.C.E. (his work is cited by Eusebius) appears acquainted with the LXX of 2 Chr 2:12ff.[27]   Thus Daniel, if translated by the same person, could not have come too many decades after 150.

(3)   The Susanna story appears to reflect a milieu in which the Jewish community possesses major powers of self-determination, and in which, in fact, the major threats are posed by internal corruption (of an occasional, not systemic nature: see chapter 4) rather than by external powers. This would seem to point toward a Hasmonean milieu (providing this version of Susanna comes from the OG translator of Daniel proper).[28]

Together, these considerations suggest a date in the late second century B.C.E., probably in the range of 120–135, for the OG translation of Daniel. Tradition locates the translation in Alexandria; modern study has produced no reasons for disputing this.[29]   As numerous

---

[25] James A. Montgomery (*A Critical and Exegetical Commentary on the Book of Daniel*, ICC [New York: Scribner, 1927], 38) summarizes the evidence, with references to earlier commentators.   Only one of the cited parallels (1 Macc 1:9 ἐπλήθυναν κακὰ ἐν τῇ γῇ = Dan 12:4 OG) points clearly to the OG rather than TH.

[26] Ibid., citing Gwyn, Thackeray, Riessler, and Torrey.

[27] Eusebius *Praeparatio evangelica* 9.31, cited by Henry Barclay Swete, *An Introduction to the Old Testament in Greek*, rev. Richard Rudsen Ottley (Cambridge: Cambridge University Press, 1914; reprint, Peabody, Massachusetts: Hendrickson, 1989), 370 (page references are to reprint edition).

[28] Those commentators who raise the question, "does the OG of the additions come from the same source as the OG of Daniel proper?" unanimously answer "yes," citing similarity of style. However, this assumption has never been subjected to the kind of testing TH has undergone (see discussion beginning on p. 33 below). For an alternative view on milieu, see Michael Heltzer, "The Story of Susanna and the Self-Government of the Jewish Community in Achaemenid Babylonia," *AION* 41 (1981), 35–39.   Those who follow Nehemiah Brüll's theory that Susanna is a *Tendenzschrift* related to legal proceedings ("Das apokryphische Susanna Buch," *Jahrbuch für jüdische Geschichte und Literatur* 3 [1877]: 1–69) usually also follow his dating of the story to the time of Alexander Jannäus (early first century B.C.E.). Since I reject Brüll's theory (see discussion below, beginning on p. 49), I feel unconstrained by his date.

[29] Thus Pfeiffer deals with the question in a single sentence: "No one doubts that the LXX of Daniel was prepared in Egypt, presumably at Alexandria." Robert H. Pfeiffer, *History of New Testament Times with an Introduction to the Apocrypha* (New York: Harper and Brothers, 1949), 440.

commentators remark, the motif of worshiping live snakes does fit well with an Egyptian milieu.

What about the date of TH? Here we face a puzzle, for although Epiphanius dates Theodotion to 180 C.E., Theodotionic readings appear in sources written *before* 180 C.E. The most famous "anachronistic" readings from TH Daniel occur in the New Testament. Heb 11:33, for instance, uses wording (ἔφραξαν στόματα λεόντων) far closer to Dan 6:23 TH (ἐνέφραξεν τὰ στόματα τῶν λεόντων) than to the OG (σέσωκέ με ὁ θεὸς ἀπὸ τῶν λεόντων). Likewise Matt 28:3 (τὸ ἔνδυμα αὐτοῦ λευκὸν ὡς χιών) seems to allude to Dan 7:9 TH (τὸ ἔνδυμα αὐτοῦ ὡσεὶ χιὼν λευκόν), rather than the OG (ἔχων περιβολὴν ὡσεὶ χιόνα). Theodotionic influence may also be seen in allusions to the coming of One Like A Human Being (ὡς υἱὸς ἀνθρώπου, Dan 7:13). In the OG this figure comes *on* (ἐπί) the clouds; in TH, *with* (μετά) the clouds.[30] Matt 24:30 and 26:64 and Rev 14:14 follow the OG. Mark 14:62 and Rev 1:7 follow TH.[31]   (For a helpful summary of lists of "Theodotionic" allusions in the Apocrypha and Pseudepigrapha, New Testament, and early Christian writings, see Schmitt.[32])

These and other clues led Dominique Barthélemy to decide, in an important 1963 study based on first-century (C.E.) fragments of the minor prophets, that the so-called Theodotion recension does not come from a late second-century translator, but belongs to the καίγε group[33] produced in the first half of the first century C.E., perhaps by Hillel's disciple Jonathan ben Uzziel.[34] The motivation for the new translation, according to Barthélemy, was an effort to combat heresies, including nascent Christianity, among Greek-speaking Jews.

Pierre Grelot developed the thesis further in a 1966 article building on Barthélemy's results. He explains the joint presence of OG and TH readings from Daniel in early Christian citations (including the New Testament and especially Revelation) as resulting from a situation in which both Greek versions were held as authoritative: the OG in its own

---

[30] Interestingly this key verse contains yet another important variation: in TH the One Like a Human Being comes *to* (ἕως) the Ancient of Days, while the OG has this person coming *as* (ὡς) the Ancient of Days (Ziegler emends, Rahlfs does not).

[31] Mark 13:26 and Luke 21:27 use ἐν, perhaps influenced by theophany traditions in which God comes *in* cloud.

[32] Armin Schmitt, *Stammt der sogenannte "Θ"-Text bei Daniel wirklich von Theodotion?*, Mitteilungen des Septuaginta-Unternehmens, vol. 9 (Göttingen: Vandenhoeck und Ruprecht, 1966), 12–14.

[33] So called because it tends to render גם as καίγε.

[34] Barthélemy, *Les devanciers d'Aquila*, VTSup 10 (Leiden: E. J. Brill, 1963), 148–155.

right as the received text of the Greek-speaking church/synagogue, and TH as a witness to the contemporary Semitic form of the book (which, Grelot argues on the evidence of TH, at this point contained the deuterocanonical additions in Hebrew and/or Aramaic).[35]

In the same year (1966) Armin Schmitt published a major study entitled *Stammt der sogennante "Θ"-Text bei Daniel wirklich von Theodotion?*[36] After minute examination of additions, omissions, alterations, translation patterns for specific Hebrew words, and a number of characteristic syntactical configurations in the "sogenannte 'Θ'-Text bei Daniel," Schmitt answers his title question with a clear "No." This comes as no surprise, given the observations already made about early citations of TH readings.

Barthélemy's work had appeared after most of Schmitt's research was done, but Schmitt does discuss Barthélemy's book briefly in the final pages (15-16) of his introductory chapter. In response to the earlier scholar's conclusions, Schmitt excludes the minor prophets and 2 Sam 11:2 to 1 Kgs 2:11 from his reference base of TH readings. Because Barthélemy's texts were excluded from Schmitt's comparative base, Schmitt's conclusion does not rule out close connection between the "Theodotion" text found in Daniel and that of the Deuteronomistic history or the prophetic texts studied by Barthélemy.

In a separate chapter devoted to the deuterocanonical portions of Daniel, Schmitt concludes that (1) "Theodotion" depends on the OG (not a new contention); (2) these portions do not come from the Theodotion who translated the portions of scripture which Schmitt uses as a reference base (again no surprise); (3) we might be looking at Symmachus's work; and (4) the uses of δεσπότης, ὑπό, δέ, γάρ, instrumental dative, conjunctive participles, οὐδέ, and the genitive of reflexive pronouns suggest that the deuterocanonical "Theodotion" material comes from a different hand than that at work in the "Theodotion" version of Daniel proper.[37]

Barthélemy responds to Schmitt in a 1977 article which charges Schmitt with presenting a special pleading rather than a balanced assessment of evidence, and with basing his argument on rare exceptions to a pattern rather than the pattern itself. He points out that by Schmitt's own evidence, TH Daniel shows the same major characteristics as other TH manuscripts. He charges that Schmitt gives insufficient weight to

---

[35] Pierre Grelot, "Les versions grecques de Daniel," *Bib* 47 (1966): 381-402.

[36] Schmitt.

[37] Schmitt, 110-12.

the recensional character of TH (as a revision of the OG, not a fresh translation) and that he conceptualizes Theodotion as a single person working with mechanical consistency, rather than realistically as a much less consistent editor or, quite possibly, different editors belonging to the same school. (If the different TH recensions come from different translators of the same school, which shall we take as the standard, the "real Theodotion"? Barthélemy, citing Origen's letter to Africanus, nominates the Daniel translator). Barthélemy explains the relatively few, but real, contradictions between readings found in Daniel TH and other Theodotionic material as points where the recensionist simply left the base version unchanged, or, more rarely, as later tampering. In this article Barthélemy also reaffirms his dating of the TH recension to 30–50 C.E.[38]

Another response to Schmitt came from J. R. Busto Saiz in 1980.[39] Busto Saiz (who published a major work on Symmachus in the Psalms two years earlier) denies Schmitt's tentative suggestion that the "Theodotion" of the deuterocanonical sections might actually be Symmachus, since the Daniel material clearly revises the OG, whereas, he says, Symmachus undertakes an entirely new translation.

Busto Saiz explains the observed differences between TH's style in Daniel proper and in the additions by positing that the recension of Daniel was guided by reference to a Semitic version, while the additions represent simple editing. This, however, introduces an awkward catch into the reasoning, for the one characteristic of "Theodotion" upon which everyone agrees is that this translator/reviser was concerned to produce a Greek edition faithful to the contemporary Hebrew/Aramaic. As Grelot and others have asked, would such a translator concern him- or herself with material not present in the Semitic text, let alone undertake major revisions of and additions to such extra material?[40]

---

[38] Barthélemy, "Notes critiques sur quelques points d'histoire du texte," in *Übersetzung und Deutung*, festschrift for Alexander Reinard Hulst (Nijkerk: Callenbach, 1977), 9–23; also published as a chapter in *Études d'histoire du texte de l'Ancien Testament*, OBO 21 (Fribourg: Editions Universitaires, 1978; Göttingen: Vandenhoeck and Ruprecht, 1978), 289–303. The first part of the article responds to a different controversy involving Frank Cross and does not concern us here. The response to Schmitt occupies pp. 17–21 of the 1977 publication.

[39] J. R. Busto Saiz, "El texto teodociónico de Daniel y la traducción de Símaco," *Sef* 40 (1980): 41–55.

[40] Note that according to Origen (*Ad Africanum* 2) Aquila did not include the additions (to Dan 3, at least). The examples of Origen and Jerome show that translators concerned with fidelity to the Semitic version might still transmit the Greek additions—but Origen and Jerome were constrained by established Christian usage. Would the same situation have obtained for a first-century Jewish translator?

On the one hand, it is difficult to explain TH's inclusion of the additions, except by their presence in a Semitic source. But if "Theodotion" had such a source for the additions, we must rule out Busto Saiz's explanation of the stylistic divergences documented by Schmitt. My own studies introduce an additional complication, for it appears probable that the TH translator of Bel and the Dragon did not use OG as a base at all. Verbatim overlap occurs in only about 20 percent of the text.[41] (This estimate is, if anything, too generous.) The verbatim repetitions are short—none involves more than a dozen contiguous words[42]—and often interrupted.[43] Most involve stock phrases.[44] Almost a third of each version[45] consists of "unique" material—phrases present in one version but not the other[46] and events which vary substantively between versions.[47] The quantity (small) and quality (brief, often interrupted, conventional expressions) of repetition suggests that the texts may be independent translations of rather different source texts, rather than an original and its revision.[48]

In Susanna we find a somewhat different situation. TH's Susanna is more than a third again as long as the OG and over a third of it presents material not present in the other version.[49] Yet almost a quarter of the OG text is repeated verbatim in TH,[50] and here the verbatim repetitions occur in long, distinctive chunks, mostly in dialogue and typically at crucial junctures of the plot.[51] This pattern suggests that TH indeed used the OG as a base, while expanding it significantly.

---

[41] Something like 184 words, of the OG's 894 and TH's 863.

[42] If we accepted the 88/SyrH reading in 5 we would have one stretch of thirteen or fourteen identical words: "[the] God who created heaven and earth, and has sovereignty over all flesh."

[43] E.g., OG 20, "And the king said, 'of men and women and children'"; compare TH 20, "And the king said, '*I see the tracks* of men and women and children'."

[44] E.g. συμβιωτὴς τοῦ βασιλέως (2); "and the king said to Daniel" (24).

[45] 282 of 894 words in the OG; 280 of 863 in TH.

[46] E.g. OG 19, "Behold the deception of the priests!"

[47] E.g. 17. In the OG Daniel asks the priests and the king to inspect the seals. In TH the king asks Daniel to inspect them.

[48] Moore (119–20) suggests that in Susanna the OG translates an early Aramaic version, and TH a later Hebrew version.

[49] About 427 of TH's 1133 words and 89 of the OG's 811 fall into this category.

[50] About 198 words.

[51] E.g., Susanna's refusal of the elders' proposition (22–23), her prayer (OG 35a, TH 42–43), and large chunks of Daniel's court speeches (52–59).

If it is true that TH's Susanna adapts OG Susanna (with or without reference to a contemporary Semitic version) while TH's Bel and the Dragon presents translates a Semitic original varying significantly from the OG *Vorlage*, without reference to the OG, then the transmission history of Greek Daniel is even more complicated than current theories suggest, and resists explication (at least, on the basis of present information). We do know, however, that it eventuated in the OG and TH collections we now have, and on that empirical basis I shall deal with each version as a single entity when I discuss the Greek books of Daniel in chapters 6 and 7.

Where did this activity take place? Irenaeus describes Theodotion as an Ephesian.[52] Barthélemy rejects this in favor of a Palestinian locale, since he identifies "Theodotion" with Jonathan Ben Uzziel,[53] but Thackeray cites linguistic evidence to support placement of at least the Samuel/Kings portion of the καίγε tradition in the Ephesian area.[54] A 1973 study by Koch which deals specifically with Daniel approaches the matter by considering the Aramaic endings of TH's transliterations, the titles used in Dan 3:2, and the promotions described in Dan 3:97. Koch's evidence points toward a Syrian location (not as far west as Ephesus?) in Roman times.[55]

Combining the evidence, we find a locale with a significant Jewish presence, where both Greek and Aramaic figure as important languages, with a history of Seleucid government and close to the eastern or southern edges of Asia Minor. Ephesus fits except for the

---

[52] ... ὡς Θεοδοτίων ἡρμήνευσεν ὁ Ἐφέσιος καὶ Ἀκύλας ὁ Ποντικός, ἀμφότεροι Ἰουδαῖοι προσήλυτοι (Irenaeus *Adversus Haereses* 3.30.5).

[53] Barthélemy, 148–156. He also cites a tomb inscription on the Mount of Olives bearing the name ΘΕΟΔΟΤΙΩΝΟΣ (156).

[54] H. St. John Thackeray, *The Septuagint and Jewish Worship: A Study in Origins*, 2nd ed., The Schweich Lectures, 1920 (London: Oxford University Press, 1923), 25–28. (Thackeray, by the way, anticipates Barthélemy in proposing that "Ur-Theodotion" must have antedated Aquila.) The argument involves a rare word for traveler, πάροδος, found in tomb inscriptions only from Lesbos, Smyrna, Laodicea, Cos, Aegiale (a Milesian colony), and on an Italian monument erected by a Laodicean. These locations are all very close to Ephesus. Sidney Jellicoe enthusiastically endorses Thackeray's location (although he prefers an earlier date), in "Some Reflections on the καιγε Recension," *VT* 23 (1973): 15–21, 1973.

[55] Klaus Koch, "Die Herkunft der Proto-Theodotion-Übersetzung des Danielbuches," *VT* 23 (1973): 362–65. In particular, στρατηγός as a civil title points to Syria, τοπάρχης for satrap seems to rule out Egypt, and ὕπατοι for city rulers indicates Roman times. Koch himself concludes that the translation comes from "der syrisch–mesopotamische Raum mit seinen hellenisierten Städten in Übergang von der seleukidischen zur römischen Herrschaft" (364).

history of Seleucid government.[56] A location such as Antioch or Laodicea answers everything but the specific association with Ephesus. One might posit a translator from Ephesus working in Syria, or vice versa, but this is sheer speculation. In my discussion I shall take Ephesus and Antioch as representative possibilities for the sorts of Hellenistic Jewish communities likely to have produced this version.

Interpretation of the Greek Daniel Legends

How did the Greek Daniel legends[57] affect the faith of those who read (or heard) them? The most straightforward way to answer this question is to see what ancient readers wrote about them, so we shall open this section of the chapter with a look at ancient comments on the stories. Then we shall see what light modern scholarship has thrown upon Bel and the Dragon and Susanna.

Ancient Readings

As we survey ancient discussions of the Greek Daniel legends, two general approaches can be distinguished. The dominant approach takes the legends at face value as stories about people named Daniel, Susanna, and so forth. Another, less common, reads the stories as elaborate allegories of events past, present, and to come.

The first (and more familiar) approach is admirably illustrated by a controversy between Origen and Julius Africanus in the late second or early third century C.E. Africanus charges that Susanna, although "elegantly written, is plainly a more modern forgery," for not only does Daniel prophesy in a style quite unlike his usual one of visions and dream interpretation, but the crucial puns on tree names in vv. 54–55 and 58–59 depend on *Greek* roots. Furthermore, charges Africanus, the living conditions portrayed in the story are quite unrealistic for exiles.[58]

Origen's reply begins with a defense of the LXX. He of all people (as he points out) is intimately acquainted with the divergences

---

[56] Ephesus was indeed under Seleucid rule at one point, but far earlier than the period which concerns us. Michael Grant, *From Alexander to Cleopatra: the Hellenistic World*, Collier Books (New York: Scribner, 1982; reprint, New York: MacMillan Publishing Company, 1990), 106. Page references are to reprint edition.

[57] Here we shall concentrate on those Daniel stories found ONLY in Greek (Susanna and Bel and the Dragon).

[58] Sextus Julius Africanus *Epistula ad Origenem*. Cited from *The Writings of Origen*, ANF (Edinburgh: T. & T. Clark, 1871) 10:369–70.

between Greek and Hebrew versions of the Old Testament. But he asks whether

> . . .when we notice such things, we are forthwith to reject as spurious the copies in use in our churches? . . . Are we to suppose that that Providence which in the sacred Scriptures has ministered to the edification of all the churches of Christ, had no thought for those bought with a price, for whom Christ died? . . . In all these cases consider whether it would not be well to remember the words, "Thou shalt not remove the ancient landmarks which thy fathers have set."[59]

Origen posits that the story's negative portrayal of elders accounts for its absence from Hebrew scripture, and cites Tobias and his brother Dachiacharus (Tobit 1), along with Mordecai and Nehemiah, as evidence of the well-being possible for Jews in exile. Likewise he appeals to scriptural examples to defend the modes of prophecy (sudden seizure, citation of scripture) used by Daniel in the story. The objection to Greek puns gives him the most difficulty; here he can say only that since his Jewish informants were unable to give him the Hebrew words for σχῖνος and πρῖνος, he can hardly rule out the possibility of a corresponding pun in Hebrew.

The arguments here sound strikingly like those of modern historical–critical scholars (which doubtless explains why this exchange is quoted so frequently). Both parties assume a link between authority and historicity; and both assess the case according to modern–sounding criteria of historical and literary probability and consistency.

At about the same time as Africanus and Origen were penning their exchange, a Christian scholar named Hippolytus produced a commentary on Daniel (packaged with the book in Codex Chisianus). Hippolytus reads the stories at two levels which we might term historical and figurative. At the historical level he takes up questions similar to those raised by Africanus, such as whether captives would have had the power to decide their own legal affairs. Here his arguments have a distinctly apologetic air.

At the figurative level Hippolytus is guided by (although not limited to) an allegorical scheme:

> Susannah prefigured the Church; and Joacim, her husband, Christ; and the garden, the calling of the saints, who are planted like fruitful trees in the Church. And Babylon is the world; and the two elders are set forth as a figure of the

---

[59] Origen *Epistula ad Africanum* 4, 5 (ibid. 371–5).

two peoples that plot against the Church—the one, namely, of the circumcision, and the other of the Gentiles.[60]

Yet the function of this scheme is less to draw arcane conclusions from the book than to help the Christian church find itself in the story of a Jewish woman:

> All these things were figuratively represented in the blessed Susannah, for our sakes, that we who now believe on God might not regard the things that are done now in the Church as strange, but believe them all to have been set forth in figure by the patriarchs of old.[61]

The final conclusion is not different than that which might be derived from a straightforward reading:

> To all these things, therefore, we ought to give heed, beloved, fearing lest any one be overtaken in any transgression, and risk the loss of his soul, knowing as we do that God is the Judge of all; and the Word Himself is the Eye which nothing that is done in the world escapes.   Therefore, always watchful in heart and pure in life, let us imitate Susannah.[62]

We need to exercise caution here, first because both Origen and Hippolytus write about two centuries later than the production of Theodotion's translation, and second because the writings of educated commentators may or may not reflect the reactions of the community at large. Nonetheless, these writings from the early centuries of the church provide a touchstone against which to test our eventual conclusions about the theological functioning of the Greek Daniel legends.

Modern Readings

The Protestants who have dominated modern biblical scholarship have paid far less attention to the Daniel additions than to the rest of the book.[63] But as interest in early Judaism has increased, these stories have received correspondingly more attention, especially since the late

---

[60] Hippolytus *Commentarium in Danielem*, English translation in ANF (Grand Rapids, Michigan: Eerdmans, 1891), 5:184.

[61] Ibid., comment on v. 18.

[62] Ibid., comment on v. 61.

[63] Two tendencies are at work here.   One is Protestant/Roman Catholic polemic, resulting in decreased attention to parts of the Roman Catholic canon which have been rejected by Protestant churches. The other is the fact that Protestants are Christian, and the apocalyptic images of Daniel loom so large in Christian thought that the book's non-apocalyptic portions, canonical or otherwise, get relatively short shrift.

nineteenth century. What have modern scholars done with the stories of
Susanna and Bel and the Dragon?

In the 1890s, Roman Catholic scholar Anton Scholz published a
set of thoroughly allegorical interpretations of Susanna and Bel and the
Dragon, as well as other canonical and deuterocanonical books.[64]
Scholz claimed, with Hippolytus as precedent, that his approach more
accurately discerned the ancient meanings of the books than did the more
straightforward readings of Protestant commentators. Like Hippolytus,
he sees Susanna as the (Christian) church, but he presses the allegory
farther and in different directions. His most novel claim, with respect to
Susanna, is that the trees named by the elders have specific
religious/messianic connotations, so that the responses given by the
elders in 54 and 58 are actually coded acknowledgments of Susanna's
innocence.[65]

Scholz takes a similar approach to Bel and the Dragon, interpreting it as "eine der veilen Darstellungen der Kämpfe des Reiches Gottes,
namentlich der letzten Zeit, wie Ezech. Cpp. 38.39."[66] The sheep,
flour, wine, and oil given to Bel become the people of God offered to
the devil, the "false door" of Bel 17 a deliberate counterpoint to the
"true door" of John 10:9, and Habakkuk's ἄριστον a symbol of the messianic banquet.[67]

While Scholz's aggressively Christian interpretations hardly suffice as explanations of the "original" (pertaining to the time of translation) meanings of these Jewish books,[68] the Targums and rabbinic
legends offer proof that this *general* approach to interpretation was not
unknown to the Jewish community. Thus, without endorsing Scholz's
program in all its details, I shall bear his readings in mind as I turn to
the tales in question.

Virtually all other modern scholars have followed the lead of
Africanus and Origen in focusing (positively or negatively) on the "plain
sense" of the stories, often advancing theories about derivation or genre
as keys to interpretation. Most seem to take it as self-evident that the

---

[64] The titles which concern us are *Commentar über das Buch "Esther" mit
seinen Zusätzen und über "Susanna"* and *Commentar über das Buch "Judith" und über
"Bel Und Drache"* (Würzburg: Leo Woerl, 1892 and 1896).

[65] Scholz, *Susanna*, 149-52.

[66] Scholz, *Bel und Drache*, 201.

[67] Ibid., 206, 213, 228.

[68] While Susanna and Bel and the Dragon are certainly Jewish in origin, I
must allow that the TH *of the additions* might possibly be Christian. Scholz, however,
applies his method to *both* versions, sometimes appealing to the OG to clarify allusions
which he feels have been obscured in TH.

"religious meaning" of the stories lies in the example of virtue and faith set by Susanna and (to a lesser extent) Daniel, or in assurance that God will protect the faithful.

Beyond these generalities, interpretations of Bel and the Dragon and Susanna have gone in different enough directions that we shall discuss the modern interpretive histories of the two stories separately. Unless otherwise indicated, the interpretations are based upon the TH version. Only a few very recent studies have attended to the OG as a distinct voice.

Modern Interpretations of Bel and the Dragon

Two issues dominate discussions of Bel and the Dragon: source and genre. Source discussion often begins with questions of historicity and almost always ends up concurring with Jerome's evaluation of the tale as a "fable."[69] Along the way, however, we may receive a great deal of interesting information about Bel, snake worship, and priestly impostures in the ancient world.[70] Source critics have also called attention to possible links between this story and the ancient tale of Marduk's battle with Tiamat. Such connection may offer the best explanation of Daniel's puzzling snake–poison recipe.[71] A final type of source criticism, which regards Bel and the Dragon as haggadic elaboration, calls our attention to other biblical texts which may have provided the stimulus for this process.[72]

These modes of approach often focus so intensely on identifying sources and previous forms that they pass quickly over features of the text as it finally stands. However, the connections pointed out by such

---

[69] Jerome, in "Preface to Daniel," NPNF, Second Series, 6:492-3.

[70] For a thorough review of these matters see Ball, 344-58. Further information on the snake question comes from Simon Landersdorfer, "Der Drache von Babylon," *BZ* 11 (1913): 1-4.

[71] Frank Zimmermann, "Bel and the Dragon," *VT* 8 (1958): 438-40. For more general discussion of the Marduk connection, Ball is again helpful. This history-of-religions approach dominates Crawford H. Toy's article "Bel and the Dragon" in *The Jewish Encyclopedia* (New York: Funk and Wagnalls, 1905), 2:650-51.

[72] Modern commentaries tend to give great credence to this approach. The seminal article is Nehemiah Brüll's "Die Geschichte von Bel und dem Drachen," *Jahrbuch für jüdische Geschichte und Literatur* 8 (1887): 28-29; Ball provides an excellent summary in English. Andres Pezard follows the process into post-biblical times in "Betrice et les soupes d'Habacuc," in *Melanges d'histoire des religions*, ed. A. Bareau (Paris: Presses Universitaires de France, 1974): 557-68.

research will prove valuable to us when we turn to investigating inter-textuality in the Greek Daniel legends (chapter 6).

More recently, a great deal of attention has been paid to the issue of genre in Bel and the Dragon. Two major hypotheses have been advanced, one focusing on the story's court setting and associated conflicts, the other on its ridicule of pagan worship.

Consideration of the story as a court tale received an important stimulus from W. Lee Humphreys's 1973 article entitled "A Life–Style for Diaspora: A Study of the Tales of Esther and Daniel." Noting the tension between the violent ethnic conflict reflected by Esther and Daniel in their final forms, and the fact that both books involve protagonists who actively participate, *and prosper*, in the affairs of foreign courts, Humphreys posits that the pre–apocalyptic form of Daniel and the pre–Purim form of Esther were both examples of "a common literary type that was quite popular in the Near East of this period: the tale of the courtier."[73] These tales, he believes, exemplify the attitude recommended by Jeremiah in his letter to the exiles (Jer 29:4–7):

> The possibilities of life in contact and interaction with things foreign is affirmed; there has been no polarization of the situation. . . . One could, as a Jew, overcome adversity and find a life both rewarding and creative within the pagan setting and as a part of this foreign world; one need not cut himself off from that world or seek or hope for its destruction.[74]

The social function of these stories would be to encourage Diaspora Jews to participate actively in the life of their new communities without giving up their Jewish identity.

In his discussion of Daniel 1–6, Humphreys distinguishes two subtypes of the courtier story. In *tales of court conflict*,

> one faction seeks the ruin of the other; the tale centers on this, and in the resolution, the due punishment of the one and the reward of the other side are noted.[75]

Daniel 3 and 6, the story of Esther and Mordecai, *Aḥiqar*, and parts of Nehemiah's story are tales of court conflict.

In *tales of court contest*,

---

[73] W. Lee Humphreys, "A Life–Style for Diaspora," *JBL* 92 (1973): 211–23, quote from p. 217. Other courtier tales he cites are the Joseph novella, *Aḥiqar*, and elements of Nehemiah's story.

[74] Ibid., 221, 223.

[75] Ibid., 219.

the form is that of a contest: the hero succeeds where all others fail. The resolution notes the reward of the hero, but not necessarily the punishment of those who fail (although this can be present at least as a threat, as in Daniel 2).[76]

Daniel 2, 4, and 5 and Genesis 40–41 provide examples.

Humphreys makes no direct mention of Bel and the Dragon. His scheme, however, is taken up and developed by Lawrence M. Wills in a dissertation entitled *The Jew in the Court of a Foreign King: Ancient Jewish Court Legends*. Wills carefully reviews the debate over the genre(s) of the biblical court legends and concludes, "The definition of genres. . .can proceed along different lines; different sets of criteria give rise to different groupings of exempla of the genre, which can be conceived, for instance, in overlapping circles."[77] He himself uses a multiplex scheme which attends not only to motifs and plot, but to theme, character, intention, and audience.[78]

Wills contends that in general the ancient Near Eastern court legend functions "as a propaganda device to assert ethnic identity."[79] The Jewish stories in particular reflect "the orientation of the administrative and entrepeneurial class."[80] Accepting Humphreys's distinction between the court contest (Daniel 2, 4, 5) and the court conflict (Daniel 3, 6), Wills discerns an emphasis in the former on mantic (specially revealed) wisdom, granted to those of the relevant ethnic group (Jews). In the conflict stories, where Jewish courtiers experience persecution rather than friendly rivalry from other courtiers, Wills finds an increasing emphasis on "witness," explicit loyalty to the ethnic practices setting the Jews apart from others. According to Wills, the Daniel corpus develops away from focus on ethnic identity (which is, however, never

---

[76] Ibid. Susan Niditch and Robert Doran criticize Humphreys for methodological looseness because he fails to specify the diachronic pattern of contest tales. They relate Daniel 2, Genesis 41, and *Aḥiqar* 5–7 to Aarne/Thompson's Type 922, the tale of "Clever Acts and Words," and propose a four–step plot outline for such tales. See Niditch and Doran, "The Success Story of the Wise Courtier: A Formal Approach," *JBL* 96 (1977), 179–93; and Antti Aarne, *The Types of the Folktale: A Classification and Bibliography*, second revision, trans. and enlarged by Stith Thompson, Folklore Fellows Communications no. 184 (Helsinki: Academia Scientarum Fennice, 1961), 320–322.

[77] Wills, 12.

[78] Ibid., 2.

[79] Ibid., 150.

[80] Ibid., 197.

quite lost) toward focus on issues of righteousness and obedience.[81]
This puts Daniel 1-6

> in an intermediate position between the bourgeois novellas—including the
> other court legends—and the pious protests of the apocalypses: the "ruled eth-
> nic perspective" for Daniel 1-6 is not that of "Jews" but of "righteous Jews."
> What is lacking in a comparison with the later Jewish apocalyptic writings is
> any accounting for unrighteous Jews.[82]

Wills's study of Bel and the Dragon has a decidedly redaction-
critical cast; he proposes "not just that Bel and the Dragon and Daniel 6
are similar and variants of the same story, but also that the story now
attested only in the Greek Bible is an *older* version of the one in the
MT."[83]   This helps explain the puzzling motifs of sealing with the
king's ring and executing the priests' families, which form logical parts
of the plot in Bel and the Dragon (where it is important to establish
whether the temple has been tampered with, and where the wives and
children participate in the fraud) but seem slightly out of place in Daniel
6 (where application of a signet to a lion pit is not merely odd, but
"practically impossible," and the wives and children are not mentioned
prior to their destruction).[84] Wills suggests that a line of development
can be discerned from Bel and the Dragon OG to Bel and the Dragon TH
to Daniel 6 OG to Daniel 6 MT; indeed he goes so far as to suggest that
Bel TH may once have stood where Daniel 6 does now.[85] Intriguing as
these suggestions are, he does not supply a proposal as to how the earliest element in his sequence, Bel OG, came to be attached to a book
containing the third element (Daniel 6 OG), while the "intermediate"
element, Bel TH, first comes to our attention in conjunction with the
most developed Greek version of Daniel (containing Daniel 6 TH).

True to his contention that genre descriptions are an attempt to
characterize multifaceted, often overlapping phenomena, Wills finds

---

81 Ibid., 148-51.

82 Ibid., 151-52. I find the last sentence here patently inappropriate with
respect to Susanna, which explicitly deals with unrighteousness within the Jewish community. Wills, however, considers Susanna representative of "a broader, pan-Jewish
perspective" (151). Wills's main treatment of Susanna is very brief (76-79); he speaks
of it as an "adaptation of the standard court legend genre to a Jewish middle-class
audience" (77).

83 Ibid., 134.

84 Ibid., 135-36.

85 Wills discusses the sequence on 137, making his suggestion about Bel TH
in n. 121.

traces of prophetic legend[86] and idol parody[87] as well as court legend in Bel and the Dragon. He summarizes the differences between the additions (with an eye primarily to the two versions of Bel and the Dragon) and the stories of Daniel 1–6 as follows:

1) Daniel 1–6 emphasize an interventionist theology while the additions do not to the same extent;

2) Daniel 1–6 are in general more negative toward the king than the additions. . . .

3) the crisis in Daniel 1–6 is not intentionally initiated by the heroes, as it is in Bel and the Dragon;

4) in Daniel 1–6 the heroes maintain their observances, while in Bel and the Dragon they destroy others'; and

5) there is no reductionistic explanation of idols in Daniel 1–6, as there is in Bel and the Dragon.[88]

Wills also offers some observations on the relations between the two Greek versions of Bel and the Dragon. The OG, he notes, emphasizes the hero more than the king, who is not named. TH uses more "up-to-date" theological language ($εἴδωλα$ $χειροποίητα$ rather than $οὐδένα$; $ζῶντα$ $θεόν$ rather than $κύριον$ $τὸν$ $θεόν$; and, possibly, omission of the oath for theological reasons). Lack of burial appears as a concern in the OG but not TH. TH has a friendlier king but a correspondingly heightened level of threat from the priests and people, "which perhaps reflects a heightened expression of ethnic competition and defensiveness."[89] This reminds one of the redactional tendency toward greater ethnic tension observed by Humphreys in the MT versions of Esther and Daniel.[90]

Mockery of idol-worship is undeniably a theme of the Bel and the Dragon story. It appears most devastatingly in Daniel's own words, first his observation with respect to Bel that "This one is clay on the inside and brass on the outside," and then his remark over the snake's blasted body: "Look at your objects of worship!"[91] Commentators can

---

[86] In the OG only, ibid., 129 n. 102.
[87] Ibid., 131–33, see below for further discussion.
[88] Ibid., 133–34.
[89] Ibid., 130–31.
[90] Humphreys, 222–23.
[91] Bel 7, 27 TH.

scarcely miss the point, so that Charles Ball, for instance, after an exhaustive source discussion, concludes that

> Jeremiah furnishes the motive, which the Haggada has developed in its own fashion, turning the prophet's poetic imagery and metaphor into coarsely concrete matter of fact; but at the same time illustrating in a highly effective manner *the prophet's own moral of the utter futility of idols*, and the sole sovereignty of the God of Israel."[92]

Similarly William Daubney remarks,

> It is evidently desired to put both idols and idolaters into ridiculous positions, not for mere amusement, but in order to destroy the confidence which was groundlessly placed in them.[93]

In 1975, Wolfgang Roth presented an argument that idol parody is not merely an occasional phenomenon, but a distinct genre. Starting with the idol parodies of Deutero-Isaiah, he describes a thee-part structure. The *introduction*, comprised of real or rhetorical questions or a provocative thesis statement, is "designed to raise unequivocally the issue with those who don't care to have that issue raised or who do not see there an issue at all." The *main section* of the idol parody focuses on the idol's production, with the idol maker the subject and the idol itself merely an object. This section bears formal resemblance to a participial hymn, but its content stresses the idol maker's need of encouragement, limited strength, profane use of associated materials, and the lifelessness of the product. The *conclusion* "describes the effect of the idol fabrication on its producers and worshipers; it 'applies' the argument to the hearers and so has like the introduction an address-like character."[94]

After exploring other early postexilic parodies in Habakkuk, Jeremiah, and Psalms, Roth turns to Hellenistic Jewish texts: Baruch, *Jubilees*, Wisdom, and Bel and the Dragon. Of Bel and the Dragon he says,

> In the literary execution of both the idol and the dragon sections (3–22/23–27), the genre of the idol parody is, next to the pattern of the paradigmatic encounter story, the formative element. 5–7 and 24–25 correspond to the

---

[92] Ball, 346, emphasis added.

[93] William H. Daubney, *The Three Additions to Daniel* (Cambridge: Deighton and Bell, 1906), 195.

[94] Wolfgang M. W. Roth, "For Life, He Appeals to Death (Wis 13:18): A Study of Old Testament Idol Parodies," *CBQ* 37 (1975): 21–47, basic structure described 22–28, quotes from 27 and 28.

introduction of the parody in that the temptation of idolatry and even more of zoolatry is sharpened into an either/or issue by the pagan king's question and by the Jew's credal affirmation. 8-20 and 26-27a correspond to the main section of the idol parody in that a narrative review of the idol's and dragon's inability to protect themselves is presented. Vss. 21-2, 27b show by way of conclusion how both the idol and the beast are left in pieces, obviously without the divine power claimed for them.[95]

In fact, Roth argues,

> the beast's death is the climax of the composition; the idol's destruction merely leads up to it. Evidently the worship of living beasts is at stake, a practice attested for Egypt and attacked in Wis. 15:18-19 and Aristeas 138. This suggests that Dan. 14 originated as a Daniel-type confrontation story in Egyptian Jewish circles where zoolatry was perceived, over and above idolatry, as a possible or real temptation.[96]

In fact, Bel and the Dragon diverges from Roth's model in several ways, the most significant of which is its narrative character—although Roth recognizes that the idol parody is here secondary: "the genre of the idol parody is, *next to the pattern of the paradigmatic encounter story,* the formative element."[97] Secondly, while Daniel does take a more aggressive role in this story than in those of Daniel 1-6, both incidents (especially that of the snake!) are, in fact, provoked by the king's questions, meaning that the king does not belong entirely to the category of "those who don't care to have that issue raised or who do not see there an issue at all."[98]

Finally, I wonder if Roth assumes too quickly that the presence of idol parody means that idol (or animal) worship was a live temptation for the story's audience. Roth himself observes that by the time of his Wisdom and *Jubilees* texts, idolatry was "not one possible temptation but *the* antithesis of Judaism."[99] If idol worship is indeed the defining characteristic of the "not-Jew," and if Wills is right about the function of the court-legend as a celebration of ethnic identity, then the parody in Bel and the Dragon may function less to dissuade Jews from idol worship than to underline the stupidity of non-Jews.[100]

---

[95] Ibid., 43.

[96] Ibid.

[97] Ibid., emphasis added.

[98] Ibid., 27.

[99] Ibid., 47.

[100] Wills discusses Roth's thesis at some length (131-33), with general approval. He does not comment one way or the other on the issue I have just raised.

While the studies reviewed here provide a great deal of helpful information about Bel and the Dragon's history, theology, and life-setting, only Wills provides fruitful comment about the effects of the differences between the two Greek versions.   Furthermore, scholars have been inclined to discuss the story in terms of a single *Tendenz*, rather than recognizing that a single narrative typically reflects and reinforces (or challenges) many different aspects of worldview simultaneously.

Finally, almost no attention has gone to the narratological functioning of the story.   For instance, the debate over genre has produced various descriptions of plot structure, but description has stopped with mere lists of the sequence of events; no one has moved beyond this to explore the effects of this sequence (or other story features) on the reader.

The lack of true narrative analysis is perhaps illustrated by Carey A. Moore's commentary, which is one of the best in its effort to explore the Daniel additions as literary phenomena and which even includes subsections entitled "Literary Merit."   Moore evaluates Bel and the Dragon TH as superior because it has "a greater use of emotive words . . . shows a preference for having its characters speak *to* the deity rather than *about* him," and "has greater precision and specificity,"[101] while he prefers the OG version of The Snake because it is "better edited (see e.g. the LXX's 'in that place' in vs. 23), and is more simple and precise in its content."[102]   Despite Moore's respect for the additions as storytelling, he does not explain why emotive words, or simplicity and precision, should be regarded as merits, or what narrative purposes may be served by their presence (or absence) in a particular version.   Ultimately, Moore's criterion for literary merit becomes "the 'test of time,' i.e. the frequency, extent, and length of times a literary work is quoted or alluded to."[103]   This criterion is, as he recognizes, awkward, since citation of a story involves other aspects besides its literary excellence.   He neglects to mention that the test of time is also subject to severe cultural bias as literary tastes and conventions change.

There remains, then, a great deal to do in exploring the narrative features of the two Greek versions of Bel and the Dragon, and their relation to the literary and theological currents of their ancient communities.

---

[101] Moore, 139.
[102] Ibid., 147.
[103] Ibid., 27–8.

Modern Interpretations of "Susanna"

Unlike Bel and the Dragon, which often seems to be treated merely as an appendix to Daniel 1-6, the story of Susanna has received a great deal of attention in its own right. A few scholarly interpreters, such as Wiederholt, have followed Origen in defending the story's essential historicity.[104] Another small minority, caught up in turn-of-the-century enthusiasm for comparative religion, saw Susanna as a secular version of a love goddess bringing destruction to human admirers.[105] More recently, Michael P. Carroll, in a quite different "mythological" approach, has argued that Esther, Judith, and Susanna are transformations of a single myth, in accordance with Lévi-Straussian theory.[106]

An influential thesis advanced by Nehemiah Brüll in the late nineteenth century related Susanna to rabbinic controversies over judicial proceeding, particularly with respect to cross-examination of witnesses and punishment of false witnesses.[107] This thesis has now fallen largely by the way, for as Walter Baumgartner forcefully points out, Daniel's approach in "Susanna" hardly provides a technically correct model for judicial proceedings.[108] Rabbinic connections and parallels discerned by Brüll nonetheless remain influential in Susanna studies. His citations

---

[104] Theodor von Wiederholt, "Die Geschichte der Susanna," *TQ* 51 (1869): 383-94. William H. Daubney's position on the matter is difficult to pin down, but at points he also seems inclined to a defense, albeit very guarded, of Susanna's basic historicity (e.g. 122-23, 142-48, esp. 148).

[105] For references see Pfeiffer, 452-53.

[106] Michael P. Carroll, "Myth, Methodology and Transformation in the Old Testament: The Stories of Esther, Judith, and Susanna," *SR* 12 (1983): 301-12. Carroll also draws in the haggadic story of Ahab and Zedekiah's attempted seduction of Nebuchadnezzar's wife. He presents his study as a methodological test for the location of transformational series; he does not discuss Susanna in terms of mediation and "meaning."

[107] Nehemiah Brüll, "Das apokryphische Susanna Buch," *Jahrbuch für jüdische Geschichte und Literatur* 3 (1877): 1-69. I have been unable to consult Brüll's work directly, so my discussion depends on secondary reports of it in Ball, 323-343 (the primary English-language explication of Brüll's thesis); Walter I. Baumgartner, "Susanna—die Geschichte einer Legende" (*ARW* 24 [1926]: 259-80, reprinted in *Zum Alten Testament und seiner Umwelt* [Leiden: E. J. Brill, 1959], 42-66); and Engel, 49-52. Brüll uses legal parallels to date Susanna to the period of Alexander Jannäus, 107-75 B.C.E., a dating which many scholars seem to retain even while discarding the juridical interpretation which underlies it.

[108] Baumgartner, 48-49. Note that Daniel condemns both elders before hearing their testimony (52-3, 56-7), and pronounces judgment on the first before hearing the second (55).

have called attention to the fact that Susanna, like Bel, involves midrashic elaboration on other scriptural traditions, especially from Jeremiah. As with Bel, however, scholars seem to accept the parallels without inquiring what bearing they have on the story's meaning—an issue we shall take up in chapter 6. The ties to rabbinic judicial procedure first indicated by Brüll have been used to clarify just how old a νεώτερος probably is.[109]

Although the "folkloric" character of Susanna's story had been noted at least since the time of Africanus, vigorous inquiry into the story's folk connections got its modern start with a 1912 article by Gedeon Huet.[110] Taking the story's essential non-historicity as given, Huet pointed out Susanna's similarity to several other stories from widely varying milieux in which children unmask falsehood by clever questions.

Walter Baumgartner picked up the folklore theme in two articles in the 1920s. Concurring with Huet that the "wise child" motif appears in Susanna, he points out that this aspect dominates only the final judgment scene, while the story as a whole reflects another folklore motif, that of the innocent woman attacked by rejected lovers.[111] But while "Susanna" may have begun life as profane entertainment, says Baumgartner, it has subsequently acquired an educational character. Thus finally he links up with the dominant interpretive line which sees in Susanna "an example of life and instruction of manners."[112]

Both the midrashic connections pointed out by Brüll and the shaping influence of international folklore motifs have now been generally accepted as part of Susanna's heritage; more recent scholarship has turned to questions about the literary art and theological nuances of their combination in the two rather dramatically different Greek versions of Susanna.

---

[109] E. Stauffer, "Eine Bemerkung zum griechischen Danieltext," in *Donum Gentilicium*, ed. E. Bammel, C. K. Barrett, and W. D. Davies (Oxford: Clarendon, 1978), 27–39.

[110] Gedeon Huet, "Daniel et Susanne: Note de littérature comparée," *RHR* 65 (1912): 277–84. Huet elaborates further in "Daniel et Susanne," *RHR* 76 (1917): 129–30.

[111] Baumgartner, "Susanna"; and "Der weise Knabe und die des Ehebruchs beschuldigte Frau," *AfR* 27 (1929): 187–88. Both are reprinted in *Zum Alten Testament und seiner Umwelt* (Leiden: E. J. Brill, 1959), 42–67. Page references are to reprint edition. Further parallels for the wise child and accused wife (Genoveva) motifs, along with references to Aarne's *Index*, appear in Bernhard Heller's "Die Suzannerzählung: Ein Märchen," *ZAW* 34 (1936): 281–87.

[112] Daubney, 173.

Robert Dunn's article on "Discriminations in the Comic Spirit in the Story of Susanna" combines Proppian analysis with literary methodology to explore the role of laughter in the two Susanna stories.[113] While the applicability of Propp's categories (derived from Russian heroic fairy tales) to a Near Eastern story with a female protagonist might well be questioned, the point Dunn develops is simply that "only in the Septuagint do we have a real 'helper' figure."[114] "This minor difference," he continues,

> makes necessary a major distinction between the sub-genres of the two versions. . . .The Septuagint is what I would call a martyr tale, or a kind of saint's legend, in that the divine controls the victim-saint's fate and directs the defense presented by Daniel. Theodotion is a wisdom tale, for here the human hero's wit, although inspired by God, is sufficient to save Susanna.[115]

Dunn goes on to explore characterization and the narrator's roles. He explains that in the OG,

> the end of human possibility is the beginning of divine action. Laughter signals the wonderful recognition that human actions do not matter and that heaven will act miraculously to defend innocence.[116]

TH's comedy, by contrast,

> is social and satiric. It is based on the ability of a zealous young person, inspired of God, to beat the corrupt system.[117]

Dunn's analysis, while very limited in scope, suggests something of the riches to be discerned through the application of modern literary criticism to these ancient texts.

Joakim Schüpphaus has also compared the OG and TH versions (of all three additions) and concludes that OG Susanna is a story about

---

[113] Robert Dunn, "Discriminations in the Comic Spirit in the Story of Susanna," *Christianity and Literature* 31, no. 4 (Summer, 1982): 19-31.

[114] Ibid., 22. Dunn justifies his use of Propp's categories by appeal to the generally recognized folkloric character of the stories. For proposals about tales with female lead figures, see Heda Jason, "The Fairy Tale of the Active Heroine: An Outline for Discussion," in *Le conte, pourquoi? comment?* ed. G. Galame-Griaule, V. Görög-Karady, and M. Chiche (Paris: CNRS, 1984), 79-97; and especially Ilana Dan, "The Innocent Persecuted Heroine: An Attempt at a Model for the Surface Level of the Narrative Structure of the Female Fairy Tale" in *Patterns in Oral Literature*, ed. Heda Jason and Dimitri Segal (The Hague: Mouton, 1977), 13-30. For Dunn's limited purposes I am inclined to say, "if Propp's scheme works, use it."

[115] Dunn, 22-23.

[116] Ibid., 24.

[117] Ibid., 25.

judges, with special stress on the opposition between the lawlessness of the old judges and the cleverness and integrity of the young man who saves Susanna.   The purpose of this story, he says, is to show the excellence of the young and call for support and utilization of their abilities, that they may in turn guarantee and guard the rights and laws of the faithful.[118]

TH, says Schüpphaus, becomes a story about *Susanna*, who in steadfast purity sets her hope on God, and is vindicated in her innocence. He sees behind this story a community pressed from without and within by the godless.   The conclusion, "They praised God, who saves those who hope in him" (60), points to the theological lesson TH hopes to instill.[119]

A similar but far more detailed study on the two versions of Susanna was published by Helmut Engel in 1985. Engel's work, like Wills's analysis of Bel and the Dragon, displays a distinct redaction-critical slant: Engel spends considerable effort in nailing down the conclusion that TH is a revision of the OG.   But, having criticized earlier studies for a tendency to take TH as normative and treat the OG only as a variation of it, Engel also attends closely to the OG as an independent piece of literature.[120]

A major question in the study of OG Susanna has been, "How did the story open?"   The Chigi manuscript (88) and the Syrohexapla both incorporate hexaplaric markings suggesting that vv. 1–5a were imported into the OG text from other versions.[121]   But most commentators have found it impossible to believe that the OG opened with περὶ ὧν ἐλάλησεν . . . Both Rahlfs and Ziegler assume that the markings are misplaced and begin their OG text at verse 6 (καὶ ἤρχοντο κρίσεις . . .); various proposals have been made as to what would have preceded this in the original.

Discovery and publication of the pre-hexaplaric Papyrus 967 have shed new light on the question, as this version, too, appears to begin with the contested περὶ ὧν ἐλάλησεν . . .[122] After discussing

---

[118] Joakim Schüpphaus, "Der Verhältnis von LXX- und Theodotion-Text in den apokryphen Zusätzen zum Danielbuch," *ZAW* 83 (1971): 68–69.

[119] Ibid., 67.

[120] Engel sets out his program in conjunction with a very illuminating review of past studies in the introductory chapter, 9–77.

[121] Manuscript 88 uses the lemniscus to mark this section and ascribes it in the margin to Aquila, Symmachus, and Theodotion. The Syriac uses obeli and ascribes the section to Symmachus and Theodotion (Ziegler, 81).

[122] Geissen, 280.

whether the story might have opened on the (missing) bottom of the previous page of the papyrus, and concluding that it probably did not, Engels appeals to 1 Cor. 7:1 as evidence that περὶ ὧν can indeed be used to open a discourse, serving to introduce the topic of discussion (that is, in the case of Susanna, the theme–text which the subsequent story will elucidate).[123]

Engel then takes the citation in 5b, along with the OG conclusion in verse 62a,b,[124] as his hermeneutical keys for interpretation of the OG story. Like Schüpphaus (whose work he quotes with approval), he concludes that the OG is a story fundamentally concerned with the abuse/preservation of justice in a community, employing a contrast of age and youth much like that reflected in *Jubilees*. TH, by contrast, propagandizes for a virtuous, Torah–revering life. TH's revision of the story, says Engels, is characterized by (1) stylistic smoothing (which in this case includes Semiticization of the language); (2) eroticizing and psychologizing; (3) individualizing and historizing; and (4) corresponding revision of the conclusion.[125]

Engel finds "wisdom narrative" an appropriate general classification for the two stories but feels that further distinction between the two is desirable: the OG is an ecclesial didactic story with a sermonic outlook, while TH is a legendary wisdom didactic story.[126]

In Chapter 2 we saw that a comprehensive narrative analysis should look at a story's plot, character, tone, and atmosphere, and that a variety of critical approaches are needed to comprehend this range of material. Engel's superb study, which combines a redaction–critical interest with fine–grained composition criticism, provides a wealth of information about tone and some good observations on character. Dunn's study too focuses primarily on tone. Each notes the structural contrast between elders and youngers but does not develop the observation with respect to other structural elements in the narrative. Neither engages in a sustained narratological look at the plot of the story (for instance, what is the effect of moving Susanna's prayer from 35a in

---

[123] Engel, 12–15.

[124] Ziegler's numbering; 63 in Rahlfs.

[125] Engel, 177–83.

[126] ". . . der-LXX Text als eine *theologische Lehrerzählung mit paränetischer Absicht* und die Th–Bearbeitung als *legendhafte weisheitliche Lehr- oder Beispielerzählung*" (ibid. 177, original emphasis, see also Engel's n. 8 on "theologische"). Prior to this Engel discusses Weimar's classification of the stories as "novellistische Erzählung" and "Lehrerzählung mit aretalogischem Gepräge," and also reviews Müller's criteria for the "weisheitliche Lehrerzählung," a category he considers more appropriate for TH's Susanna than for the OG (175–77).

the OG to 42–43 in TH?).   While both acknowledge the presence of intertextual "tags" in the story, neither attempts to elucidate the interplay between Susanna and related texts such as Jeremiah.

Thus, while Engel's work (and, to a much more limited extent, Dunn's) provides a solid foundation upon which to build, a great deal remains to be explored, especially with respect to Susanna's plot, characters, and narrative horizons.

Chapter 4

BEL AND THE DRAGON

Having surveyed methodological issues and reviewed previous studies of the Greek Daniel legends, we turn to the stories themselves— Bel and the Dragon in this chapter, Susanna in chapter 5. I shall begin by presenting translations of Bel and the Dragon in its two versions. I organize subsequent discussion by the levels of Mieke Bal's paradigm:[1] "fabula," "story," and "text." To avoid duplication, I do not present a verse–by–verse close reading. Instead, I incorporate observations on composition into the translation notes and narratological analysis.[2] Intertextual dynamics and narrative horizons will be dealt with later (chapters 6 and 7).

Bel and the Dragon in English

Base Texts

The standard critical texts of Bel and the Dragon appear in the Göttingen Septuagint, edited by Joseph Ziegler.[3] As noted in chapter 3, however, Ziegler's text was prepared before Geissen's publication of the

---

[1] Presented in Mieke Bal, *Narratology: Introduction to the Theory of Narrative* (Toronto: University of Toronto Press, 1985).

[2] See especially the section on "tone" in the text–level analysis.

[3] Joseph Ziegler, ed., *Susanna, Daniel, Bel et Draco*, in *Septuaginta*, Vetus Testamentum Graecum auctoritate Societatis Gottingensis editum, vol. 16, no. 2 (Göttingen: Vandenhoeck & Ruprecht, 1954). Ziegler's text of Bel and the Dragon agrees very closely with that prepared by Alfred Rahlfs, *Septuaginta*, 2 vols. (Stuttgart: Deutsche Bibelgesellschaft, 1935; combined volume 1979). (The one major difference is Rahlf's retention of ὁ βασιλεύς in TH 17.) Unfortunately, the two editions number verses differently; I follow Ziegler.

Bel and the Dragon portions of Papyrus 967 (OG).[4] Table 1 shows the points at which I depart from Ziegler's OG text (for discussion, see the notes). I adopt Ziegler's TH text unchanged.

Table 1.—Bel and the Dragon: Departures from Ziegler's Old Greek.

Verse	Change
5	Delete καὶ ἔχοντα πάσης σαρκὸς κυριείαν
21	εὗρον for εὗρε
28	Add πάλαι before 'Ιουδαῖος
34	Delete σοι Κύριος
36	Delete second αὐτοῦ
37	Delete Κύριος

Note: Minor variations in word order and spelling differences (e.g. addition or deletion of movable ν) are not included in this table.

Translations

The following translations use fairly colloquial language, conveying something of the Greek's own odd mixture of folk style and formal religious jargon. Subsequent discussions will introduce more "literal" translation as needed to clarify technical points. Notes begin on page 61.

---

[4] Angelo Geissen, *Der Septuaginta-Text des Buches, Daniel: Kap. 5–12, zusammen mit Susanna, Bel et Draco, sowie Esther Kap. 1,1a–2,15, nach dem Kölner Teil des Papyrus 967*, Papyrologische Texte und Abhandlungen (Bonn: Rudolf Habelt, 1968).

Old Greek

1. From the prophecy of Habakkuk (Jeshua's son, from the tribe of Levi).

2. There was a certain man, a priest, named Daniel (Abal's son), who was a companion of the king of Babylon. 3. And there was an idol, Bel, which the Babylonians revered. Every day twelve barrels of fine flour, four sheep, and six barrels of oil were consumed by it. 4. The king revered it. The king went every day and worshiped it; but Daniel prayed to Lord.

So the king said to Daniel, "Why don't you worship Bel?"

5. Daniel answered the king, "*I* revere none but the Lord God, Creator of heaven and earth."

6. The king asked him, "This is a god, isn't it? Haven't you seen how much is supplied to it every day?"

7. Daniel answered him, "Certainly not! Don't let anyone fool you: this is pottery on the inside, bronze on the outside; and I swear to you by Lord the God of Gods that this has never eaten anything."

8. Then the king got mad and called for the temple administrators. He said to them, "Show who eats Bel's provisions! Otherwise, you die—9. or Daniel, who says they aren't eaten by him."

They said, "Bel himself is the one who eats them!"

Theodotion

1. King Astyages was gathered to his fathers, and Cyrus the Persian took over his kingdom. 2. Daniel was a companion of the king, honored above all his friends. 3. And the Babylonians had an idol named Bel, and every day twelve barrels of fine flour, forty sheep, and six barrels of wine were supplied to it. 4. The king revered it, and went every day to worship it; but Daniel worshiped his own God.

So the king said to him, "Why don't you worship Bel?"

5. He answered, "I don't revere idols made with hands, but rather the living God, Creator of heaven and earth, who has dominion over all flesh."

6. The king asked him, "You believe Bel's a living god, don't you? Haven't you seen how much he eats and drinks every day?"

7. Daniel said, laughing, "No way, Your Majesty! This is clay on the inside, bronze on the outside, and has not eaten or drunk, ever."

8. Then the king got mad and called for his priests. He said to them, "If you don't tell me who eats up these supplies, you die—9. but if you show that Bel eats them up, Daniel dies, since he blasphemed against Bel."

And Daniel said to the king, "Let's do it this way: if I don't show you that it's not Bel who eats them, I'll die, and my folk with me."

And Daniel said to the king, "Let it be just as you've said."

10. Now, there were seventy Bel priests, aside from their wives and children. They led the king to the temple. The food was set out in front of the king and Daniel; mixed wine was brought and set out for Bel. Daniel said, "Your Majesty, you have seen for yourself that things are laid out. Let's have *you* seal the sanctuary doors, when it's locked." And it seemed a good idea to the king.

10. Now, there were seventy Bel priests, besides their wives and children.

The king went with Daniel to Bel's home. 11. And the Bel priests said, "Look. We're going outside. Your Majesty, let's have you set out the food yourself, mix the wine and put it out, lock the door and seal it with your own ring. 12. Then come early in the morning, and if you don't find everything eaten by Bel, we'll die—or Daniel, who's lying about us!"

13. Now, they knew they'd made a hidden entrance under the table, and they'd always come in through it and consume everything.

14. But Daniel ordered his folk that when they'd put everyone out of the sanctuary they should sprinkle the whole sanctuary with ashes, without anyone beside him knowing. Then he ordered the sanctuary sealed with the king's ring and the rings of some of the most important priests—and that's what happened.

14. So when they had gone out, the king set out food for Bel. But Daniel gave his servants orders, and they brought ashes and sprinkled the whole sanctuary, in front of the king alone. Then they went out, locked the door, sealed it with the king's ring, and left.

15-17. Now, the next day they arrived at the place—but the Bel priests had come in through secret doors and eaten up all Bel's provisions, and drunk down the wine. Daniel said, "Inspect your seals, priests, to see if they're still there. You too, Your Majesty. See if anything's gone wrong."

15. But the priests came in the night, as usual—their wives and children, too—and ate and drank everything up.

So the king got up very early, and Daniel was with him. He said, "Are the seals OK, Daniel?"

And they checked the seal's condition, and took the seal off.

And he said, "OK, Your Majesty."

Old Greek

Theodotion

18. When they opened the doors, they saw everything that was set out had been consumed, and the tables empty! The king was delighted, saying, "Bel is great! There's no trickery about him!"

19. But Daniel laughed uproariously and said to the king, "Look! See the priests' trickery!" Then Daniel said, "Your Majesty, whose tracks are these?"

20. And the king said, "Men's, women's, and children's!"

21. So he went to the house where the priests lived, and they found Bel's food and wine, and Daniel showed the king the hidden doors that the priests used to go in through and consume the things set out for Bel. 22. Then the king led them out of the Bel temple and handed them over to Daniel, and gave the supplies to him. But Bel, he overturned.

23. Now, there was a serpent in the same place, and the Babylonians revered it. 24. The king said to Daniel, "You can't say this one's bronze, can you? See, it lives and eats and drinks—worship it!"

26. Daniel answered, "Your Majesty, give me permission, and I'll do away with the serpent—without steel or stick!"

The king agreed. "You've got it!"

27. So Daniel took thirty measures of pitch, fat, and hair, boiled them together, made a ball, and put it in the serpent's mouth. It ate it and blew up.

18. And then, when the doors were opened, the king peeked in at the tables and shouted, "You're great, Bel! There's no trickery about you, not any!"

19. But Daniel laughed and held the king back from going inside. He said, "Look at the ground and realize whose tracks these are!"

20. And the king said, "I see the tracks of men, women, and children!"

21. Then the king got furious, and arrested the priests and their wives and children, and they showed him the hidden doors, that they used to go in through and eat up what was on the tables. 22. And the king killed them, and handed Bel over to Daniel, and he overturned it and its temple.

23. There was also a big serpent, and the Babylonians revered it. 24. The king said to Daniel, "You *can't* say that this isn't a living God—so worship it!"

25. Daniel answered, "I worship Lord my God, because *he* is a living god. 26. But you give me permission, Your Majesty, and I'll kill the serpent—without sword or stick!"

And the king said, "I'm giving it to you."

27. So Daniel took pitch, fat, and hair, boiled them together, made balls, and put them into the serpent's mouth. The serpent ate them and blew up. He

He showed it to the king. "Weren't you all revering these things, Your Majesty?"

28. Then the country's people gathered against Daniel, saying, "The king's become a Jew already—he overturned Bel and killed the serpent!"

30. The king, seeing the local crowd gathered against him, called for his companions. "I'm giving Daniel up to destruction."

31–32. Now, there was a pit in which they kept seven lions, and they handed traitors against the king over to them, providing them with two condemned bodies every day. So the crowd threw Daniel into that pit, that he might be consumed and never buried. And Daniel was in the pit for six days.

33. On the sixth day, Habakkuk had bread broken in a bowl of stew, and a skin of mixed wine, and was going to the field to the reapers. 34. Lord's angel spoke to Habakkuk and said, "Thus says God: 'Take that lunch you have to the lions' pit in Babylon, for Daniel'."

35. Habakkuk said, "Lord God, I've never seen Babylon. I don't know where the lion pit is!"

36. So Lord's angel took Habakkuk by the hair of his head and set him above the pit in Babylon.

said, "Look at these things you all have been revering!"

28. When the Babylonians heard, they got very upset and rallied against the king, saying, "The king's become a Jew—he smashed Bel, killed the serpent, and destroyed the priests!" 29. When they came to the king they said, "Hand Daniel over to us. If you don't, we'll kill you and your family."

30. The king saw that they were pressing him hard, and being in a bind, he handed Daniel over to them.

31. Now, they threw him into the lions' pit, and he was there six days. 32. There were seven lions in the pit, and every day they used to give them two bodies and two sheep, but now they didn't give them to them, so that they'd eat up Daniel.

33. Now, the prophet Habakkuk was in Judah, and he himself had boiled a stew, broken bread into a bowl, and was going out to the field to take it to the reapers. 34. But Lord's angel said to Habakkuk, "Take that lunch you have to Babylon, to the lions' pit, for Daniel."

35. Habakkuk said, "Lord, I've never seen Babylon. I don't know the lion pit!"

36. So Lord's angel took his head, and grabbing him by the hair of his head, whooshed him to Babylon above the pit.

Old Greek	*Theodotion*
37. Habakkuk said to Daniel, "Get up! Eat the lunch God's sent you!"	37. Habakkuk shouted, "Daniel! Daniel! Take the lunch God's sent you!"
Daniel answered, "Yes, Lord God remembered me! He doesn't forget people who love him."	Daniel answered, "Yes, you remembered me, God! You don't forget people who love you."
39. Then Daniel ate, and Lord's angel returned Habakkuk to where he'd taken him from that same day. So the Lord God remembered Daniel.	39. So Daniel stood and ate, and God's angel took Habakkuk back instantly to his own place.
40. Now afterwards the king went out, grieving for Daniel. He peered into the pit—and saw him sitting there! 41. The king shouted, "The Lord God is great, and there isn't any other than he!" 42. Then the king led Daniel out of the pit. But he threw the folks that caused his destruction into the pit in front of Daniel, and they were eaten up.	40. On the seventh day, the king went to grieve for Daniel. He came to the pit and looked in, and—look! Daniel, sitting there! 41. He yelled, "You are great, Lord, Daniel's God! There isn't any other than you!" 42. Then he pulled him out. But he threw the folks that caused his destruction into the pit, and they were eaten up instantly, right in front of him.

Notes

verse 1: The OG titles our story a prophecy of Habakkuk. Anton Scholz posits the existence of a "Habakkuk collection" containing Bel and the Dragon, Susanna, other stories about the two elders, Esther, the Midrashim of Daniel, Judith, Tobit, Habakkuk, and possibly other books.[5]

verse 3: Both tellers, but especially TH (καὶ ἦν Δανιηλ . . . καὶ ἦν εἴδωλον), make Bel a grammatical counterpart of Daniel. I render αὐτῷ/αὐτόν as "it" since the narrator clearly wishes to portray the idol as inanimate. "Revere" for σέβομαι distinguishes it from προσκυνέω; otherwise I would prefer "worship."

---

5 Anton Scholz, *Commentar über das Buch "Esther" mit seinen Zusätzen und über "Susanna"* (Würzburg: Leo Woerl, 1892), 136, which in turn references an article by Scholz in the *Tübinger TQ* (1890): 257. Sidney B. Hoenig suggests that "insertion of the Habakkuk element may be due to a gematria חבקוק = גור אריה, thus connecting the lion legends. This is found in a thirteenth-century record of R. Eleazar of Worms." Hoenig, "Bel and the Dragon," *IDB* 1:376.

verse 4: Both versions refer to the king's worship with a verb, προσκυνέω, that also appears in Exodus's prohibition of idolatry.[6] The OG uses a different word for Daniel's worship: "pray" (προσεύχομαι).

The OG here, and TH later, use κύριος as a proper name without article (much as Jews use the directly related "Adonai," Christians use "Christ," and both use "God"). I follow suit with anarthrous "Lord." I capitalize God (TH) for the same reason I refer to Bel as "it"—because for the ancient narrator, this one was clearly The (Only) God.

verse 5: Esther 13:10–12 also links Lord's creatorship to Jewish monolatry. SyrH and 88 add, with TH, "who has dominion over all flesh."[7] Since such a striking phrase is more likely to have been added in transmission than deleted, I follow 967's reading in the OG.

verse 6: As Moore observes, the OG shows faulty logic: "From what the king says in the LXX one might infer more about the great devotion of Bel's followers than about Bel's existence."[8] Attempting to show Bel's clear divinity, the king reveals his own gullibility.

An alternate translation for the king's question in TH, "Bel seems to be a living god, doesn't he?", leaves σοί implicit but captures the sense of εἶναι.[9] Ball finds irony in the king's argument: "a necessity of eating is proof not of divinity but of mortality."[10] Ancient pagan audiences might not have seen it this way, but the conventions of idol parody suggest that Jewish audiences concurred with Ball.

verse 7: In the OG Daniel responds to the king's implied argument (Bel eats what is supplied), not to his actual words (have you seen what is supplied?). Daniel does not (at this point) question "eating and drinking" as criteria for divinity. "God of gods" may have a polemic thrust since this was also a title of Marduk/Bel; or it may simply be a Semiticism for superlative divinity.[11]

I owe the phrase "Your Majesty" (TH) to Carey Moore.[12] Daniel is pushing it here, but not as much as the bare English vocative "king" would suggest.

---

[6] Exod 20:4–5, LXX. As presented in Exodus, of course, the prohibition is not addressed to foreigners.

[7] Note that these (SyrH and 88) are not independent witnesses since they both follow Origen.

[8] Carey A. Moore, *Daniel, Esther, and Jeremiah: The Additions*, AB 44 (New York: Doubleday, 1977), 135.

[9] Cf. BAGD, s.v. δοκέω 2a,b, and 3a.

[10] Charles James Ball, "The Additions to Daniel," in *Apocrypha of the Speaker's Commentary*, ed. by Henry Wace (London: John Murray, 1888), 2:353.

[11] On Marduk, ibid. On this construction as a superlative, Ronald J. Williams, *Hebrew Syntax: An Outline*, 2nd ed. (Toronto: University Press, 1976), 47.

[12] Moore, 130.

verse 8: Why does the OG refer to Bel's personnel as "temple administrators" here? (Later it uses "priests.") TH's king seems defensive and angry, stating the potential outcome negatively and interpreting Daniel's words as blasphemy. This is a little surprising since Daniel's own preceding statement is milder in this version. Perhaps his laughter accounts for the king's ire.

verse 9 : "Folk" (OG) in the sense of family or household, not in the sense of an entire people. Cf. v. 14.

verse 11: The wine might have been mixed with water (a Greco–Roman custom)[13] or spices (a Jewish custom).[14]

verse 14 (OG): Daniel's "folk" (τοὺς παρ᾽ αὐτοῦ) may be the same people Daniel put on the line at the end of v. 9. While a first-time reader would be baffled by the sprinkling (this version has not tipped us off to the priests' activities), this may be a story whose life lies in the re-reading (or re-hearing).[15]

verses 15-17 (TH): Nominative plus δὲ marks v. 15 as a narrator's aside (cf. 13, 31; nearly every other sentence in TH's narrative begins with καὶ). The verb for eating (κατεσθίω/κατέφαγον) echoes the king's challenge (8).

In v. 16, the king arrives "early," just as the priests instructed (12). The rare adjective σῷοι ("intact") may punningly remind us that the test is to show if Bel is a living (ζῶν) god.

verses 15-17 (OG): The text shifts from "seals" (Daniel's order to the priests) to "seal" (narrator's report). Perhaps the second σφραγίς means "lock" rather than seal, or the narrator's report refers specifically to the *king's* seal.

verse 18: TH's accent on σοί (normally enclitic) shows stress on the pronoun: "no trickery in *you*."[16] The superfluous "not one!" at the end of the king's statement helps convey his emotion.

---

13 Otto Fridolin Fritzsche, "Zusätze zu dem Buche Daniel," in the *Kurzgefasstes exegetisches Handbuch zu den Apokryphen des Alten Testaments*, ed. Otto F. Fritzsche and C. Grim (Leipzig: Weidmann'sche Buchandlung, 1851), 1:148.

14 Otto Zöckler, "Die erzählenden Zusätze zu Daniel," in *Die Apokryphen des alten Testamentes*, Kurzgefasstes Kommentar zu den Heiligen Schriften (München: Oskar Beck, 1892), ad loc. He cites Prov 9:2,5. Witton D. Davies points out Jewish dislike for the Greek custom (Isa 1:22) and adds Isa 5:22 to Zöckler's list ("Bel and the Dragon," *APOT* 1:660).

15 Cf. "The Three Little Pigs" or, on a more biblical note, Isaiah's "Song of the Vineyard."

16 Of course, this represents later interpretation of the originally unaccented Greek.

verse 19: Carey Moore, noting the Vulgate rendering of ἐγέλασεν as "smiled," translates "chuckled" here and in TH 7.[17] The verb ordinarily denotes stronger emotion—Jerome's translation softens the outrageousness of Daniel's behavior. In the OG, Daniel picks up the word "trickery" from the king's comment in v. 18. Bel is so impotent that even trickery must come from the priests, not the idol!

verse 21: I follow 967 and SyrH ("they found") rather than 88 ("he found"), because the former is more difficult. Divergence between SyrH and 88 increases the suspicion that 88's reading is a scribal correction.

Narratively, the OG slips here—according to vv. 15-17, the food and wine were consumed in the sanctuary. Both versions use vocabulary (δαπανάω, παρατίθημι) associated with the king's and Daniel's points of view, not the priests'.

verse 22: Neither version is absolutely clear about who destroys Bel. In the OG it is probably the king (subject of other verbs in sentence, parallel construction) but in TH it seems to be Daniel (since Bel has been handed over to him). Either way, the declaration conflicts with ancient historians' reports on destruction of the great temple of Bel.[18]

verse 23: Traditionally, δράκων has been translated by its English cognate, "dragon." Moore prefers "snake," arguing that the story clearly refers to a flesh–and–blood creature.[19] I choose "serpent," which combines reference to actual snakes with a mythological, "olden days" nuance.

While Bel was indeed a Babylonian god, the serpent presents more of a problem. A few argue that the Babylonians indeed engaged in live snake worship.[20] Others see a connection with the Babylonian creation legend, *Enuma Elish*, for it portrays Marduk/Bel in close association with the dragon or sea monster Tiamat. A hazy remembrance of this association may suffice to explain the juxtaposition of Bel and the serpent.[21] But this serpent is an actual snake rather than a long–dead mythological one—a feature reflective of Egyptian practice.

---

[17] Moore, 135-36.

[18] Moore (138) cites Herodotus 1.183, Strabo 16:1,5, and Arrian *Expedition of Alexander* 7.17.

[19] Ibid., 141-42.

[20] For a review of the controversy, see ibid., 122-25.

[21] This would explain the stories' stress on Lord's status as creator (5). For more on the serpent and its possible connections to Tiamat, see the discussion of "pitch, fat, and hair," p. 66.

verse 24: For the first time, the OG introduces "living" as a criterion for godhead. Explicit mention of eating and drinking strengthens ties to the Bel story in this version.

verse 26: Daniel responds (in both versions) by introducing a new criterion—can the object of worship be destroyed "without sword or club (ἄνευ μαχαίρας καὶ ῥάβδου, TH)"? Why these weapons? Is there a tradition of destroying serpents with swords/clubs?[22] Or are swords/sticks the obvious weapons for serpent–killing because they can be wielded from a distance?[23]

The OG's expression, "without iron[24] or a stick (ἄνευ σιδήρου καὶ ῥάβδου)," suggests another possibility. Many cultures attribute magical properties to iron. In the Hellenistic world, a stone related to iron was used as a remedy for snake–bite.[25] ῥάβδου, meanwhile, can mean not simply "stick" but "[magic] wand."[26] Thus Daniel's strange allusion may possibly mean (in the OG) that he proposes to dispose of the serpent without resort to magical arts, but if so, TH does not pick up on it.

verse 27: Thirty minas (OG) would be almost 38 pounds. If πίσσα refers to naphtha (rather than tar), the ball would be highly flammable. Did Greek serpents breathe fire? Again we wonder whether the narrators envision an ordinary snake, or a dragon–like being.

Marshall explains the ingredients of the cake on the basis of a presumed connection with the Tiamat story, arguing that "pitch" resulted from confusion of the Aramaic *wêpiʾ* (pitch) with *waʿapiʾ*(south wind,

---

[22] Ball and Zimmerman suppose some connection with the destruction of Tiamat, but Tiamat was destroyed by an arrow. Ball, 2:348-9; and Frank Zimmermann, "Bel and the Dragon", *VT* 8 (1958): 438-40.

[23] This would mean that the hard part of Daniel's deed was not making the concoction but administering it—something one does wonder about, but in which the storyteller exhibits no interest. (Also, were this the issue, we would again expect arrows to be the weapons of choice.)

[24] In the running translation I render σίδηρος as "steel," often used metonymically for sword in English (as in Greek here?). Steel may in fact have been used in this time. Robert A. Coughenour, "Iron," *HBD*.

[25] LSJ, s.v. σιδαρίτας. The definition cites Orphica *Lithica* 361, 390, 419.

[26] Ibid., s.v. A search for juxtapositions of "iron," "sword (μαχαίρα)," or "stick (ῥάβδος)" with δράκων in the Greek texts of the TLG CD-ROM produced a string of references to Moses's confrontation with the Egyptian priests (Ex. 7), which would tend to support the magical interpretation but does not explain the iron. *Pilot CD ROM #C*, copyright Thesaurus Linguae Grecae and the Regents of the University of California (Irvine, California: University of California, Irvine, 1987); searched with L-base for CD-ROM (Version 4.5e, Dallas, Texas: Silver Mountain Software, 1990).

used by Marduk/Bel to vanquish his foe).[27] Zimmermann presents a similar argument, contending since a human protagonist couldn't use wind, "wind" (סערה) was read in Aramaic as "barley" (סערתא—hence the μάζα or barley-cake), and in turn by the Greek translator as "hair" (סערה, סער). "So we have the unhappy translation that Daniel after mixing fat, pitch and hair made barley cakes to feed the dragon. The dragon, however, 'burst' from the original *sâru*."[28] One might also posit a connection with the legend of Alexander's destruction of a sacred snake using poison and tar.[29]

These speculations may historically clarify the odd ingredients, but if the Hellenistic storytellers were so far from the sources as to commit the posited confusions, we can hardly claim efficacious reference to the windy defeat of Tiamat. In the stories as they stand, Daniel's use of such unlikely—but successful—ingredients simply confirms his superior knowledge and ability.

Having eaten, the serpent dies not of constipation but by bursting.[30] (TH's report has a satisfying aural resonance: καὶ φαγὼν διερράγη ὁ δράκων). Daniel subsequently refers to objects of worship (plural, both versions[31])—perhaps because of the snake's exploded condition, or perhaps suggesting a more general question: "Your deities are this sort of thing?" He addresses a plural "you."

verse 28: I accept 967's "already" as a more difficult reading. For the third time, TH uses the word "Babylonians" in the first verse of a sequence (cf. 3, 23).

The people's opening charge introduces new information: we have had no previous hint of anything so drastic as the king's conversion.[32] While Daniel grouped the king with the people (plural "you"

---

[27] John T. Marshall, *Hastings Dictionary of the Bible* (New York: Scribner, 1901), s.v. "Bel and the Dragon."

[28] Zimmerman, 440. About pitch and fat, Zimmerman says only that they are "probably the proper ingredients to do away with the dragon" (438).

[29] References given ibid., 439 n. 3.

[30] διαρρήγνυμι. According to Liddell & Scott, this verb is also used for bursting from eating too much in Xenophon's *Institutio Cyri* 8.2.21, Anaxilas 25, and Phoenicides 3.

[31] The OG's *narrator* uses the singular, "it."

[32] Or, in the OG where they have gathered against *Daniel*, are they saying, "A Jew has become the king"? (Note that at least one of the following actions was Daniel's, not the king's.) Usual Greek syntax would make "the king" subject and "Jew" a predicate nominative, but *koine* Greek may sometimes have departed from this rule. For a recent survey of discussion (with references) on anarthrous nouns as subjects (although focused on εἰμί, not γίνομαι), see D. A. Carson, "The Purpose of the Fourth Gospel: John 20:3 Reconsidered," *JBL* 106 (1987): 642–43.

in 27), the people identify the king with Daniel—in the OG they credit the king with killing the serpent (which Daniel did); in TH he gets credit for destroying Bel as well (which Daniel seems to have done in this version). The people's report also seems (even more) unreliable in TH because they introduce new vocabulary: "hauled down" (κατασπάω) and "slaughtered" (κατασφάζω).

verse 30: "They pressed hard against him" is a strikingly physical, tactile metaphor in an overwhelmingly visual and verbal story. In the OG, the king's perception adds an additional preposition to the narrator's verb (συνάγω, ἐπισυνάγω) suggesting that he perceives the situation as even worse than it is.[33] With his own well-being at stake he switches to an active δίδωμι (cf. 26). This version displays a class-consciousness lacking in TH: the king perceives "those from the country" as "the crowd (ὁ ὄχλος)." He does not speak to them directly, but summons courtiers (τοὺς συμβιωτὰς αὐτοῦ, holders of Daniel's erstwhile status) to receive his decision.

verse 31: Once again TH uses nominative plus δέ (cf. 13, 15) to swing focus from the king and Daniel to their opponents. TH's definite article with "lions' pit" suggests that the reader already knows about it.[34] For those with a penchant for mythic patterns, "pit" suggests descent to the underworld or at least mortal danger, an association supported by the uses of the word λάκκος in the Psalms.[35]

verses 31-32: The OG's "eaten up and never buried," recalls in idea, though not in precise vocabulary, the prophetic curses of the Deuteronomistic history.[36] Concern with proper burial continued and even intensified in Hellenistic Judaism.[37]

verse 33: Habakkuk's stew (or "boiled stuff," ἕψημα) recalls Daniel's "boiling" (ἕψω) of the serpent-porridge in v. 27; "mixed wine" (OG only) recalls that set out for Bel in v. 11.[38] αὐτός (TH) may give

---

[33] The lexica do not indicate such a distinction between the overtones of the two verbs, but the use of freestanding ἐπί as "against" in 28 and 30 surely affects its tone when applied to the verb in the latter verse. Although the king feels helpless, we discover in 42 that he still has full command of the crowd.

[34] For the effect of a definite article used without antecedent mention of the item, compare Walter J. Ong's discussion of Hemingway's style in "The Writer's Audience is Always a Fiction, *PMLA* 90 (1975): 9-21; reprinted in *Contemporary Literary Criticism: Literary and Cultural Studies*, 2nd ed., ed. Robert Con Davis and Ronald Schleifer (New York: Longman, 1989), 83-99.

[35] See Pss 27(28):15, 29(30):3, 39(40):2, 87(88):4,6, and 142(143):7.

[36] Ezek 39:4 does use καταβιβρώσκω in such a curse.

[37] Cf. Tobit and 2 Macc 9:15 and 13:7.

[38] Anton Scholz sees reference to an eschatological banquet (*Commentar über das Buch "Judith" und über "Bel und Drache"*, Würzburg: Leo Woerl, 1896), 228.

special emphasis—as if it were unusual for a prophet to "boil stew and crumble bread into a bowl"—or perhaps we should simply ascribe it to biblical Greek's free use of pronouns.

verse 34: My OG translation follows 967 and omits SyrH/88's "Lord" since divine titles are more likely to be added than dropped (cf. 5). "To you" is probably an explanatory addition as well. This is the first time TH's narrator uses "Lord" as a proper name.[39] The angel is a stand-in for Lord; note how Habakkuk addresses his reply (both versions).[40]

verse 35: In Habakkuk's mind the problem appears to be finding the pit, not getting to Babylon. Evidently he knows who Daniel is.

verse 36: I follow 967 in omitting SyrH/88's second αὐτοῦ ("his" after hair) but this does not affect the sense (it reappears in translation). TH's angel sets Habakkuk down ἐν τῷ ῥοίζῳ τοῦ πνεύματος αὐτοῦ. πνεῦμα may mean spirit, wind, or breath; ῥοίζος can mean a rushing motion or, more often, the whistling or whizzing noise that comes from such motion.[41] I take it as the sound of rushing air rather than as "fast-moving spirit" or the angel's breathing.[42] This sensual detail is atypical of TH's emphasis on dialogue and simple action.

verse 37: As in v. 34, SyrH and 88 add "Lord."

verse 38: γάρ functions emphatically here, like Hebrew כִּי. "Remember" carries a Jewish sense of solicitude and care.[43]

verse 40: Double expressions of perception (OG "peered into and saw," TH "looked in and—behold—") show us the wonder through the king's eyes—Daniel sitting![44] Scholz suggests that this is "ein

---

[39] One of many clues that the Habakkuk episode is a relatively late addition to the story.

[40] Cf. the here-again gone-again alternation of angels with God in classical Hebrew narrative.

[41] LSJ, s.v.

[42] Common usage of the words, even in Greek scripture, suggests air noise, although the Vulgate translates "through the vehemency of his spirit" and Bereshith Rabba says "by the might of the Holy Spirit." Susan Niditch comments on the frequency of this image in shamanic journey experiences. (Susan Niditch, "The Visionary," in *Ideal Figures in Ancient Judaism*, ed. John J. Collins and George W. E. Nickelsburg, Septuagint and Cognate Studies [Chico, California: Scholars Press, 1980], 161.) I admit that my rather free "whooshing" fails to incorporate the text's αὐτοῦ.

[43] BAGD, s.v.; LSJ, s.v.

[44] TH's ἰδού functions like Hebrew הִנֵּה, introducing the visual equivalent of a direct quotation. See Adele Berlin's discussion in *Poetics and Interpretation of Biblical Narrative* (Bible and Literature Series, Sheffield: Almond, 1983), 62-3.

königliches Sitzen," a possibility supported if not guaranteed by other uses of κάθημαι in biblical and Hellenistic literature.[45]

verse 41: The king's expression in TH, "Lord God of Daniel," has an odd flavor. Who belongs to whom? We may interpret this as subtle acknowledgement that godness doesn't count for much without worshipers.[46] Or we may simply regard it as demonstration that this story takes the king (to whom Lord is "Daniel's god") as its point of reference.

verse 42: Interestingly, the tales conclude with no special reward for Daniel, although Lord receives the expected acclaim and the evildoers are punished. Here we find a narrative slip, evident in both versions but particularly egregious in the OG: does the king actually execute the entire population (cf. 28)? The lions' appetite confirms the miraculous nature of Daniel's survival—in TH, "instantly" suggests that their hunger now may be more than natural as well (cf. 39).

Fabula

We turn now to analysis of the narratives, beginning at the fabula level. A fabula is "a series of logically and chronologically related events that are caused or experienced by actors."[47] It includes events presumed but not described by the story ("Lord saves Daniel from the lions"). Events entail actors, time, and location; so these too are elements of the fabula. Reducing a narrative to its fabula helps us understand its plot structure and logic, actor alignments, and treatment of time and place. It may also help us determine similarity to other narratives.[48] Later, we shall use our fabula description as a basis for assessing story-level displacements.

---

[45] Scholz, *Bel und Drache*, 232. Compare uses of Hebrew ישׁב.

[46] Cf. Danna Nolan Fewell's literary observations in *Circle of Sovereignty: A Story of Stories in Daniel 1-6*, Bible and Literature Series (Sheffield: Almond, 1988), and Jon D. Levenson's historical analysis of creation mythology in *Creation and the Persistence of Evil* (San Francisco: Harper & Row, 1988).

[47] Bal, 5. In our case, the events are those underlying a narrative.

[48] Proppian-type analysis focuses in effect on the fabula, as is easily seen in Vladimir Propp's own seminal work, *Morphology of the Folktale*, 2nd ed., ed. by Louis A. Wagner (Austin: University of Texas Press, 1968).

Events

To describe *every* event in a narrative easily produces an "abstract" longer than the source text.   It is far more helpful to focus on turning points, actions which determine plot direction.   Bal suggests three criteria for identifying such essential events: (1) change, (2) choice, and (3) confrontation.[49]   The *change* criterion arises from the definition of an event—"the transition from one state to another state."[50] *Choice* directs our attention to events involving alternatives that affect the fabula's outcome.   *Confrontation* restricts us to events involving interaction between actors (rather than actors and objects).[51]

Applied to Bel and the Dragon, these criteria[52] yield the events shown in table 2.   Each event is phrased with the actor causing the transition as subject and the actor undergoing transition as object.

Strikingly, when we restrict attention to these critical events just one difference appears between the versions: in OG 28 it appears that *Daniel* has angered the people, while in TH 28–29 they direct their anger at the *king*.   Even this may not be a significant variation, since Daniel and the king are functionally one at this point.[53]   The similarity of fabulas suggests that our analysis has correctly identified the narrative core (one expects variation to concentrate in "fringe" events).   It also suggests why casual readers scarcely notice the differences between versions.

---

[49] Bal, 13–18, drawing heavily on the work of Roland Barthes and William O. Hendricks.

[50] Ibid., 5.   Such change may or may not be marked by an active verb at the text level (ibid., 14–15).

[51] Thus "Tom burns Paula" would probably be significant; "Tom burns supper" would not (although the resulting interaction between Paula and Tom might be). Technically, Bal's definition of an "actor" rules out the actor/object distinction (combining the definitions of event, action, and actor on p. 5 reveals that anyone or thing which causes or undergoes transition—e.g. a burned supper—is an actor), but practically speaking it remains useful.

[52] In fact, Bel and the Dragon forces at least one exception to the confrontation criterion; see the discussion of actors beginning on p. 72 below.

[53] At the fabula level one deals with "actors" (as defined by their role in events) rather than the "characters" who will emerge at story level.

Table 2.—Events in Bel and the Dragon.

Daniel's religion makes king curious/angry
    King tests priests and Daniel
        Daniel makes secret preparations
            Priests make secret preparations
            Priests' preparations persuade king
        Daniel's preparations persuade king
    King punishes priests, rewards Daniel

Daniel's religion angers king (implicit)
King threatens Daniel's religion
    Daniel/king test king's religion
    Daniel discredits king's religion
King accepts Daniel's religion (?) (implicit)

Daniel's/king's religion angers people
People frighten king
    King gives Daniel to people
        People try to kill Daniel (lions)
        Lord saves Daniel from lions (implicit)

        People try to starve Daniel (implicit)
        Lord feeds Daniel (via angel via Habakkuk)
    King recovers Daniel
King adopts Daniel's religion
Daniel/king punish people

Returning for a moment to the basic definition of a fabula, we recall that its events are "logically and chronologically related."[54] Table 2 shows such relations between events by vertical (chronological) and horizontal (logical) patterning. We see that the fabula falls into three main sequences, which I shall title "Bel," "The Serpent," and "The Lion Pit." Within each sequence, embedded event-series form chiastic patterns.

---

[54] Bal, 5. At the fabula level we deal with absolute chronology, not sequence-as-told. For more on event relationships see ibid., 19-23. Bal draws heavily on Claude Bremond, *Logique du récit* (Paris: Seuil, 1973).

The head series of each sequence involves Daniel's religion. This leads, in all three cases, to tests authorized by the king. (If the king indeed embraces Daniel's religion after the serpent's death, then all three tests concern "the king's god"—though a different deity each time.) In the Bel and serpent tests, Daniel's human actions discredit Babylonian religion (or its representatives). Yet the Bel sequence leaves the head series (the king's feeling about Daniel's religion) unresolved. Even in the Serpent sequence, royal acceptance of Daniel's religion remains implicit, inferred from the people's words in v. 28.

In the Lion Pit test, Daniel becomes object rather than subject, and Lord self, with considerable flourish, brings about the desired outcome. Only now, after divine intervention, do we get firm closure. Evildoers are punished and the king *explicitly* recognizes Daniel's God.

Actors and Aims

From Table 2 we derive the following collection of actors (agents, human or otherwise, who cause or undergo transition):

> Daniel
> the king
> the priests
> the people
> Lord
> Daniel's religion
> the king's religion
> Daniel's and priests' preparations

Appearance of "the king's religion" on this list requires special comment, for it never appears as subject of a fabula event (nor do its embodiments, Bel and the serpent). Thus technically, it should not appear as object, either—the confrontation criterion rules out events in which the objects are not also, elsewhere, subjects. Yet I could find no way to phrase the decisive event of the serpent's death without including Babylonian religion or the serpent itself as object. (One could similarly argue that in the Bel story as well the king tests his own religion, not "the priests and Daniel.") This object–only status belittles Babylonian religion. Daniel's religion, by contrast, appears several times in the subject role.

An important feature of the relationship between actors is their alignment relative to the *telos* or guiding aim of the fabula. This aim may usually be expressed as the wish or fear of some "primary subject."

Some fabulas are driven by more than one aim because they have more than one primary subject. In such a case, the fabula's unity derives from the interaction of aims.[55]

With respect to a specific subject's aim,

> there are always powers who either allow it to reach its aim or prevent it from doing so. ... One may, consequently, distinguish a class of actors – consisting of those who support the subject in the realization of its intention, supply the object, or allow it to be supplied or given – whom we shall call the *power*. ...

The power is in many cases not a person but an abstraction.[56]

Often, the *object* of the aim is *subject* of the power relationship.[57]

A primary subject typically interacts not only with powers, whose support or opposition spans the entire fabula, but with incidental[58] *helpers* and *opponents*. A helper's assistance "forms a necessary but in itself insufficient condition to reach the aim. Opponents must be overcome one by one, but such ... overcoming does not guarantee a favourable ending."[59]

Identification of primary aims and the associated powers, helpers, and opponents is not a mechanically exact process. Often a given fabula may be described in more than one way (as any preacher knows!); different descriptions highlight different features of the narrative.[60]

Bel and the Dragon offers two obvious candidates for primary subject: Daniel and the king.[61] Daniel wishes to pursue his own religion. (He does *not* display missionary zeal—he discusses his religion only when asked, and makes no overt attempt to convert the king, though he does discredit the king's religion.) With respect to Daniel's aim, the negative power[62] is Babylonian religion, aligned with several

---

[55] Bal, 26-27, 32-33.

[56] Ibid., 28. "Power" corresponds to Greimas's *destinateur*. A "receiver" (*destinataire*) role also exists but is often combined with that of subject.

[57] For instance, the primary aim, "John (subject) wants to marry Mary (object)," usually puts *Mary* in the power position of allowing or preventing realization of the aim (but in an older narrative, Mary's father might be the power). Ibid., 28-30.

[58] In the literal sense: appearing in incidents.

[59] Bal, 31.

[60] Compare the problem of describing natural processes: descriptions of "wavelength" and "frequency" call attention to light's wavelike qualities; speaking of "photons" prompts us to think about it in more "particular" ways.

[61] I shall later introduce a third, less obvious candidate.

[62] In the technical narratological sense—the tale clearly wishes to say that Babylonian religion is impotent in an ultimate sense.

opponents: the priests and their preparations, the people and their lions, and sometimes, the king.

But what is Daniel's supporting power? Lord acts only in the Lion Pit sequence, and thus appears more a helper than a power (unless, under pressure of the hypothesis, we assume hidden support from Lord in the Bel and Serpent sequences). The king, while certainly definable as one who will "either allow it [the subject, Daniel] to reach its aim or prevent it from doing so,"[63] vacillates between positions—first opposed to Daniel's religion, then (reportedly) supportive, then withdrawn, and finally firmly supportive again. With Daniel as primary subject, the positive power role is difficult to assign.

Another problem with taking Daniel as primary subject is that his desire to worship Lord plays only a minor role in the Bel sequence (where Daniel's own religion is never threatened—unless, convinced that this is the central issue, we read threat into the king's remarks about Bel). More problematically, the overall denouement (40–42) focuses on the *king's* acclaim of Lord—not Daniel's.

Might the king, then, be primary subject? What does he wish or fear? He wishes, in the first two stories, the glorification (or fears the repudiation) of his own god. In the third he seems caught by conflicting desires for Daniel's well–being and his own.

More generally, we might say the king desires "the best religion." Initially he defines this in terms of dramatic cult ("haven't you seen how much is supplied to it every day?") and wide recognition ("so worship him!"). At the end of the Serpent sequence he (apparently) refocuses his aim on Daniel's religion, but must now battle popular opposition and his own cowardice.

With the king's desire for the best religion as a starting point, Babylonian religion again appears as a negative power. Daniel becomes a positive power, since it is he who can supply "the best religion." (In this case, the object, Lord, is *not* the supplying power.) This interpretation highlights the role of deception and misunderstanding in the narrative: only after seeing through the priests' deception (Bel), the error of the "eating" criterion (Serpent), and the impotence of the crowd's threats (Lion Pit) can the king truly embrace the object of his search. But while the king's desire for true religion explains the Bel and Serpent sequences very well, we must strain a little to fit the Habakkuk episode into this pattern.

Since neither the king nor Daniel unambiguously occupies the "primary subject" position, I now present another candidate: Lord.

---

63 Bal, 28.

Lord is an unusual candidate for two reasons: first, because primary subjects are ordinarily human;[64] second, because the *textual* layer shows Lord as subject only in dialogue and the narratorial assertion of OG 39.[65] Lord does, however, supply an aim which motivates events throughout the fabula.

Lord aims to be worshipped by the king (or everyone).[66] The king can grant this aim and thus functions as supportive power (!).[67] Babylonian religion is the opposing power, aligned as usual with Bel's priests and their plans and the crowd (with their lions). But where does Daniel fit? He does not (so far as we know) desire that the king worship Lord, yet his actions consistently support and never contradict Lord's aim. His presence throughout the story argues against calling him a helper. Instead he seems to be a second supportive power, whose assistance Lord's aim requires.

What conclusions can we draw from this discussion of actors and aims? We have examined three possible primary subjects: Daniel, the king, and Lord. In every case, Babylonian religion, although only an object in the fabula as described, appears as the opposing power. If we orient on Daniel's desire to worship Lord, the king's words about Bel and events of the Bel and Serpent sequences acquire new nuances (we interpret the king as threatening and assume Lord's involvement in the discrediting of Bel and the serpent). A focus on the king emphasizes themes of deception and illusion. Lord's aim seems to motivate the fabula most fully, perhaps because it incorporates both the king's and Daniel's aims.[68] It seems odd, however, to have a primary subject so inactive at the textual level.

These options represent varying interpretations of the same material; each has merits and demerits. Perhaps (recalling that a fabula may have more than one primary subject) adequate description requires more than one of the proposed aims. We shall take up these questions

---

[64] "Taking as basis the presupposition that *human* thinking and action is directed towards an aim . . ." Ibid., 26, emphasis mine.

[65] We find a similarly restrained deity in Esther, Judith, Ruth, and (to a lesser extent) the Joseph stories and Succession Narrative. Except for Ruth, all these narratives are set in circles of power.

[66] If Lord wants to be worshipped by everyone, then the Lion Pit rescue takes place partly for Daniel's own sake, not just because of his instrumental value. The argument against "everyone" is that the stories allow pagans other than the king to go their own way (to destruction). It does *not* suffice to say only that "Lord wants to be worshipped by Daniel." This fails to account for too much of the action.

[67] Fewell discerns the same pattern in Daniel 1–6: the divine sovereign depends on earthly ones for acclamation.

[68] An interesting observation in itself.

again as we turn to other levels of the narratives. First, however, we must examine two final aspects of the fabula: time and location.

Time and Location

Bel and the Dragon's fabula presents crisis events rather than gradual developmental processes; events unfold in compact, exciting sequences.[69] The Bel sequence takes up one day and the next, the Serpent sequence one day (apparently), and the Lion Pit episode about a week, only two or three days of which are described in detail. The unspecified intervals between sequences reinforce the tri-partite structure suggested by the embedding pattern.

Spatially, the fabula is located in a city; more specifically in its royal and temple precincts. Events taking place in the idol temple(s)[70] involve only human action. The third sequence focuses on a place of mortal danger, the lion pit. Only here does Lord act, in a way which links Babylon to far-distant Judah (suggesting that for this actor space is no object). The Lion Pit sequence may also hint at court/non-court tension.[71]

Stories

Story, in Bal's scheme, occupies a middle level between the rather abstract fabula and the concrete text. The story (1) tells the fabula's events in a certain sequence (not necessarily chronological, and not necessarily including every event); (2) creates a "tempo" by summarizing some events quickly and drawing out the telling of others; (3) fleshes out the actors into "characters"; (4) correspondingly characterizes locations as specific places; (5) develops symbolic, allusive, and other relationships; and (6) adopts a particular point of view.[72]

Our two versions of Bel and the Dragon, which were nearly identical at the fabula level, vary more significantly as we move to the

---

[69] On crisis versus developmental fabulas, see Bal, 38-41.

[70] In the OG, Bel and the serpent appear to share a temple, since the second act takes place ἐν τῷ αὐτῷ τόπῳ (23). TH, which specifies destruction of Bel's temple in 22, lacks this phrase.

[71] Especially in the OG: οἱ ἀπὸ τῆς χώρας πάντες, ὁ ὄχλος τῆς χώρας (28,30).

[72] Bal, 7, 49-118. Obviously stories vary in the degree to which they carry out these different tasks. In chapter 2 I discuss some of my reservations about treating "story" as a distinct level.

story level. We shall first examine their temporal features (sequence and rhythm), then discuss characterization and focalization together since they interact so strongly. The symbolic handling of space in these stories suggests combining the topics of space and symbol as well.

Sequence

In presenting Bel and the Dragon's fabula, I arranged events in "absolute" chronological order. We now turn our attention to the departures our storytellers make from that sequence. In both versions, most anachronies occur in dialogue (second degree anachrony). They do not "feel" anachronistic, since people naturally talk about things that have happened or are going to happen. The main (first–degree) narratives also contain brief forward and backward references (e.g. TH 21, "they showed him the hidden doors through which *they used to enter and consume the things on the table*"). Most of the anachronies at both levels concern events within the main storyline (internal anachrony) and indeed, within the same *sequence*. These unobtrusive references give each sequence a sense of cohesion. The predominance of internal reference also reinforces the "crisis" nature of the fabula, suggesting that major events emerge suddenly and are resolved just as quickly, uninfluenced by long–term processes of development.

Most of the forward references in dialogue involve commands or associated conditional statements (e.g. OG 8, "show . . . or you die").[73] Their proleptic reference gives them a foreshadowing function, but their peculiar linguistic status differentiates them from ordinary indicative prolepses. They allude to past and future events which may or may not actually occur in the fabula.

Only two internal anachronies span sequence gaps: the king refers to the Bel episode at the beginning of the Serpent story (v. 24), and the people mention both Bel and the serpent as the Lion Pit story begins

---

[73] Second–degree (conversational) prolepsis occurs in OG 8, 9, 11, 26, 34, and 37, and TH 8, 9, 11, 25, 26, 29, 34, and 37. Conversational analepsis (reference to past events) occurs in OG 6, 7, 9, 11, 24, 28, 37, and 38, and TH 6, 7, 9, 24, 28, 37, and 38). Often a statement's status is unclear. Δέδοται σοι (OG 26) grammatically points to a past event, but I have interpreted it as performative speech which accomplishes an action by the process of naming it (and thus, not analeptic). I have taken ἀπέστειλέ σοι ὁ θεός (OG 37), by contrast, to refer to a past (albeit not by much!) event.

(v. 28).[74] These cross-references appear in both versions and function to knit the sequences together.

Both stories also contain external anachrony in Daniel's (second-degree) reference to Lord as "creator of heaven and earth" (v. 5). Daniel's statement that God "does not abandon those who love him" also seems to refer to events beyond (though inclusive of) the present story.[75] Thus the stories show Lord as bridging not only space (the Habakkuk incident) but time.

The versions also share iterative[76] references to Babylonian custom toward the beginning of each sequence (vv. 3-4, 23, 32). These set the stage for specific incidents of interest and are scarcely noticeable as anachronies.

We turn now to three relatively striking, version-specific instances of anachrony. The first two involve Bel's priests and their consumption of the offerings. The OG places its report of the night's events between folks' arrival in the morning and their breaking of the seal (15-17). This subtle displacement (it departs from absolute chronology by less than a sentence) serves to focus attention and build suspense.[77]

TH alerts us to the hidden entrance several verses earlier (12). Access to the priests' thoughts informs us of both their past behavior (analepsis) and their probable plans for tonight (prolepsis), so that when Daniel orders ashes scattered (14) we immediately understand his purpose. Placing the anachronous information in the priests' thoughts (subjective anachrony) allows TH to give it to us without violating strict story sequence—after all, the priests *would* have been thinking this at just the point where the story mentions it.

Finally, we turn to OG 39, where the narrator repeats Daniel's assertion (38) that Lord remembered him. As in OG 15-17, the anachrony performs a highlighting function; as in vv. 5 and 38, it focuses on Lord.

---

[74] If Daniel's plural at the conclusion of the Serpent story (OG 27 "these," TH 27 "objects of worship") refers to Bel's fragments as well as the serpent's, it provides a third link.

[75] OG 38. TH 38 uses second person. Technically we might describe this as a "mixed, complete anachrony:" mixed because it combines external and internal anachrony, "complete" in that it spans the entire duration between its farthest reference and the (narrative's) present moment.

[76] Imperfect verbs, the phrase "every day."

[77] Bal, 52. A similar but less striking inversion occurs in TH 31-32, which puts Daniel in the pit, *then* tells us how the lions have usually been fed.

Rhythm and Frequency

In telling events, a narrator imposes *rhythm* on them. Ratios of fabula time to story time lie on a spectrum between the zero of pause (fabula time remains frozen while text continues, as in description) and the infinity of ellipsis (time passes in fabula with no corresponding text coverage). Scenic presentation, in which narrative time approximates fabula time (e.g. dialogue), occupies the center of this continuum.[78]

Narrative pacing also involves *frequency*: the ratio of fabula events to their narrative treatments. Ordinarily each fabula event is narrated once, but sometimes a single description summarizes a series of events, or we find multiple narrations of a single event.[79]

Biblical narrative typically consists of scenes linked by brief summarizing bridges, with heavy use of quoted speech in the scenes. Slowdowns and pauses usually occur only in introductory material. Scenic structure and dialogue distribution in Bel and the Dragon (shown in table 3) follow this typical biblical pattern.[80]

Table 3.—Scenes in Bel and the Dragon.

		Verses	Dialogue
Introduction		1–2	—
Bel			
	Introduction	3–4a	—
	Scene 1: proposing the test	4b–9	4b–9
	Scene 2: arrangements	10–14	11
	Scene 3: results	15–22	17–20
The Serpent			
	Scene 1: the test	23–27	24–27
The Lion Pit			
	Scene 1: proposing the "test"	28–32	28–29/30
	Scene 2: rescue by Habakkuk	33–39	34–5,37–8
	Scene 3: results	40–42	41

[78] Ibid., 68–79. Notice how dependent the description of "story" is upon the

Such rhythmic segmentation has a fractal–like quality, recurring at successively finer levels of detail. For instance, scene 1 of the Bel sequence contains two subscenes (4b–7 and 8b–9) divided by a brief lapse into summarizing narrative (8a).[81] The single scene of The Serpent contains (like Bel) an introduction (23), test proposal (24–26), arrangements (27a), and results (27b). The Habakkuk scene contains its own introduction (33), a subscene centered on dialogue (34–35), a narrative bridge (36), another subscene with dialogue (37–38), and a summary conclusion (39).

Table 3 shows that although the two versions of Bel and the Dragon allocate dialogue differently (e.g., the king speaks in TH 17; Daniel at the corresponding spot in the OG) its distribution remains the same. Quantitative comparison (table 4) confirms that although TH lays a slightly greater stress on dialogue throughout, the distribution of dialogue follows the same pattern in each version.

Table 4.—Dialogue Distribution in Bel and the Dragon.

	Total Words	Words Dialogue	Percent Dialogue
Old Greek			
Bel (3–22)	483	169	34
The Serpent (23–27)	98	32	32
The Lion Pit (28–42)	301	77	26
Theodotion			
Bel (3–22)	455	165	36
The Serpent (23–27)	95	38	40
The Lion Pit (28–42)	291	85	29

---

actual text. The rhythmic spectrum also includes summary (between scene and ellipsis) and "slow–down" (between scene and pause).

[79] Ibid., 77–79.

[80] For examples of stress on dialogue, see TH 17's portrayal of an essentially non–verbal act (examination of seals) entirely through dialogue, or 19–20 (both versions) where we learn about the tell–tale tracks in the same way.

[81] A switch to singulative action (aorist verbs) marks the scene's beginning in 4b; previous introductory actions are iterative (imperfect). For the imperfect as charac-

In both versions, the sequences focused on pagan religion (Bel and The Serpent) have relatively high proportions of dialogue. In the sequence dominated by Lord's action, the proportion of dialogue drops noticeably—a narrative reflection of shifting focus.

With respect to rhythm and frequency, verse 28 is the most complex part of Bel and the Dragon. First, it seems to report a series of events as a single typical instance ("and the kind of thing they were saying was . . ."). Here scenic presentation invades even a summary introductory passage.

This verse also points to one of the narratives' most important ellipses—the king's response to what Daniel says in 27.[82] It is not a total ellipsis, since the crowd tells us what the narrator did not. But the crowd's questionable reliability leaves us unsure how the king really responded.

Focalization and Characters

At the story level, the fabula's actors (defined by their roles) become *characters* with distinctive personal attributes.[83] In addition to its human cast (Daniel, the king, the priests, the crowd,[84] and Habakkuk), Bel and the Dragon presents us with three non-human characters: Bel, the serpent, and Lord.[85] The narratives seem to presume some prior acquaintance with Daniel, Habakkuk, and Lord; possibly also with Cyrus (in TH), Bel, and the serpent.

While ancient Greek literature makes generous use of explicit characterization, classical Hebrew narrative typically avoids or subverts

---

teristic of introductions, see Robert W. Funk, *The Poetics of Biblical Narrative*, FFNT (Sonoma, California: Polebridge, 1988), 67.

[82] Lord's restraint of the lions is the other major ellipsis.

[83] Bal defines a *character* as "an actor with distinctive human characteristics. . . . An *actor* is a structural position, while a *character* is a complex semantic unit" (79).

[84] The courtiers mentioned in TH 2 play no further role in the story (unless we identify them with Bel's priests); those mentioned in OG 30 collapse into the crowd, for all practical purposes.

[85] Lord's angel and the lions are not really characters. The angel stands in for Lord (neither Habakkuk nor Daniel recognize it as a separate entity), while the lions are merely a mode of execution. Contrast the delightful treatment of the lions in Aphraat's version (cited in translation by Louis F. Hartman and Alexander A. Di Lella, *The Book of Daniel*, AB 44 [Garden City: Doubleday, 1978], 22).

epithets.[86] Table 5, which lists the explicit characterizations in each version of Bel and the Dragon, shows that both versions incline toward biblical chariness in this respect.

Table 5.—Explicit Characterization in Bel and the Dragon.

Character Speaking	Character Described	Old Greek Characterizations		Theodotion Characterizations	
narrator	Habakkuk	1:	son of Jesus, Levite	33:	Judean prophet
narrator	king	—		1:	Persian
narrator	Daniel	2:	priest, Abal's son, companion	2:	companion, most honored
Daniel	Lord	5: 7: 38: 38:	god, creator; god of gods; rememberer rememberer	5: 25:	god, living, creator, ruler; living
Daniel	Bel	7:	clay and bronze, not eater	5: 7:	made by hands; clay and bronze, not eater
Daniel	priests	19:	deceivers	—	
king	Bel	6: 18:	god, receiver of goods; great, without deceit	6: 18:	living god, eater; great, without deceit
king	Daniel	—		9:	blasphemer
king	serpent	24:	living, eating	24:	living god
king	Lord	41:	great, unique	41:	great, unique
priests	Bel	9:	eater	—	
priests	Daniel	—		12:	liar
crowd	king	28:	a Jew	28:	a Jew

The narrators provide identifying data—no more—about a few key figures (the king, Daniel, Habakkuk). "Characterizing" epithets come mostly from Daniel and the king and mostly describe objects of worship (Bel, the serpent, Lord). Bel receives the greatest variety of characterizations: positively as god, receiver of goods, eater, great, and without deceit,[87] negatively as a creature of clay and bronze who eats nothing.[88] Lord attracts a much more consistent and positive set of epithets: creator, rememberer (of those who love him), great, and unique.[89] Overall, explicit characterizations reinforce the story's focus on the question "whom shall one worship?"

Holding our focus on speech but shifting attention to implicit characterization, we note first that by implicit contrast with Bel and the serpent, Lord is *not* deceitful or easily overcome.

Looking further, at the distribution of dialogue among characters (table 6), we see that Daniel and the king generally dominate the stories' speech. But in the Lion Pit sequence, where Daniel plays a passive role, his share of dialogue drops accordingly, while Lord's agents (the angel and Habakkuk) assume a conversational prominence echoing Lord's active role. Lord's opponents (priests, crowd) are given little voice.

Table 6 also shows some significant differences between the versions. Daniel dominates the OG dialogue, at the expense of the priests and crowd (collectively designated "Lord's enemies").[90] TH grants Lord's enemies relatively greater voice (although still only about a quarter of the total dialogue), thus making them seem a more significant threat.

---

[86] For a detailed discussion of epithets and characterization in classical Hebrew narrative, see the chapter on "Proleptic Portraits" by Meir Sternberg in *The Poetics of Biblical Narrative: Ideological Literature and the Drama of Reading*, Indiana Literary Biblical Series (Bloomington: Indiana University Press, 1985), 321-64.

[87] OG. TH substitutes "living" for "receiver of goods."

[88] TH adds "made by human hands."

[89] The OG adds "God of gods"; TH adds "ruler" and "living."

[90] The OG assigns Daniel a greater role in both the Bel and Lion Pit sequences. In the Serpent sequence, the OG's Daniel speaks *less* than his TH counterpart; the slack is taken up by the king.

Table 6.—Words Per Character in Bel and the Dragon.

	Character	Old Greek		Theodotion	
Bel	Daniel	106	(62%)	56	(34%)
	king	56	(33%)	67	(41%)
	priests	7	(4%)	42	(25%)
		169	(100%)	165	(100%)
The Serpent	Daniel	17	(53%)	24	(63%)
	king	15	(46%)	14	(36%)
		32	(100%)	38	(100%)
The Lion Pit	crowd	11	(14%)	28	(32%)
	king	16	(21%)	13	(15%)
	angel	13	(17%)	14	(16%)
	Habakkuk	24	(31%)	19	(22%)
	Daniel	12	(15%)	11	(12%)
		76	(100%)	85	(100%)
Total	Daniel	140	(49%)	91	(32%)
	king	87	(31%)	94	(33%)
	Lord's allies	37	(13%)	33	(11%)
	Lord's enemies	18	(6%)	70	(24%)
		282	(100%)	288	(100%)

Note: Partial percentages may not add up to 100 due to rounding error.

Insights into characters' perceptions and feelings affect characterization directly (telling us what kinds of things go on within character's minds), and indirectly (because, in general, sharing a character's viewpoint creates sympathy with that character). Table 7 shows the points in Bel and the Dragon where narratorial "focalization," or adoption of the perspective of a particular character, becomes clear through perception of information not accessible to an outside observer.[91]

Table 7.—Focalization Through Characters in Bel and the Dragon.

	Old Greek			Theodotion	
Vv.	Focalizing Character	Object of Focalization	Vv.	Focalizing Character	Object of Focalization
8	king	anger	8	king	anger
11	king	agreement			
			13	priests	hidden door
18	"they"	empty tables	18	king	tables
			21	king	anger
26	king	agreement			
30	king	crowd danger	30	king	crowd danger
32	crowd	purpose	32	crowd	purpose
40	king	Daniel	40	king	Daniel

Note: this table describes only focalizations involving non-perceptible objects.[92]

While this analysis inevitably involves some judgment calls,[93] a pattern is evident: the narrator uses only foreigners as focalizing agents

---

[91] For a discussion of the differences between focalization and "point of view," and a defense of the former term, see Bal, 100-2. My discussion here involves only focalization through characters. Discussion of *narratorial* points-of-view begins on p. 96, below.

[92] On non-perceptible objects, see Bal, 109-10. In 18, the non-perceptible object is actually *sight of* the empty tables—a camera-eye could record that the tables were empty, but only access to the observers' consciousness lets us know that the tables were *seen*. Compare the ash-spreading in 14. This is probably focalized through the king's or Daniel's eyes, but because the object is perceptible it is difficult to determine focalization precisely.

[93] For instance, reports of the king's agreement (26), the crowd's purpose (31), and the king's anger (TH 21) might be interpreted as narratorial summaries of conclusions reachable by observation, rather than privileged access to characters' thoughts.

for nonperceptible objects.[94] The greatest number and clearest instances of focalization take the king's perspective.

In both versions, epithets, dialogue, focalization and action combine to yield the following characterizations:

The king is active and interactive—asking questions, threatening, ordering, permitting, and punishing. He shows more emotion than any other character in the story—anger, fear, grief, joy. Most of his words and actions concern religion, showing him pious in a broad sort of way. He is willing to learn.

Daniel is a more controlled, urbane character than the king, showing emotion only in his laughter. His piety is more focused than the king's, as he consistently worships Lord and rejects Babylonian gods. Daniel's entrapment of the priests and destruction of the serpent suggest wisdom.[95] In the Lion Pit sequence Daniel plays an essentially passive role.

As non–deities, tools of human trickery, *Bel* and *the serpent* are characterized primarily by others' words. Each "acts"[96] only in its destruction; hitherto they are not even objects, let alone agents.

Lord, too, appears first in the words of others. Not until the Lion Pit sequence does Lord act, but Lord then proves very active indeed.[97] Lord redefines divinity, shifting its terms from eating (which Bel could not do and the serpent died by) to feeding. Lord's implicit and explicit characterizations coincide to provide a firm portrait. Yet the closing word on Lord comes from the king, suggesting that even Lord's dominion somehow requires human recognition.[98]

The priests are minor players, presented as plotters, deceivers, and consumers.

The crowd implicitly characterizes itself as hasty and ill–informed (its statements in 28 are not quite accurate), acting only to destroy, subject finally to destruction. While the crowd shows awareness of its own deities, it perceives Daniel's religion in ethnic terms ("the king has become a Jew!"), not religious ones.

---

[94] A possible exception is OG 39: "and Lord God remembered Daniel." I interpret this as a non–narrative, discursive comment, rather than a report of Lord God's thoughts. See below, however, on coincidence between Lord's and the narrator's points of view.

[95] This wisdom includes both superior information and the ability to maneuver in court.

[96] In the technical fabula sense of causing *or undergoing* transition.

[97] More precisely, Lord's agents prove very active.

[98] See the note to v. 41.

Habakkuk appears as a provider (of food and words), dependent (on Lord/the angel for guidance and transportation) and obedient. *The angel* functions as a narrative cipher for Lord self.

The versions also show some significant differences in characterization. Daniel presents a stronger figure in the OG, closely aligned with the king. The OG priests are correspondingly less prominent. However, it characterizes the Lion Pit crowd a bit more fully than TH does.

In TH the king plays a more important role and the opponents seem stronger. TH also uses more theological language to characterize Lord and Bel. Table 8 summarizes these differences and lists supporting observations—some subtle, some very striking.

Table 8.—Characterization in Bel and the Dragon Versions.

Daniel more prominent in Old Greek

Daniel gets greater percentage of dialogue (table 6)
Daniel's name mentioned more times (OG 32x, TH 26x)
gives information about Daniel's ancestry (2)
rival courtiers not mentioned (2)
response to king has polemic thrust: "*I* worship none . . ." (5)
Daniel ups ante on king's proposal (9)
Daniel supervises preparation, priests unmentioned (11)
Daniel can order his servants to clear temple (14)
Daniel commands closing of doors (including ordering the priests to use their seals, 14)
Daniel directs inspection of seals (15-17)
Daniel calls priests deceivers (19)
Daniel shows king hidden doors (21)
priests are not destroyed, following Daniel's plan (9b) rather than the king's (8).[99]
king hands priests and Bel's ration over to Daniel (22)
crowd rallies against Daniel (28)
angel's syntax stresses Daniel, not location (34)
Lord God remembered Daniel (39)
evildoers punished "before Daniel" (42)

---

[99] Or one could argue that technically the priests *did* fullfill the king's order by showing "who eats the things supplied for Bel"—although it wasn't Bel.

Table 8.—*continued*

Daniel more closely aligned with king in Old Greek

king reports Daniel's statement descriptively (not as "blasphemy," 9)
"the king and Daniel" supervise preparations (11)
Daniel's suggestion pleases king (11)
king speaks to Daniel about empty tables (18)
"they" find Bel's supplies (21, P967 reading)
king concurs with Daniel (26)

More attention to rabble in Old Greek's Lion Pit sequence

more terms for crowd (28–32)
crowd differentiated from king's attendants (30)
(but TH's crowd gets more dialogue, table 6)

King more prominent and emotional in Theodotion

king's percentage of dialogue approximates Daniel's (table 6)
opens with accession report, king is named (1)
Lord described from king's viewpoint (4,41)
king sets out food rather than observing (13)
king observes strewing of ashes (14)
king directs inspection of seals (17)
more emphatic acclamation of Bel (18) (but emotive verb missing)
reported anger at deception (21)
king destroys priests (22)
king gives permission (1st person, 25)
crowd rallies against king (28)

Priests more prominent in Theodotion

priests get more dialogue (table 6)
priests direct preparations (11–12)[100]
priests call Daniel a liar (12)
access to priests' minds (13)
priests show king hidden doors (21)
crowd angry about priests as well as idols (28)

---

[100] Note the rhetorical deftness of the priests' speech. They keep the king center stage in their proposal—he himself will arrange everything, how can he have doubts? They also make a subtle logical jump as they say, "if you do not find everything eaten by Bel." Technically speaking, the king will be able to observe only whether the provisions have been eaten, not whether they have been eaten *by Bel*, but the priests' words equate the two. Finally, the king accused Daniel of blaspheming

Table 8.—*continued*

Theodotion uses fancier theological language

ruler of all flesh (5), living God (5,25)
idol "made by human hands" (5)
oath omitted (7)
theological speech by Daniel (25)
(but "God of Gods" OG 7)

With all this information in hand, we may ask, "who is the hero of Bel and the Dragon?"[101]   Bal suggests the following criteria for 'heroism':

> *qualification*: comprehensive information about appearance, psychology, motivation, past
> *distribution*: the hero occurs often in the story, his or her presence is felt at important moments in the fabula
> *independence*: the hero can occur alone or hold monologues
> *function*: certain actions are those of the hero along: s/he makes agreements, vanquishes opponents, unmasks traitors, etc.
> *relations*: s/he maintains relations with the largest number of characters[102]

In the OG, Daniel (and Habakkuk) receive the most historical qualification, but the king is better described psychologically.   TH describes the king more thoroughly than any other character.   Daniel is present more than the king in both versions (since the king disappears during the Habakkuk episode); neither character appears alone to any noticeable degree.   Daniel performs many vital functions in the Bel and Serpent sequences (although he does not have a monopoly on them) but remains unheroically passive in the Lion Pit segment.   Except for Daniel's very brief relation to Habakkuk, Daniel and the king engage in comparable relationships.

Bel, but the priests see his attack aimed at themselves (betraying their own knowledge and lack of respect for the idol).

[101] This is a loaded question, to be sure. Observers may differ about the identity (and likeability) of a narrative's major character. Yet we feel an urge to locate a character with whom we can identify and through whose viewpoint we may regard events.

[102] Bal, 92, emphasis added.

Distribution, I suggest, proves the deciding criterion. "On the grounds of distribution, for instance the fact that a character focalizes the first and/or the last chapter, we label it the hero(ine) of the book."[103] The OG opens with information on Daniel, gives him a more prominent role throughout (see table 8), names God from Daniel's perspective (Lord) and mentions Daniel by name twice in its final verse.

TH, by contrast, takes the king as its starting point and gives him greater prominence throughout (table 8). It refers to Lord from the king's perspective: "Daniel's god." TH's narrative concludes with a firm focus on the king, relegating Daniel to a pronoun. We may tentatively say, then, that while both Daniel and the king play important roles in both narratives, Daniel is the OG's hero, and TH's is the king.[104]

Spaces and Symbols

In some narratives, space is only a frame, a place of action. Others 'thematize' space, presenting it as an object of interest for its own sake. Space may also be fixed or dynamic, the latter allowing for movement of characters. Such movement often has symbolic value, frequently involving contrast between spaces.[105]

The main spatial frame of Bel and the Dragon is Babylon—not the historical Babylon (of either Cyrus's or Hellenistic times), nor yet the demonic Babylon of Daniel 7-12 and Revelation, but a legendary Babylon, closely akin to Joseph's Egypt, Esther's Persia, Tobit's Assyria, and the Babylon of Daniel 1-6. It harbors both danger and high professional and religious opportunity.[106] TH lays slightly more stress on Babylon than does the OG, naming its king (1), referring to the people as "Babylonians" (rather than "the country's people") in 28, and emphasizing Babylon in the angel's syntax (35).

While both versions specify locations within the frame only sketchily (where *do* 4b-9 and 28-30 take place?), the OG tends to

---

[103] Ibid., 105.

[104] Earlier we noted that one may also designate Lord as a primary subject of the narrative. I do not nominate Lord for the hero position because of Lord's withdrawn status during most of the narrative, and because this particular narrative does not invite us to identify *with* Lord, as subject, but to take a position vis-à-vis Lord as object.

[105] Bal, 93-9.

[106] Esther provides the closest parallel, with its extremes of pogrom and מִתְיַהֲדִים (Esth 8:17; cf. Bel 28). The motif of general public dislike is weaker in the Joseph, Tobit, and even Daniel 1-6 stories. More will be said about Babylon in chapter 6's discussion of intertextuality.

slightly greater precision.[107] It shows Bel residing in a sanctuary (ναός) within a temple (ἱερόν, εἰδωλεῖον). The οἶκος in which the priests live appears to be located within the same building, since the king, after confronting them there, leads them out of the Βήλιον (22). (This allows the hidden doors to be *doors*, rather than a tunnel.) The serpent resides in the same edifice ("in the same place," OG 23, cf. 15).[108]

TH does not clearly differentiate the οἶκος τοῦ Βηλ, ναός, and ἱερόν (although again ναός may refer specifically to the sanctuary), nor does TH say anything about a priestly residence. TH specifies no location for the Serpent story, but it cannot take place in the same temple since that was destroyed in verse 22.

Both versions tell us that the ναός contains table(s), a floor, a hidden entrance, and has doors which can be sealed, because these elements figure in the plot. Though physical description is sparse, the place is symbolically loaded, associated with secrecy (hidden doors), deception (public doors whose unbroken seals do not guarantee inviolateness), and embezzlement.

Neither version specifies that Bel is in the ναός—only that food is set out τῷ Βηλ (presumably, but not necessarily, in the idol's physical presence). I suspect that Bel *was* in the room, but it is interesting to see how the narratives downplay the idol's presence.

The lion pit, like Bel's sanctuary, is characterized by its contents: seven lions (plus occasional bodies, soon devoured). The word "pit" and associated verbs (ἐμβάλλω, ἐγκύπτω, ἐμβλέπω, ἀνασπάω) suggest an enclosure sunk in the ground.[109] Lord's action converts this place of danger and disrepute to one of vindication.

The final space mentioned by our stories is Judah,[110] a place of fields, food, prophets, and reapers. Here Lord's angel appears, speaks, and returns at the end of the story. Distance between Judah and Babylon is conspicuous by its absence: the angel takes Habakkuk's hair in Judah and sets him in Babylon with no mention of intervening space; the return trip occurs with comparable alacrity ("the same day" in the OG, παραχρῆμα in TH). For Lord, Judah and Babylon are contiguous.

---

[107] In addition to being spatially vague, TH seems to have less grasp of real court etiquette—see the discussion beginning on page 95 below.

[108] The temple was not destroyed in this version, contra Moore, 142.

[109] The verbs for "peeping" suggest that it may be covered as well—or is Daniel 6 influencing my perception? It is open enough for Habakkuk to converse with Daniel and deliver lunch.

[110] Named in TH 33, implicit in the OG (which assumes more knowledge of things Jewish) as Habakkuk's residence. Judah, like Babylon, will receive further consideration in chapter 6.

Texts

We turn now to the most concrete level of narration, the text. We shall first survey how specific features of vocabulary, style, and content combine to create each narrative's tone, then look at technical features of each narration: (1) narrator's position; (2) employment of description and argumentation; and (3) relations between the primary narrative and others embedded within it.[111]

Narrative Tone

When we look at the words of Bel and the Dragon, one of the first things we notice is how different the versions are. As discussed in chapter 3, verbatim overlap accounts for only about 20 percent of the chapters, and its pattern suggests that it may result from the use of stock phrases, rather than direct dependence.

It is also interesting to note the vocabulary size of each version. Carey Moore comments that the OG "evidences a slightly greater variety in its vocabulary" and is, for this reason among others, "the more 'literary'."[112] For instance, OG 4 uses three words for worship (σέβομαι, προσκυνέω, and προσεύχομαι) while TH uses only two, and OG 10 uses the technical term εἰδώλιον while TH says simply "Bel's house."

A simple count confirms that the OG does use a larger vocabulary (251 words) than TH (245 words);[113] however, the OG text is also slightly longer.[114] To correct for differing lengths we shall compare *rates* of vocabulary introduction (figure 1).[115]

---

[111] Bal, chapter 3 (119–149).

[112] Moore, 139.

[113] These figures were reached using Lbase and data files derived from the Morphologically Analyzed Greek Jewish Scriptures (compiled by R. Kraft, Computer Assisted Tools for Septuagint Studies Project [CATSS]) included on the *PHI/CCAT CD-ROM 1* (published by cooperation of the Center for Computer Analysis of Texts [CCAT, University of Pennsylvania], and the Packard Humanities Institute [Los Altos, California], 1987). I modified the files to match my text and combined fields 11 (lemma) and 12 (prefix) of the records so that items with the same lemma but different prefixes (e.g., καθίστημι and ἀνίστημι) register as different words.

[114] The OG has 894 words; TH, 863.

[115] Simple percentages (number of dictionary forms divided by total number of words) are misleading when comparing texts of different lengths, because new words occur more frequently toward the beginnings of texts (a first sentence will use mostly new words, while most of the vocabulary of a last sentence will already have been introduced). Thus the need to compare *rates* of vocabulary introduction. The Bel and

Lemmas

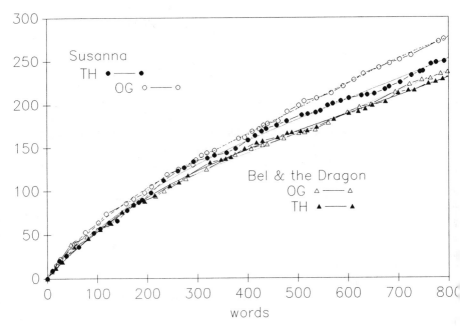

Fig. 1. Vocabulary Introduction Rates.

The two Bel and the Dragon curves virtually coincide (as do the Susanna curves), showing that there is no significant difference in vocabulary size, despite the fact that the versions share only about two-thirds of this vocabulary.[116] Surprisingly, vocabulary size is more a trait of the story material than of the teller.[117] It would be interesting to investigate how story types and genres correlate with vocabulary intro-duction—is a specific pattern of vocabulary breadth a hitherto undocu-mented part of genre expectation?

the Dragon texts are so close to the same length that this refinement may seem super-fluous, but we need it when we begin to consider the Susanna texts.

[116] 164 words appear in both versions, comprising 65 percent of the OG's 251-word vocabulary and 66 percent of TH's 245 words.

[117] That is, the curves for different versions of the same story resemble one another more closely than curves for different stories from the same version.

Because the fabula and story levels are, in the end, deduced from and dependent upon the words of a tale—its textual level—we have already had occasion to comment on many compositional subtleties of our stories. We saw that fabula patterns, narrative rhythm, anachronies, and dialogue work together to divide Bel and the Dragon into three main sequences (Bel, The Serpent, and The Lion Pit, with vv. 1–2 serving as a general introduction), some including several scenes (table 3). Character distribution and temporal and spatial transitions reinforce this structure. At the textual level, conventional signals such as introductory formulas (καὶ ἐγένετο), summaries, praise of God, punishment of evildoers, and departures further mark the structural transitions.[118]

In arguing for three main structural divisions I violate a tradition at least as old as the Peshitta, which divides the chapter into two sequences titled "Bel the Idol" and "Then Follows the Dragon."[119] English translations usually insert a typographical break between (and only between) vv. 22 and 23.[120] Carey Moore expresses scholarly consensus when he begins his commentary with the statement that

> "Bel and the Snake" consists of two "confrontation narratives" in which Daniel, a confidant of King Cyrus of Persia, courted his own destruction by deliberately setting out to disprove the "divinity" of two revered Babylonian gods, the idol called Bel and a very large snake.[121]

However, the spatial and temporal break between vv. 27 and 28 is clearer than that between vv. 23 and 24. In vv. 23–27 Daniel and the

---

[118] For a very comprehensive treatment of structure in Greek biblical narrative see Funk. Narrative segmentation forms the primary focus of his book. Funk describes his method as one of surface analysis (15), although he makes generous use of criteria (e.g. time, space, and participants) which would seem more related to the fabula and story ("content") levels. My disagreement with his methodological self-characterization has not prevented me from finding his observations very helpful. Funk draws heavily upon Propp; Seymour Chatman, *Story and Discourse: Narrative Structure in Fiction and Film* (Ithaca: Cornell University Press, 1978); Gérard Genette, *Narrative Discourse: An Essay in Method* (Ithaca: Cornell University Press, 1980); and Shlomith Rimmon-Kenan, *Narrative Fiction: Contemporary Poetics* (London and New York: Methuen, 1983). On "terminal functions" such as praise of God, see 126–132. His "illustrative rather than exhaustive" (127) list does not show punishment of evildoers as a terminal function; however, such a function forms a clear part of the court legend genre.

[119] W. O. E. Oesterley, *An Introduction to the Books of the Apocrypha* (New York: MacMillan, 1935), 287.

[120] RSV, NRSV, and REB all show this single break in the chapter, placed between vv. 22 and 23. NJB divides the chapter into three parts, but puts the second division after v. 30.

[121] Moore, 117.

king play roles like those of vv. 3–22, not vv. 28–42. Although The Serpent lacks punishment of evildoers (there were none) and praise of God (Bel also lacks this), it contains two closing functions: the serpent's destruction and Daniel's conversation–stopping question/remark.[122] The subsequent Lion Pit story builds equally upon the Bel and Serpent sequences, as the people's words make clear (28).[123]

The importance of this three–part structure lies in the parallels and contrasts it sets up between the first two sequences and the third. The first two implicitly and explicitly mock the impotence of false gods. Here, Daniel's wisdom suffices for a successful outcome. But when Lord is put to test, Daniel fades to passivity (a subtle corrective to his self–sufficiency in the previous stories). Daniel's survival in the Pit, and the king's long–awaited acclaim of Lord, come through Lord's own action, not human effort.[124] A quite different narrative feature, the manipulation of direct characterizations (table 5), supports this stress on Lord's action.

Both stories seem a little out of touch with courtly reality (surely a real king, sponsor of the national cult, would be well aware of the disposition of offerings),[125] but satiric lampoons are noted for neither accuracy nor sympathy. Beyond assuming the king's ignorance (which is essential to the plot), TH's tale heightens details and ignores the niceties of etiquette for an extravagant, almost fairy–tale flavor (table 9).

Table 9.—Extravagance in Theodotion's Bel and the Dragon.

Verse	Feature
4	more offerings (40 sheep, plural verb)
7	Daniel laughs
8	Daniel physically restrains king
24	a BIG snake
29	crowd threatens king
32	two sheep in addition to two bodies
36	more extensive description of airlift
37	Habakkuk shouts
39	Habakkuk returned home INSTANTLY
41	King shouts LOUDLY
42	evildoers eaten INSTANTLY

We have noted (table 8) that TH's king is a strong figure presiding over a relatively equal rivalry between Daniel and the priests. Court competition is suggested by the comparative of TH 2, the priests' statement in TH 12 (they stress Daniel's attack on themselves, not the question of Bel's legitimacy), execution of the priests (22) and inclusion of that execution in the crowd's complaint.[126]

The OG, with Daniel as its central figure,[127] puts greater stress on the deceptiveness of Babylonian religion, introducing the idea of deception in v. 7 (where TH's Daniel treats the king as merely ignorant), referring to the doors as "false," not merely hidden (15, 21; cf. TH 13, 21), and including an extra statement about the priests' trickery (19). These many differences in detail produce the overall effect noted by Wills: the stories combine features of the idol parody and court legend genres, but the OG leans more toward idol parody while TH accents court legend features.[128]

Technical Features

One of the most obvious questions to ask of a story is, "who tells this?"[129] The narrators of both Bel and the Dragon tales speak from

---

[122] On the "conversation stopper" as a concluding technique, see Funk, 130.

[123] If the three-fold division is so obvious, why have so many missed it? Probably because it results in a middle sequence of only four verses—but those four verses make an elegant, self-sufficient little pericope (see p. 80).

[124] Compare the dual stress of Deutero-Isaiah, who mocks the impotence of Babylonian gods on the one hand, and affirms the active sovereignty of Lord on the other.

[125] Nor would a pagan king be likely to acclaim *just* one god (41, "there isn't any other") although he might well honor one *alongside* others.

[126] One wonders whether TH 28's *Vorlage* used "Chaldeans" in the court-magician sense rather than the citizen-of-Babylon sense; this would make throwing them all to the lions (42) a more feasible proposition.

[127] The OG accordingly uses Jewish points of reference (note esp. the opening verses and the terminology for Lord) in contrast to TH's orientation on the Baylonian court.

[128] Lawrence M. Wills, *The Jew in the Court of a Foreign King: Ancient Jewish Court Legends*, HDR (Minneapolis: Fortress, 1990), 129-37. Wills also finds elements of prophetic legend in the OG (129 n. 102).

[129] Here, I shall deal with the question from a literary point of view: what *literary* features characterize each narrator? One may also ask the question historically: what real person(s) wrote these narratives? See chapters 3 and 7 for discussion of the narrators' historical positions.

what used to be called a "third–person omniscient" viewpoint. We cannot clearly identify them with any story characters and they do not indulge in affective remarks or refer to themselves (external, nonperceptible narrators). They are spatially independent of the narrative actors (e.g., they can observe the events of both 15 and 33-36).[130] In addition to observing actions, they have access to characters' perceptions, thoughts, and feelings.[131]

Both narrators exercise their powers with great discretion. We have seen how sparingly they employ their ability to peep into minds and feelings (table 7). While they occasionally summarize characters' speech or thoughts,[132] they avoid locutions which would confuse their words (primary level) with characters' words or thoughts (second level) and thus weaken dramatic effect.[133]

They also avoid extensive description, using few adjectives (table 10).[134] Most of the adjectives we do find are distributive—e.g. $\pi \hat{\alpha} \varsigma$ and $\check{\epsilon} \kappa \alpha \sigma \tau o \varsigma$—or function as substantives—e.g. $\phi \acute{\iota} \lambda o \varsigma$ in TH 2. ("Big" and "hidden" are TH's main sensory adjectives; the OG uses "big" and "empty.") We have already noted the paucity of explicit characterization (table 5, mark how few characterizations come from the narrators) and spatial detail.

---

130 More precisely, they are independent of the *human* actors. Their standpoints are indistinguishable from that of Lord (who might be also present in all scenes and have access to all minds)—a point to which I shall return.

131 Bal remarks that "when an utterance which is narrated at the second level is not perceptible, this is also an *indication of fictionality*" (136). Meir Sternberg contends that this is a culturally relative statement. "Omniscience in modern narrative attends and signals fictionality, while in the ancient tradition it not only accomodates but also guarantees authenticity" (34).

132 E.g., OG 12, "it seemed a good idea to the king." These summaries tend to occur at transition points.

133 Such confusion does occur in 31-32 (statement of the crowd's purpose), which might be a free summary of the crowd's speech, a report of their thoughts, or the narrator's external assessment of their intentions. Indirect quotation (another cross-level form) occurs in OG 14.

134 TH consistently uses even fewer adjectives than the OG—note v. 7, where TH's Daniel speaks of bronze and clay ($\pi \eta \lambda \acute{o} \varsigma$ and $\chi \alpha \lambda \kappa \grave{o} \varsigma$) while the OG's Daniel uses adjectival forms, "of bronze" and "of clay" ($\pi \acute{\eta} \lambda \iota \nu \acute{o} \varsigma$ and $\chi \alpha \lambda \kappa o \hat{\upsilon} \varsigma$). A preference for nouns belongs to TH's more Hebraizing style.

Table 10.—Adjectives in Bel and the Dragon and Susanna.

	Old Greek			Theodotion		
	No. Adj.	No. Words	% Adj.	No. Adj.	No. Words	% Adj.
Bel and the Dragon	28	894	3.1%	25	863	2.8%
Susanna	59	811	7.2%	73	1133	6.4%

In lieu of overt description, the narrators incorporate information into the narrative flow, most often via reported action.[135] For instance, Bel's provisions are described in context of their being supplied. Description also occurs in conversation—Daniel's words tell us that Bel is made of clay and bronze; the king's words tell us who left tracks on the floor. Description by focalization is limited to a few key events—notably, the king's discovery of Daniel in v. 40.

This style, heavily weighted by dialogue and economical with description, argument, intrusion into character's thoughts, and rhetorical figures, may well be termed "dramatic." It has much the flavor of a theater piece performed on a bare stage with only essential props.[136] Words, and a few key actions, carry the weight of the story. The characters, not the narrators, dismiss Babylonian religion, exalt Lord, and affirm Lord's intervention.

The one exception to this rule comes in OG 39, "Lord God remembered Daniel," which functions primarily as a boundary marker for the end of the Habakkuk episode (an ancient equivalent of "they lived happily ever after") but also as narratorial confirmation of Daniel's assertion in v. 38. Other signs of greater narratorial presence in the OG are its anachronies (TH's anachronies occur only at the second level) and occasional narrative comments in verses where TH employs only

---

[135] "Fabula level" motivation, as compared to description through focalization (motivation at the story level) or a character's words (motivation at the textual level). Bal, 132.

[136] We might even envision a mime, since the narratives tell us so little of how the props look or feel.

dialogue (17, 27). Overall, however, even the OG narrator operates covertly.

Such presentation appears "objective," allowing us to observe and draw our own conclusions. In fact, of course, the narrator determines what we perceive and manipulates us toward the desired impressions. This combination of virtually divine power and resolute anonymity characterizes most biblical narration. Meir Sternberg argues that it allows each situation to be presented in the way which most effectively justifies the deity, while maintaining human and artistic interest. Restrained use of narratorial power combines with anonymity to veil the narrator's ideological alignment and avoid overshadowing of Lord's powers.

> Poised between God and people, then, the narrator in effect claims to draw on both sides, to represent both and to have the interests of both at heart, of which the most vital is to bring their viewpoints into alignment . . . . The building of supernatural premises into the action, the preference of the dramatic method over commentary, the foreshadowing-fulfillment structure of repetition, the manifold patterning of redundancy, speech as creative act, the manipulation of sequence in units ranging from the entire Bible to a verse, similarly variable play of perspective, forms of serialization, shifts between overt and covert providence, spatiotemporal bounding, and so on: the strategy coordinating such an array bespeaks an ideological crux of the first magnitude . . . . Above all, their ideological imperative accounts for the narrator's drastic self-effacement in the handling of a plot that foregrounds God's omnipotence.[137]

Such is the process we see at work in Bel and the Dragon, in both the OG and TH tellings.

---

[137] Sternberg, 118.

Chapter 5

SUSANNA

We turn now to the story of Susanna, as told in the OG and TH. The versions vary more strikingly here than in Bel and the Dragon: as we noted in chapter 3, TH's Susanna is significantly longer than the OG and over a third of it is new material, yet the two versions also contain a significant amount of verbatim overlap,[1] involving long and distinctive expressions at key junctures.

I shall first present translations of the two versions, then discuss them at the successive levels of fabula, story and text. As in chapter 4, observations from close reading will be incorporated into the translation notes and narratological discussion.

Susanna in English

Base Texts

For Susanna as for Bel, the standard critical text (Ziegler's Göttingen Septuagint edition) was prepared prior to Geissen's publication of the Papyrus 967 fragments.[2] Helmut Engel has revised Ziegler's text in light of the papyrus readings (see table 11 for a list of Engel's

---

[1] About 198 words, of the OG's 811 and TH's 1133.

[2] Joseph Ziegler, ed., *Susanna, Daniel, Bel et Draco*, in *Septuaginta*, Vetus Testamentum Graecum auctoritate Societatis Gottingensis editum, vol. 16, no. 2 (Göttingen: Vandenhoeck & Ruprecht, 1954). Ziegler's text varies only slightly from that of Alfred Rahlfs (*Septuaginta*, 2 vols. [Stuttgart: Deutsche Bibelgesellschaft, 1935; combined volume 1979]) in verse numbering and content. Angelo Geissen, *Der Septuaginta-Text des Buches, Daniel: Kap. 5-12, zusammen mit Susanna, Bel et Draco, sowie Esther Kap. 1,1a-2,15, nach dem Kölner Teil des Papyrus 967*, Papyrologische Texte und Abhandlungen (Bonn: Rudolf Habelt, 1968).

changes), and I adopt this revised text for the OG.[3] My TH translation follows Ziegler's edition.

Table 11.—Susanna: Engel's Departures from Ziegler's Old Greek

Verse	Change
5	Begin with περὶ ὧν ἐλάλησεν . . .
9	διεστρέψαντο for διέστρεψαν
21	ἐξεβιάσαντο for ἐξεβιάζοντο
22	αὐτό for τοῦτο
34	πρεσβύτεροι <u>οἱ</u> καὶ κριταί
35	add τῷ before κυρίῳ
35a	ἄνθρωποι ὁμοῦ for ἄνομοι; ἐν for ἐπ'
36	delete δύο
45	συνετάγη for προσετάγη; ὀνόματι for ὄντι
48	delete καί before στάς; μέσος for ἐν μέσῳ; add οἱ before υἱοί; ἀπεκτείνατε for ἀπεκρίνατε
55	σήμερον at beginning of verse, not end (relocate γάρ accordingly)
56	μικρά for μιαρά
57	τὸ νόσημα for τὴν νόσον

Translations

The following translations lean more toward dynamic than grammatical equivalence, although I preserve both when possible. Subsequent discussions will sometimes employ different wording in order to clarify the points being made. Notes begin on page 108.

---

[3] Helmut Engel, *Die Susanna-Erzählung: Einleitung, Übersetzung und Kommentar zum Septuaginta-Text und zur Theodotion-Bearbeitung* (Freiburg: Universitätsverlag, 1985; Göttingen: Vandenhoeck & Ruprecht, 1985), 78-84.

Old Greek	*Theodotion*

1. There was once a man named Joachim, and he lived in Babylon. 2. He married a woman named Susanna, Hilkiah's daughter. She was very beautiful, and devoted to the Lord, 3. for her parents were good people and taught their daughter according to Mosaic law. 4. As for Joachim, he was very rich. His house had fenced grounds, and the Jews gathered around him because he was the most distinguished of them all.

5. Now, about what the Master said: "Lawlessness came from Babylon" (from elders, judges who only seemed to steer the people)— 6. Cases were brought to them from other cities.

5. That year they appointed two elders from the people as judges—about whom the Master said, "Lawlessness came from Babylon" (from elders, judges who only seemed to steer the people). 6. They used to spend a lot of time at Joachim's house, and all the people with lawsuits would come to them.

7. They saw a good-looking woman, wife of one of their Israelite brothers, named Susanna (she was Hilkiah's daughter, married to Joachim), as she was walking around her husband's estate in the evening.

7. Now, when the people went away in the middle of the day, Susanna used to go and stroll about her husband's estate. The two elders saw her coming in and strolling every day, and fell into lust for her.

8. They lusted for her, 9. and perverted their understanding, turning their sights away from heaven and forgetting about fair judgment. 10. Both were hurting over her, but they pretended to each other that they had no evil thoughts about her. The woman knew nothing about the matter.

9. Then they perverted their understanding, turning their sights away from heaven and forgetting about fair judgment. 10. Both were hurting over her, but they didn't tell each other their pain, 11. because they were ashamed to reveal their lust, their desire to have her. Each day they watched intently to see her.

12. When dawn came, they approached secretly, hurrying to be first to show up and speak to her. 13. And she—there she was, walking about as usual. One of the elders came, and then—there came the other! They questioned each other. "How come you went

13. So they said to each other, "It's lunchtime. Let's go home." But after they left they split away from each other 14. and turned back, and ran into each other again. They interrogated each other about the reason, and confessed their lust. Then they made an appointment with each

Old Greek

out early like this and didn't bring me along?" 14. Then they confessed their agony to each other . . .

. . . 19. and said to each other, "Let's approach her." So, having decided, they went to her and grabbed her.

22. The Jewish woman said to them, "I know if I do this, it's death, and if I don't, I still won't escape your hands. 23. But it's better for me to fall into your hands, not having done it, than to sin in Lord's sight."

Theodotion

other for a time when they would be able to find her alone.

15. Now while they were seeking an opportune time, she came into the grounds, just as always, with just two maids, and wanted to take a swim there, since it was hot. 16. No one was around except the two elders—hidden and spying on her. 17. She said to the maids, "Bring me some oil and lotion, and shut the estate gates, please, so I can swim." 18. They did just as she said, shutting the estate gates and going out through the side doors to bring the things she'd asked them for. They didn't see the elders, since they were hidden.

19. When the maids went out, the two elders got up and ran at her, 20. saying, "Look, the estate gates are closed and nobody can see us. We want you, so cooperate and do it with us. 21. If you don't, we'll testify that a young man was with you and that was why you sent your maids away."

22. Susanna groaned. "I'm in a bind! If I do this, it's death, and if I don't, I still won't escape your hands. 23. It's better for me not to do it, and fall into your hands, than to sin in Lord's sight." 24. Then Susanna screamed, but the two elders also yelled at the same time, 25. and one of them ran and opened the estate gates.

26. When the household heard the uproar out on the grounds, people ran through the side doors to see what had happened to her, 27. and when the elders had their say, the servants were real embarrassed, because no one had ever said such a thing about Susanna.

Old Greek	*Theodotion*

28. So the criminals went away, blustering to themselves and plotting her death.

When they came to the assembly of their home town, they held council with those who were there, all the Israelites. 29. The two elders, who were judges, stood up and said, "Send for Susanna, Hilkiah's daughter, who's married to Joachim." Right away they summoned her.

30. The woman came, with her father and mother. Her servants and maids also came (there were five hundred of them), and Susanna's four children. 31. And this woman was extremely good-looking.

32. Then the criminals ordered that she be uncovered, so they could sate their lust for her beauty. Meanwhile, everyone with her and all who knew her cried.

34. Then the elder judges stood and laid their hands on her head. 35. But she trusted firmly in the Lord her God. Looking upward, crying inside, she prayed, 35a. "Lord, Eternal God, who knows everything before it happpens, you know I didn't do what these men conspire to charge me with." And Lord heard her plea.

36. The elders said, "We were walking around on her husband's estate 37. and as we came around the path we saw this one lying with a man. We stood and watched them having intercourse with each other. 38. They didn't know we were standing there. Then we went along with each other, saying, 'Let's find out who these people are.' 39. And when we approached we recognized her, but the

---

28. The next day, when the people gathered around her husband Joachim, the two elders came, full of wicked intent against Susanna, to cause her death.

They said, in the presence of the people, 29. "Send for Susanna, Hilkiah's daughter, who's married to Joachim." And they sent for her.

30. She came, as well as her parents and children and all her relatives. 31. Now Susanna was extremely good-looking, a pleasure to behold.

32. Then the criminals ordered her uncovered (she was veiled) so they could sate themselves with her beauty. 33. Meanwhile, her household and all who saw her were crying.

34. Then the two elders stood in the midst of the people and laid their hands on her head. 35. But she, crying, looked up toward heaven, because she trusted firmly in the Lord.

36. The elders said, "While we were walking by ourselves around the estate, this one came in with two maids, shut the estate gates, and dismissed the maids. 37. Then a young man came to her—he'd been hidden—and lay down with her. 38. We, being in the corner of the grounds and seeing this lawlessness, ran to them. 39. But although we'd seen them doing it, we couldn't get hold of the

Old Greek	*Theodotion*
young man fled, completely covered up. 40. So we caught this one, and asked her, 'Who's the man?' 41. But she didn't tell us who he was. To this we swear." And the whole assembly believed them, because they were elders, and the people's judges.	man because he was stronger than we—he opened the gates and ran away. 40. But this one we caught, and asked who the young man was, 41. and she wouldn't tell us. To this we swear." And the assembly believed them, because they were the people's elders and judges. So they condemned her to death.
	42. Susanna screamed. "Eternal God, who understands hidden things, who knows everything before it happens, 43. you know they've given false testimony against me. Look! I'm going to die, although I haven't done any of the things these men have wickedly accused me of!"
44-45. Then—Lord's angel came! As she was being led away to be executed, Lord's angel (following orders) gave an insightful spirit to a young man named Daniel.	44. Lord heard her cry. 45. As she was being led away to be executed, God began to stir the saintly spirit of a boy named Daniel. He shouted, "I'm innocent of this woman's blood!"
	47. All the people turned toward him. They asked, "What is this, that you've just said?"
48. Cutting through the crowd, Daniel took the stand and said, "Are you such idiots, Israelites? Have you really killed an Israelite woman without investigating and finding out the facts? . . .	48. Taking the stand he said, "Are you such idiots, Israelites? Have you really condemned an Israelite woman without investigating and finding out the facts? Go back to the court, for these men have given false testimony against her."
	50. Everyone rushed back. The elders said to him, "Come, sit with us and enlighten us, since God has given you eldership."
. . . 51. Now, separate them well from each other for me, so I can test them."	51. Daniel said to them, "Separate them well from each other, and I'll question them."
51a. When they had been separated, Daniel said to the assembly, "Now, don't focus on the fact that these are elders, saying, 'Surely they wouldn't lie!' I will	

Old Greek	*Theodotion*

<table>
<tr><td>

ask them whatever questions occur to me."

52. Then he summoned one of them. They led the elder to the young man, and Daniel said to him, "Listen up, you who've grown old in evil times! Now your past sins have caught up with you— 53. you who were trusted to hear and decide cases involving the death penalty— you condemned the innocent, but let the guilty go free, even though the Lord says, 'You shall not kill the innocent or the righteous'! 54. Now, then—under which tree and in what sort of part of the estate did you see them doing it?"

And the godless fellow said, "Under a clove."

55. The young man said, "Right! You've perjured yourself, and this very day Lord's angel will cleave your soul from you."

56. Then, having removed that one, he said to bring him the other one. And to him he said, "How did your genes get twisted to be like Sidon's and not like Judah's? Beauty has led you astray— petty lust! 57. You dealt this way with Israel's daughters, and being afraid, they had intercourse with you. But Judah's daughter refused to give illegal consent to you two's sickness. 58. Now then, tell me: under what tree, and in what kind of place in the grounds did you catch them having intercourse with each other?"

And he said, "Under a yew."

59. Daniel said, "Sinner, Lord's angel stands now with a sword, waiting for the people to destroy you two, that he may hew you."

</td><td>

52. When they had been separated from each other, he summoned one of them and said to him, "You who've grown old in evil times, now your past sins have caught up with you— 53. judging cases unfairly, condemning the innocent and letting the guilty go free, even though the Lord says, 'You shall not kill the innocent or the righteous'! 54. Now, then, if you really saw this woman, say: under what tree did you see them having intercourse with each other?"

And he said, "Under a clove."

55. Daniel said, "Right! You've perjured yourself, and already God's angel has gotten orders from God to cleave you down the middle!"

56. Then, having removed him, he ordered them to bring the other. He said to him, "Offspring of Canaan, rather than Judah, beauty seduced you and lust twisted your mind! 57. You dealt this way with Israel's daughters, and being afraid, they had intercourse with you. But Judah's daughter didn't submit to you two's lawlessness. 58. Now then, tell me: Under what tree did you catch them having intercourse with each other?"

And he said, "Under a yew."

59. Daniel said to him, "Right! You too have perjured yourself! God's angel waits with a sword to hew you down the middle, to destroy you two."

</td></tr>
</table>

Old Greek   *Theodotion*

60–62. Then all the assembly shouted about Daniel, how with his own words he had made them both confess to being false witnesses. Then they dealt with them (just as the law commands) as they had plotted to deal with their sister. They gagged them, led them away, and threw them into a ravine. Then Lord's angel threw fire between them. So innocent blood was saved that day.

60. Then all the assembly yelled and shouted, praising God who saves those who trust in him. 61. They rose up against the two elders, since Daniel had shown them through their own word to be false witnesses. Following Mosaic law, they dealt with them as they had plotted to deal with their neighbor, and killed them. So innocent blood was saved that day.

62a. Thus, in their sincerity, young men are Jacob's beloved. 62b. As for us, we must see that young men become men of worth, for when young men are pious, an insightful and understanding spirit will always be in them.

63. Hilkiah and his wife gave thanks that their daughter had been exonerated from the shameful charge, as did her husband Joachim and all the relatives. 64. As for Daniel, he acquired an impressive reputation from that day on.

Notes

verse 1 (TH): Possible identities of Joachim and Hilkiah will be discussed in chapter 6.

verse 3 (TH): The Greek reads simply, "*and* her parents were good people . . . ," but I judge this to be a case where biblical Greek follows Hebrew style in using a simple coordinating conjunction to express a more complex syntactical relationship. I translate δίκαιοι as "good" because of the problematic overtones "righteous" has acquired in Christian circles. (Carey Moore's "religious" also has much to commend it.)[4]

verse 4: "Estate grounds" is probably our closest equivalent to παράδεισος. "Garden" would preserve the connection to Jeremiah 29 (see chap. 6) but has too horticultural an overtone; "park" describes the landscape more accurately but has a public connotation that makes Susanna's desire to bathe there seem quite inappropriate.

verse 5: I follow 967 and the hexaplaric notations of 88/SyrH in starting the OG here rather than with v. 6. περὶ ὧν thus functions as an introduction of subject matter,[5] rather than an ordinary relative statement

---

[4] Carey A. Moore, *Daniel, Esther, and Jeremiah: The Additions*, AB 44 (New York: Doubleday, 1977), 93.

[5] Cf. 1 Cor 7:1. Josef–Tadeusz Milik, "Daniel et Susanne à Qumrân?," chap. in *De la Tôrah au Messie* (Paris, Desclée, 1981), 345–46; Engel, 12–14. See also my discussion in chapter 3.

(as in TH). Verses 5-6 still read as if they have been torn from context. In chapter 6 we shall look at possible sources for the quote and a context which would allow the elders to be spoken of in this resumptive fashion. It is not clear where the quoted statement ends—I opt for the shortest reasonable length and take the rest of the sentence as an explanatory addition.

Delcor translates πρεσβύτεροι with *anciens* rather than *vieillards*, explaining "Il s'agit ici d'une institution" (a conclusion with which most interpreters seem to agree).[6] The parallel uses of πρεσβύτεροι and κριταί in vv. 5 and 41 (also OG 29, 34) and especially the usage of πρεσβύτεροι in TH 50 do suggest that it connotes formal authority in addition to age, so I translate "elders" rather than "old men."[7]

Both versions use δεσπότης (Master) rather than κύριος (Lord) in this verse only. δοκέω in the final clause is ambiguous: did they *appear* to be steering (a nautical term) the people (people's perception), or did they *think* they were steering the people (elders' perception)? I opt for the former, on the assumption that the elders knew their own perfidy perfectly well.

verse 7: Notice the order in which the OG tells us what the elders notice about Susanna: first her beauty, only then that she is "wife of their brother." Ἀστεῖος can mean "urbane," but here it seems to refer more to physical beauty (cf. Jdt 11:23, although the context there also praises Judith's wisdom and culture).[8] Here as in v. 29 Susanna's father is named before her husband. Papryus 967 lacks τὸ δειλινόν. Milik omits it as an adaptation to TH; Engel hesitates.[9]

verse 9: Natural-sounding English requires fairly free rendering in this verse. The first phrase has a reflexive sense (middle aorist in the OG, ἑαυτῶν in TH): "they perverted *their own* understanding." The plural verb with singular νοῦν conveys the elders' individual responsibility as well as their union in villainy.

---

[6] Matthias Delcor, *Le livre de Daniel* (Paris: J. Gabalda, 1971), 263.

[7] But see Emil Schürer, *The History of the Jewish People in the Time of Jesus Christ: A New English Version*, 3 vols., rev. and ed. Geza Vermes, Fergus Millar, and Martin Goodman (Edinburgh: T. & T. Clark, 1973-86), 1:101-2. According to this source, "the earliest clearly dated evidence [for use of the title πρεσβύτερος in the Diaspora] is . . . from the synagogue of Dura-Europos, from AD 244-5 . . . . The inscriptions on which the title occurs all seem to be relatively late . . . . It is also open to question whether *presbyteros* in the inscriptions is everywhere meant as a title, and not on occasion simply as a designation of age."

[8] The OG does seem interested in Susanna's aristocratic standing; note its enumeration of her servants in v. 30.

[9] Milik, 341 n. 10; Engel, 78.

verse 10: The OG seems to say, "they did not pretend (to one another) the evil they had about her," but that does not fit the situation. My interpretation follows the general line suggested by Bissell.[10] Note "their" (plural) pain and lust, in both versions.

verse 11 (TH): Kay gives a lovely (if now quaint) translation of συγγενέσθαι αὐτῇ as "to have to do with her."[11]

verse 14: Both versions use language with strong judicial overtones.

verse 15 (TH): In Greek, Susanna requests lotion and soap because she wants to take a bath, but outdoor bathing is so risqué in our culture that readers quickly conclude that Susanna is "looking for trouble." Culturally, taking a swim provides a better equivalent.[12] The phrase translated "just as always" seems to originate in the Hebrew כִּתְמוֹל שִׁלְשׁוֹם (Gen 31:2, 2 Kgs 13:55).[13]

verse 20 (TH): γενοῦ μεθ᾽ ἡμῶν may reflect the Hebrew idiom הָיָה עִם (cf. Gen 39:12, 2 Sam 13:20, and Tob 3:8).

verse 22: TH's phrase, στενά μοι πάντοθεν, also occurs in 2 Sam 24:14. I have not found any examples of this idiom outside of biblical contexts.

verse 24 (TH): Delcor notes the judicial significance of Susanna's cry (cf. Deut 22:24).[14] The elders shout κατέναντι αὐτῆς, which might be applied to the content of their shout—thus "against her" (both Moore and Kay)—or taken in the sense of creating a counter-ruckus, thus my "at the same time."[15]

verse 28: Papyrus 967's OG text lacks ἐν ἑαυτοῖς, but it should probably be retained as the more difficult reading.[16]

verse 32: Does the uncovering have significance beyond the reason stated in the text ("that they might sate themselves with her beauty")? Ezek 16:39 and rabbinic parallels suggest that it may have been customary to bare a convicted adulteress as part of her punishment;

---

[10] Edwin Cone Bissell, *The Apocrypha of the Old Testament: With Historical Introductions, A Revised Translation, and Notes Critical and Explanatory* (New York: Charles Scribner's Sons, 1903), 457.

[11] David M. Kay, "Susanna," *APOT* 1:648.

[12] The same problem arises in connection with Bathsheba's rooftop lustration (2 Sam 11:2), although that text indicates the woman's innocence less clearly.

[13] Theodor von Wiederholt, "Die Geschichte der Susanna," *TQ* 51 (1869): 297.

[14] Delcor, 267.

[15] Moore, 94; Kay, 648.

[16] So Milik, 342, and Engel, 100.

if so, this represents one more perversion of judicial process: Susanna has not yet been accused, let alone convicted.[17]

verse 34: Here we see the truth of Susanna's words, "I will not escape your hands" (22). This laying-on of hands is another gesture the implications of which are hotly debated; attempts have been made to connect it with procedures prescribed for cases of blasphemy (Lev 24:14) and adultery (Deut 17:7).[18] None of the proposed parallels exactly matches the phraseology of this passage, although it does seem quite possible that it refers to a standard courtroom procedure.

verse 35: The implications of καρδία are sufficiently different from English "heart" that I drop the word entirely (thus implicitly interpreting it as "self," or that part of the self which trusts). Milik points out that only here does biblical literature speak of Lord as a woman's personal God.[19] Note the contrast between the elders who looked away from heaven (9) and Susanna who looks toward it.

Does the OG's "inwardly" apply to Susanna's weeping, her prayer, or both? Engel argues, by parallel with Sarah's laughter in Genesis 18, that the crying and prayer are *both* internal,[20] giving Susanna a more self-disciplined appearance. (To avoid confusing the issue, I translate λέγουσα, often used for thoughts, as "prayed" rather than "said.") Her inward weeping corresponds to the inward threats of the elders in OG 28.

verse 35a (OG): Papyrus 967 reads ἄνθρωποι ὁμοῦ where the OG and SyrH have ἄνομοι. "Conspire" picks up the senses of both wickedness and joint action.[21]

verse 36: TH's shift from κορασίων (narrator, 15, 17, and 19; elders, 21) to παιδισκῶν (36, twice) is one of many subtle clues that the elders are lying.

---

[17] Frank Zimmermann, "The Story of Susanna and its Original Language," *JQR* 48 (1957-58): 236-37 n. 2.

[18] For discussion of these and other possible parallels, see Otto Fridolin Fritzsche, "Zusätze zu dem Buche Daniel," in *Kurzgefasstes exegetisches Handbuch zu den Apokryphen des Alten Testaments*, ed. O. Fritzsche and C. Grim (Leipzig: Weidmann'sche Buchhandlung, 1851), 1:138; Otto Zöckler, "Die erzählenden Zusätze zu Daniel," chap. in *Die Apokryphen des alten Testamentes*, Kurzgefasstes Kommentar zu den Heiligen Schriften des alten und neuen Testamentes sowie zu den Apokryphen (München: Oskar Beck, 1892), 9:218; Bissell, 458; Charles James Ball, "The Additions to Daniel," in *Apocrypha of the Speaker's Commentary*, ed. Henry Wace (London: John Murray, 1888), 2:337. Engel gives a nice summary of the evidence in his excursus on the problem, 137-141.

[19] Milik, 342 n. 27—but Ruth 1:16?

[20] Engel, 106.

[21] The papyrus also reads ἐν where SyrH and 88 have ἐπ'.

verse 37: The OG's ὁμιλοῦντας can refer to either conversation (see Dan 1:19) or sex. (It is perhaps less "loaded" toward the latter than its English analogue "intercourse.")

verse 39: The elders' explanation in the OG seems inherently suspicious: "completely covered" is not what we expect in light of the activity the young man flees from.

verse 41: A number of biblical texts (Lev 20:10, 21:9, Deut 22:22, Ezek 16:38-40, John 8:5) speak of capital punishment for adultery.

verse 43: I like the briskness of Moore's "they have framed me," but I prefer "false testimony" for its resonance with the Ten Commandments (this passage does not use precisely the same language as Exod 20:16, but the latter surely lurks close by).

verse 44/45 (OG): Papyrus 967 reads ὀνόματι Δανιηλῳ rather than ὄντι Δανιηλ—perhaps reflecting a stage less accommodated to the book of Daniel. The nuances of νεώτερος are discussed below, beginning on page 130.

verse 45 (TH): τὸ πνεῦμα τὸ ἅγιον is used for God's spirit in Ps 51:13 (LXX 50:13), Isa 63:10-11, and Wis 9:17, and of Daniel's spirit in Dan 4:4 and 5:11,14 (LXX 4:8, 5:12, 6:3).

verse 48: Standing "in the midst" may have legal overtones (cf. Sir 1:30), thus my translation "taking the stand." μωροί may connote religious obtuseness rather than simple stupidity.[22] In the OG I (following Engel) follow the Chigi manuscript, Syrohexapla, and Papyrus 967, which all read ἀπεκτείνατε, rather than Ziegler and Rahlfs, who both emend to ἀπεκρίνατε. Technically speaking, of course, Susanna has not yet been killed—but in light of the verdict and the fact that she is even now being led to execution, Daniel's reference to the killing as a *fait accompli* is easily understandable.

verse 49 (TH): κριτήριον, like "court," may refer to either a place or the tribunal which sits there.

verse 50 (TH): Evidently the speakers here are the "elders" in general—not the two elders who have accused Susanna—but the text, like my translation, refers to them simply as "the elders." Scholz reads the turning as "repentance" and argues that it is indeed Susanna's assailants, overcome by conscience, who now invite Daniel to teach them.[23]

verse 53: In the OG, Daniel says the elder has condemned (aorist) the innocent one (singular) while he has been letting (imperfect)

---

22 Engel, 117.

23 Anton Scholz, *Commentar über das Buch "Esther" mit seinen Zusätzen und über "Susanna"* (Würzburg: Leo Woerl, 1892), 174-76.

the guilty ones (plural) go free—a description strikingly applicable to the affair at hand.[24] Both versions quote Exod 23:7 (LXX) verbatim.[25]

verse 54: The σχῖνος is usually identified as a mastich tree (*Pistacia Lentiscus*), but the pun seems more important than the actual species.[26] Since at least the time of Julius Africanus, folk have argued that this paronomasia proves that the story was written in Greek. Others respond that the Greek may reflect word-play in a Hebrew or Aramaic original.[27]

In the OG, Daniel asks *two* questions, although he receives only one answer. Milik argues that an Aramaic original would have contained a *quadruple* word-play here, involving the type of tree (ערבא), its location in the garden (בערבא or במערבא), and two meanings of the verb ערב.[28]

verse 55: My thanks to Carey Moore for the elegant rendering, "you've perjured yourself." My treatment of the paronomasia here and in v. 59 follows a suggestion by Ball.[29]

verse 56: I read μικρὰ ἐπιθυμία, as in all three OG manuscripts, rather than μιαρὰ ἐπιθυμία as proposed by Rahlfs and Ziegler. Milik argues that "Judah" here refers specifically to the patriarch, not generally to nationality, and posits several parallels with the pseudepigraphal *Testament of Judah*.[30]

verse 57: Daniel uses a second-person plural in his accusation, as indicated by "you two."

verse 58: Again my translation stresses the upcoming pun rather than botanical identification.[31]

---

24 I owe this observation to Engel, 122.

25 ἀσεβής in OG 54 may continue the allusion to Exod 23:7, while the verb διαστρέπω (used for the other elder in 56) might possibly echo Exod 23:6.

26 LSJ, s.v. Scholz, against virtually all other interpreters, insists that the actual species is important. He identifies the trees here and in v. 58 as the בְּרוֹשׁ and תְאַשּׁוּר, which he interprets (on the basis of Isa 60:13 and Hos 14:9) as symbols of the Realm of God. According to Scholz, when the elders name these trees, they symbolically confess Susanna's innocence, and it is on this basis that Daniel can declare the first to have condemned himself before hearing the answer of the second. Scholz, *Susanna*, 144.

27 E.g. Zimmermann, 237. The Vulgate brings the pun into Latin here (*sub schino—Ecce enim Angelus Dei scindet te medium*) but not in 58-59.

28 Milik, 350-53.

29 Moore, 107; Ball, 341 (followed by Moore as well).

30 Milik, 344 nn. 49, 51-52.

31 But see note 26 on Scholz's argument that the botanical reference is important.

verses 60–62 (OG), *verse 62* (TH): The commandment referred to is presumably Deut 19:19.[32] The OG's "sister" may correspond to "brother" in the Deuteronomy text, but is highly ironic in view of its use elsewhere as a romantic term of endearment.[33] (TH's "neighbor" appears in an alternate Greek Deuteronomy tradition.)

The OG's reference to "gagging" or silencing is puzzling; this custom is not otherwise attested.[34] Engel relates the hurling to the punishment prescribed for blasphemers in Lev 24:14. The subsequent punishment by fire may relate to Lev 21:9 and Jer 29:22 (LXX 36:22)— I shall have more to say about this in chapter 6.

verses 62a–b (OG): This section poses a number of problems.[35] The Greek text reads:

Διὰ τοῦτο οἱ νεώτεροι ἀγαπητοὶ Ιακωβ ἐν τῇ ἁπλότητι αὐτῶν καὶ ἡμεῖς φυλασσώμεθα εἰς υἱοὺς δυνατοὺς νεωτέρους εὐσεβήσουσι γὰρ νεώτεροι καὶ ἔσται ἐν αὐτοῖς πνεῦμα ἐπιστήμης καὶ συνέσεως εἰς αἰῶνα αἰῶνος.

Several questions arise. Are young men Jacob's beloved, or (as suggested by SyrH, which transposes ἀγαπητοί and Ιακωβ) are Jacob's young men beloved, and in any case, what does that mean? I understanding "Jacob's beloved" in the sense of "those of Jacob who are beloved," the "true Israelites."[36] Note the contrast with v. 56, where the second elder has "genes like Sidon's rather than Judah's."

Next we must ask the meaning of φυλασσώμεθα εἰς . . . . Fritzsche suggests reading ὡς for εἰς: "und lasset uns bewachen, schützen wie Söhne die mächtigen, vornehmen Jugendlichen," or, as Bissell puts it in English, "let us watch over, as sons, mighty young

---

[32] During the reign of Alexander Janneus the interpretation of Deut 19:19 was hotly debated—should one punish the false witness as the victim had actually *been punished*, or as the witness *had intended* for the victim to be punished? Many mid-twentieth century commentators regard "Susanna" as a propaganda piece related to this controversy, e.g. Robert H. Pfeiffer, *History of New Testament Times With an Introduction to the Apocrypha* (New York: Harper and Brothers, 1949), 435. TH's specification of *Mosaic* law may indicate the importance of other civil law in its time.

[33] Engel, 129.

[34] For discussion see Zimmermann, 240–41. Scholz (180–81) relates it to texts about the binding of demons or Satan.

[35] Fritzsche (144) calls the Greek "unexampled and intolerable." Ball (342) says, "It is difficult to imagine that Greek was the original language of this closing sentence. As Greek it is intolerable as well as unintelligible." He continues, ". . . as a bald rendering from a Semitic tongue its peculiarities are intelligible enough."

[36] Engel (85) translates, "Deshalb (sind) die Jungen die (von Gott) geliebten Jakobs (söhne) wegen ihrer Ganzheit."

men."[37]   Others, I think correctly, separate υἱοὺς δυνατούς from νεωτέρους and take εἰς as indicative of purpose or product, thus Kay, "Let us watch over young men so that they may become men of worth."[38]

Finally, we must figure out how the final statements about young men (they "are pious, and an insightful and understanding spirit will be in them forever") relate to the watching/guarding. Some, appealing to a presumed Semitic original, give a resultative sense to γάρ—thus Kay ("for *so* young men will be God-fearing") and Pfeiffer ("so that they may become valiant, pious, and understanding").[39] MacKenzie, by contrast, takes the first clause as condition and the second as result: "if young men are pious, a spirit of discernment and understanding will remain in them."[40]   This fits the Greek more comfortably. In this reading, piety evidenced by the young guarantees their future wisdom and makes them proper candidates for community leaders.

verse 63 (TH): Note that Susanna's family celebrates her innocence (or perhaps the recognition of such), rather than her survival. The phrase ἄσχημον πρᾶγμα also appears in Deut 24:1 (LXX).

Fabula

We turn now to an analysis of the Susanna narratives at the fabula level. The fabula, the reader will recall, is the sequence of events presumed by a narrative. These events involve various actors (subjects and objects of action) and take place in time and space. We shall look at each of these elements in turn.

Events

In chapter 4, I used the criteria of change, choice, and confrontation to identify central events of Bel and the Dragon's fabula.[41]   I apply

---

[37] Fritzsche, 144; Bissell, 457.

[38] Kay, 651, with a list of Hebrew parallels in the accompanying note. See also Ball, 342, and Roderick A. F. MacKenzie, "The Meaning of the Susanna Story," *CJT* 3 (1957), 213. These interpreters take υἱοὺς δυνατούς as a Greek equivalent of בנ חיל (cf. 2 Sam 2:7).

[39] Kay, 651; Pfeiffer, 436.

[40] MacKenzie, 213. Engel (85) takes a similar tack: "denn (wenn) die jungen (Leute) gottesfürchtig sind, dann wird ihnen Geist von Wissen und Einsicht zuteil zu aller Zeit."

[41] Mieke Bal, *Narratology: Introduction to the Theory of Narrative* (Toronto: University of Toronto Press, 1985), 13–18.

the same criteria to the Susanna narratives, but with the further observation that key events tend to occur in triads: first an event which poses a choice, second the making of that choice, and third the outcome of the decision.[42] For instance, when the sight of Susanna awakens lust in the elders (7-8) a choice opens: will they give rein to their desire? They do, "perverting their understanding" (9), and this leads to individual efforts to meet Susanna. We can summarize this triad with the question, "will the elders control their lust?"

Table 12 presents the key event–series of each Susanna version in such question form. The two fabulas contain the same core events, although TH orders the fourth and fifth series differently than does the OG.

Table 12.—Event Series in Susanna.

Series #	Controlling Choice	Outcome Value
Old Greek		
1	Will the elders control their lust?	(+)
2	Will they confide their lust to each other?	(+)
3	Will Susanna accede to their wishes?	(−)?
4	Will God respond to Susanna?	(−)
5	Will the assembly believe the elders?	(+)
6	Will the assembly listen to Daniel?	(−)
7	Will the elders be able to answer the questions?	(−)
Theodotion		
1	Will the elders control their lust?	(+)
2	Will they confide their lust to each other?	(+)
3	Will Susanna accede to their wishes?	(−)? (+)
4	Will the assembly believe the elders?	(+)
5	Will God respond to Susanna?	(−)
6	Will the assembly listen to Daniel?	(−)
7	Will the elders be able to answer the questions?	(−)

Note: outcome values determined with respect to the elders' aim. (See discussion on page 118.)

The first series (will the elders control their lust?) deserves special note, because Susanna can be read as a "blame the victim" story—what did she expect, bathing in the garden?[43] Indeed, both versions treat the elders' lust as a natural consequence of seeing Susanna—they saw her and wanted her. What the tales do not assume is that desire must automatically lead to perversion. Instead, both present the perversion as a separate event, an action performed by the elders themselves (not inflicted on them by the woman).[44]

In TH's fabula, series of events follow one another in a single continuous chain. In particular, Susanna's prayer (42-43) comes as a natural response to her conviction (41). God's decision to attend to it (44, resulting in Daniel's agitation, 45) leads smoothly to the next sequence (Daniel's outcry and the assembly's response, 46-50). God thus makes a point intervention in a straightforward sequence of events.

The OG presents a more complex picture. Here, Susanna's prayer—and God's reported attention to it—occurs between her arraignment (to which it is an understandable response) and the elders' testimony. The earthly chain of events continues—the elders testify, the assembly condemns, and Susanna is led away for execution. But the prayer has initiated a second, ultimately decisive sequence in which God hears the prayer and orders the angel to inspire Daniel (who successfully challenges Susanna's conviction). This double-stranded fabula suggests a world in which divergent causal chains twist back upon one another. Even as human perfidy works its evil, a salvific impulse, prompted by prayer, propagates through layers of agents and ultimately leads the evildoers to work their own downfall.[45]

---

[42] Ibid., 19-20, building on the work of Claude Bremond.

[43] Thus my preference for the translation "swim."

[44] See the note to v. 9. This attitude runs counter to the Greco-Roman culture's general assumption that lust aroused leads more or less automatically to action (oral communication from Brian Grant). Commentators have asked how TH can use ἐπιθυμέω for an innocent wish in v. 15 when the noun ἐπιθυμία carries such negative freight elsewhere in the narrative. The answer may lie partly in this distinction between desire per se and subsequent perversion of the will.

[45] Robert P. Dunn, although generally a sensitive reader, fails to note this significant plot difference between the versions. His oversight may result from the fact that he uses Proppian event-categories (drawn from Russian heroic fairy tales) for his analysis. Dunn, "Discriminations in the Comic Spirit in the Story of Susanna," *Christianity and Literature* 31, no. 4 (Summer, 1982): 20-21. Engel, 164, likewise fails to attribute any significance to the differing placements of the prayer.

Actors and Aims

Who is the principal subject of Susanna? Two candidates come immediately to mind: Susanna herself, and the elders (considered collectively as a single actant). Susanna aims to live a virtuous life.[46] The elders wish to possess her sexually—a desire evident in series 1–3 and in their command to expose Susanna during the trial. This wish, when frustrated, transmutes into a wish for Susanna's death, the motivating (if ultimately denied) aim of event series 4–7 in both stories. Susanna's counter-aim correspondingly takes two forms: in series 1–3 she seeks to live *virtuously*; in series 4–7 she struggles to *live* virtuously.

Thus the relationship of life and virtue stands at issue. The elders want Susanna to believe that sexual acquiescence will preserve life, while virtuous refusal will bring death. Susanna denies the first part of their equation, asserting in both versions that "if I do this, it is death to me" (22). But she accepts the second part: ". . . if I do not, I will not escape your hands."

In the fabula structure, by contrast, sexual acquiescence in the first part corresponds to death in the second; virtue in the first to life in the second. In preserving her virtue, Susanna preserves her life as well. We may summarize these relationships as follows:

Elders:	Sex = Life	Chastity = Death
Susanna:	Sex = Death	Chastity = Death[47]
Fabula structure:	Sex = Death	Chastity = Life

Phrasing the aims in terms of sex/chastity and death/life gives valuable insight into the relationships of these terms, but also leaves a sense of disjuncture between the first and second parts of the tales. This can be overcome by phrasing the aims more broadly in terms of control: the elders want to control Susanna; Susanna wants not to be controlled by them.[48] Clearly, then, the elders' aim determines the fabula; Susanna's is reactionary to theirs.[49]

---

[46] Is the "virtue" chastity, or fidelity? I suspect the former, on the basis of Hellenistic trends toward the idealizing of virginity (c.f. *Joseph and Asenath*) and the near–invisibility of Susanna's husband Joachim.

[47] More precisely, Susanna argues that sex = death and not-sex = not-life.

[48] To say that Susanna wants to control herself would inject a modern agenda in the text; the story does not tell us that she desires self-determination, only that she resists determination by the elders. Susanna's response to the elders suggests that she is content to be controlled by Lord; the characterization of her as virtuous daughter, wife, and mother suggests that she also acquiesces to control by her husband and parents. Esther evinces a similar pliability.

This leaves us with the following list of participants:

The elders are primary subjects who desire to control Susanna, the object.

Susanna, as object, nonetheless holds power to grant or withhold that which the elders desire.

The assembly helps the elders in the OG series 5 (TH series 4) but opposes them in the chain initiated by Susanna's prayer (series 6 and 7). The assembly aligns itself with whoever plays the subject role in a given series.

Daniel and *Lord*, by helping Susanna, act as opponents of the elders. This may seem theologically troubling: we expect Lord to be a "power." But in Susanna Lord's help is incidental, necessary but not sufficient to determine the tales' outcome.[50]

Conspicuous by their absence from the list of actors are Susanna's household and especially her husband, Joachim. These characters provide scenic interest but do nothing to affect the tales' outcome. It comes as no great surprise that the Syriac version makes Susanna a widow (having been married for only a few days before her husband's death).[51] Joachim's insignificance is one reason for suspecting that the tellers think of Susanna's virtue more in terms of chastity than of fidelity.[52]

An actor's effectiveness in achieving (or opposing) aims depends on the actor's possession of various competences, which we may broadly categorize under the headings of determination, power, and skill.[53] Table 13 shows the distribution of competences among Susanna's primary actors.

---

[49] This designation of the elders as primary subjects does not mean that they are the "heroes" with whom our sympathy lies. Clearly Susanna takes that role.

[50] Bal, 31. Dunn (22–23) makes a great deal of the angel's presence as a Proppian "helper" in the OG and the fact that the angel gives Daniel something, while in TH God merely "somehow inspires Daniel to counteract the villains." I feel that Dunn overlooks the stand-in quality of angels in biblical narrative (compare the angel's role in Bel and the Dragon) and ignores the functional equivalence of the angel's action in the OG with God's in TH.

[51] William H. Daubney, *The Three Additions to Daniel* (Cambridge: Deighton and Bell, 1906), 155.

[52] This celebration of chastity in a story that turns on sex recalls parallels such as Judith, *Joseph and Asenath*, and the Hellenistic romances—not to mention early Christian hagiography, which Thomas Häag views as successor to the romances. Thomas Häag, *The Novel in Antiquity* (Berkeley and Los Angeles: University of California Press, 1983), 154–165.

[53] Bal, 33–34, drawing on the work of A. J. Greimas.

Table 13.—Competences in Susanna.

Actor	Competence(s)
Elders	Determination, power, skill
Susanna	Determination
Assembly	Power
Daniel	Skill
(Lord)	(Delegates to Daniel)

The table shows very clearly why the elders cannot be defeated until determination, power, and wisdom are aligned against them by the alliance of Susanna, Daniel (with Lord's help), and the assembly, for the elders alone possess all three types of competence. It is also interesting to note how competences are passed between actors. The assembly possesses power but consistently delegates it—first to the elders, then to Daniel. The other character who delegates is Lord. Lord, in the OG, supplies Daniel's wisdom. In TH, Lord might be seen as supplying wisdom, or determination to complement an already–possessed wisdom.[54]

Note also that while the elders clearly function as a single actant (neither version even names them individually), they do not always act in concert. Initially they deceive one another about their desires and plans, but after unexpectedly encountering each other on the estate grounds they begin to cooperate. Collusion ends when they are separated for questioning. While cooperating they are effective; acting singly they seem impotent. For the villains as for the heroes, success in this fabula world depends on cooperation with others.

This fabula, like Bel and the Dragon's, enmeshes the actors in various relationships of falsehood and secrecy. The elders appear as protectors of virtue; in fact they violate it. The assembly appears to exercise judgment; in fact it easily yields to manipulation. Susanna appears easy prey; in fact she and her supporting powers bring the elders to destruction. Daniel appears a youth, but possesses the wisdom of

---

[54] TH 45 tells us that Lord was "rousing up" (ἐξήγειρεν) Daniel's spirit. In v. 50 the assembly asserts that God has given eldership (πρεσβεῖον) to Daniel, which might be seen as either wisdom or power.

eldership. Lord does not appear at all, but exists and exercises decisive influence.

In general, the worldly rulers of the fabula (elders, assembly) appear powerful and virtuous, but are weak and corrupt. They are deceitful. Susanna and her helpers (Lord and Daniel), seem powerless but can mobilize the resources needed to prevail. They have secret power—and in this treacherous fabula world, they need it.[55]

Time and Location

The Susanna fabulas present an interesting mix of development and crisis in their use of time. Both versions make clear that the villainy of the elders has been brewing over a long period of time (52-53, 57). The actual events of the fabulas, however, take place within a short period. The OG's action begins with an evening stroll by Susanna[56] and extends through her trial which seems to take place the following afternoon.

TH's fabula develops over a somewhat broader time period than the OG's. This version alludes at the beginning to the long and careful training which Susanna has undergone (3). In the story proper, the elders' lust simmers for some days between seeing Susanna and their confession to one another.[57] First sight, confession and conspiracy, and the actual proposition all take place in mid-day, its heat providing a metaphor for lust as well as occasion for Susanna to disrobe.

Divergence between appearance and reality, which we noted in the fabulas' actor relationships, occurs again in their handling of space. Two locations dominate the OG's fabula: Joachim's estate and the assembly-place of the elders' city. The estate, seemingly under Susanna's husband's control, is in fact a place of assault by strangers, where occur the plot events associated with the elders' lust (series 1, 2, and 3). The assembly-place, ostensibly a place of justice, turns out (at least initially) to be the place where an innocent woman is condemned while the guilty go free. Here occur the plot events associated with the elders' desire to condemn and kill (series 4, 5, 6, and 7). The ravine

---

[55] For the definitions of "lie" and "secret" see Bal, 34-36.

[56] If we follow 88 and SyrH rather than Papyrus 967, which omits τὸ δειλινόν.

[57] καθ᾽ ἡμέραν they see her (8) and seek to behold her again (12). It is not quite clear whether a further period elapses between their mutual confession and the seized opportunity (14-15).

into which the condemned are flung figures only briefly as a site of punishment at the end of the fabula.

TH places the entire fabula at Joachim's house: there Susanna is initially accosted and there she is later tried.[58] The expected protective quality of the estate is symbolized by the closing of its gates when Susanna wishes to bathe, but those closed gates become symbols of entrapment in the presence of the elders (20). Since this fabula centers on a single location, a change in time (28, τῇ ἐπαύριον), rather than location, separates the lust sequence (series 1, 2, and 3) from the death sequence (series 4, 5, 6, and 7).

Both versions contain a final spatial contrast between heaven above and the earth below. These realms are linked by eyesight. When earthlings turn their eyes from heaven (9), trouble results. When eyes look up (35), heaven responds to right the injustices of earth.

Stories

We turn now from the relatively formal, functional level of fabula to the level of story, which encompasses tellers' decisions about chronological sequence, rhythm and frequency, and characterization and focalization.[59] At story level, the OG and TH diverge much more markedly than they did in their fabulas.

Sequence

One way a story may differ from its fabula is in the ordering of events. OG Susanna has no temporal displacements at the narratorial level, and TH has only a few (vv. 3, 5, 27, and 63). Of these, only one (27, "such things had never been said") occurs in the main body of the story, and it, like TH's anachrony in Bel 12, conveys information from characters' thoughts, so we do not experience it as a violation of story sequence. (A similar argument could be made for 63's comment that "no shameful thing had been found.")

The characters, by contrast, engage in a great deal of retrospection and anticipation. They enunciate questions, comments, and

---

[58] One cannot tell whether the trial takes place in the house or outside on the grounds.

[59] We shall not devote a separate section to space, since the presentation of space in the stories does not differ greatly from its valence in the fabulas. Story segmentation will be discussed in conjunction with rhythm.

allegations about past events; they offer orders, threats, and speculation about future ones. We shall return to some of these utterances later, for the relationship between characters' narration and the narrators' creates noteworthy effects at the textual level of the narratives.

For now, we observe that the characters of the Susanna stories are historically conscious beings. Past and future, made present in words, control their lives. This verbalized history is shifting and unstable, being recounted now one way, now another. Words remake reality in the elders' testimony; more words explode that illusion in Daniel's cross-examination. Words control history.

Lord is the one actor independent of this captivity to history-in-words, as Susanna (OG 35a, TH 42–43) so clearly states: "Lord, Eternal God, who knows everything before it happpens . . ."[60] Lord alone has knowledge apart from temporal sequence, knowledge independent of oh-so-fallible verbal reports of that sequence.[61] The TH version of the prayer makes Lord's cognitive independence even more explicit by adding the epithet, "who knows hidden things."

Most of the stories' temporal displacements refer to events within the primary span of the fabula. Exceptions are TH's reports of Susanna's upbringing (3) and spotless reputation (27) and Daniel's accusations of a long history of perfidy by the elders (52–53, 56–57, both versions). These extradiegetic references suggest that virtue (in TH) and vice (both versions) are character qualities developed/exhibited over a long period of time. This gives a sense that the crisis events of the fabula proper are representative rather than exceptional.

One other set of references in the stories reaches beyond the primary span of the fabula: the allusions to scripture in vv. 5, 53, and 62, as well as TH 3.[62] The stories set up a subtle but strong contrast between the ancient, prophetic (time-spanning), and fixed Word of the tradition (compare Lord's own independence from time and testimony) and the transitory, often deceptive quality of contemporary speech.[63]

---

[60] OG 35a, similarly TH 42-3.

[61] The prayer's use of οἶδα for "know" might be significant in this respect.

[62] I identify these as scriptural references on the basis of the way they are presented in Susanna itself. In chapter 6 we shall take up the question of what specific texts the storytellers may have had in mind (5 is particularly problematic), and how these texts interact with the Susanna story itself.

[63] Susanna's prayer is an interesting intermediate case, strongly situational but able to reach the divine ear.

Rhythm and Frequency

In Bel and the Dragon, we saw a close association between dialogue and scenic presentation: dialogue dominated the scenes of the narrative, while the more rapidly paced connective sections were composed entirely of narration.

The Susanna stories also contain a great deal of dialogue,[64] but most of it is concentrated in a few long speeches (esp. 36–41, 52–54, and 56–58), so that overall the Susanna stories contain fewer pieces of quoted dialogue (14 in the OG, 19 in TH) than does Bel and the Dragon (24 pieces in the OG, 23 in TH).[65] By contrast Susanna contains *more* indirect quotations and reported speech acts than Bel and the Dragon.[66] Such speech forms tend to fall midway between the scenic pace of quoted dialogue and the summarizing pace of connecting narrative. Their employment in Susanna yields a broad, variably paced narrative flow. Bel and the Dragon had three speeds: Scene, summary, and ellipsis.[67] The Susanna stories seem to have infinitely variable transmissions.

Within this variable flow, we can nonetheless distinguish broad regions of slower movement and greater emphasis, and these vary between the versions. We have seen that the OG concentrates the primary fabula events (from the elders' first sighting of Susanna to their execution) into a two–day period, and presents the development of the elders' lust (7–10) singulatively (aorist verbs, one–day time span). Descriptive material about Susanna which appears *within* the report of their seeing (7) prolongs the narration of this key moment. Verse 9 with its multiple phrases for capitulation to temptation creates a similar effect. Imperfect verbs in vv. 10 and 12 mark a transition to the next scene.

---

[64] OG Susanna is 42 percent dialogue, TH 37 percent. (The Bel and the Dragon narratives were 31 [OG] and 33 [TH] percent dialogue.) About two–thirds of the verbatim identity between versions occurs in dialogue at key points in the story (Susanna's refusal, the elder's testimony, Susanna's prayer, Daniel's cross–examination)—at the "punch lines," so to speak.

[65] OG Susanna thus has one piece of quoted dialogue per 58 words, and TH one per 60, while Bel and the Dragon had one per 37–38 words in each version.

[66] Indirect discourse gives the content of speech, although not in the actor's own words—e.g. v. 32, "They commanded that she be revealed." In reported speech the narrator tells us that someone spoke, but does not cite the words even indirectly—e.g. 52, "He called one of them." Bal discusses these forms as an aspect of text (137–142), and we too will return to the topic when we examine the textual level. I mention it here because of the close association between speech forms and pacing.

[67] Similar patterns typify classical Hebrew and New Testament narratives.

The OG report of the elders' encounters with one another and Susanna the next day shows scenic elements combined with summarizing ones.[68] ἰδού (twice-repeated) gives visual sharpness and we find three pieces of quoted dialogue. In this version, the elders' conference and their assault on Susanna comprise a single scene in which the elders hold center stage.

From here the OG moves quickly to Susanna's trial. Verses 30–33 use description to retard the narrative pace.[69] Dialogue dominates 35–59. Only twice in the OG do actors respond to quoted speech with more quoted speech; both instances occur in the trial scene.[70]

Although the trial (29–59, or 28–62 if we include introduction and conclusion) is continuous in time and space, the angel's intervention in verses 44–45 marks a significant break, before which the elders dominate and after which Daniel controls the action.

If we combine these observations about narrative pacing and dialogue distribution in OG Susanna with earlier ones about its use of time and space, we arrive at the structure shown in table 14. While the elders' sighting and pursuit of Susanna (7–23) are scenically presented, this part remains subordinate (in length and detail of presentation), to the trial. The court scene, especially the second segment (dominated by Daniel) takes up the most verses, has the most dialogue, and demonstrates the greatest slowing of narrative pace—all signs that the central focus of the OG narrative lies here.[71]

Table 14.—Scenes and Dialogue in Old Greek Susanna.

Text Division	Verses	Number of Words	Words of Dialogue	Percent Dialogue
Prologue	5b–6	26	—	—
Part 1: Lust				
Desire	7–11	76	—	—
Action	12–28a	120	42	35
Part 2: Death				
False Justice	28b–41	239	96	40
True Justice	44–62	319	188	58
Epilogue	62a,b	31	—	—
		811	326	40

Note: Dialogue figures do not include biblical citations ("the Lord said . . .").

Table 15 outlines a similar structure for TH's Susanna. A long introductory section (1-6) introduces all significant characters except Daniel. Action begins with development of the elders' lust (7-12).[72] TH presents this as an iterative process (imperfect verbs, the phrase "every day"), although in the story it is described only once. Thus this section has a higher ratio of fabula time to story space (is more summarizing) in TH than in the OG—even though the two sections are about the same length and use many of the same words.

Table 15.—Scenes and Dialogue in Theodotion's Susanna.

Text Division	Verses	Number of Words	Words of Dialogue	Percent Dialogue
Prologue	1–6	106	—	—
Part 1: Lust				
Desire	7–12	84	—	—
Action				
Elders	13–14	43	8	19
Susanna	15–18	87	14	16
Proposition	19–25	117	74	63
Discovery	26–27	41	—	—
Part 2: Death				
False Justice	28–43	265	124	46
True Justice	44–62	348	194	55
Epilogue	62a,b	42	—	—
		1133	414	37

Note: Dialogue figures do not include biblical citations ("the Lord said . . .").

[68] In particular, their mutual confession and their approach to Susanna ("having agreed, they approached and seized her") are described in summarizing fashion.

[69] Again I note that Susanna's household functions as "local color" rather than playing an active role in the fabula.

[70] Vv. 52–55 and 56–59. Vv. 35–41 juxtapose quoted speeches, but since Susanna's prayer is not pronounced aloud, the elders' speech is not a response to it.

[71] The trial scene (excluding prologue) occupies twenty–seven of the OG's forty verses.

[72] The transitional verse 12 both concludes this scene and introduces the next.

TH's first true scene portrays the elders' pursuit of Susanna.[73] It contains four subscenes marked off by their character sets and type of action. The first relates the elders' maneuvering, encounter, and alliance. The second, beginning while the first is still in progress, stretches from Susanna's entrance to the maids' departure. The third and most important, using direct–response dialogue (which does not occur in the LXX's depiction of this scene), reports the elders' proposition/threat and Susanna's response. The fourth, a narrative recounting of the confrontation's aftermath, concludes both the garden scene and the larger "lust" section of the story.

TH, like the OG, gives greatest space to the trial; at v. 44 it moves, as the OG does, from action dominated by the elders to action controlled by Daniel. Both versions give increasing prominence to dialogue as the story moves toward its climax. There are three important differences, two obvious, one subtle, between their handling of the trial. The obvious differences are the placement of Susanna's prayer (already discussed) and TH's dialogue between the assembly and Daniel (46–50), which underscores the drama of Daniel's outburst and allows the assembly to attest Daniel's authority.

The subtle difference is TH's use of an inceptive imperfect, ἐξήγειρεν, to describe God's action on Daniel. For TH, arousal of a saintly spirit is, like perfidy's growth, progressive rather than punctual.[74]

Focalization and Characters

At the story level, the fabula's actors become full–fledged characters. Explicit narratorial description is the most blatant vehicle for such characterization, and we find quite a bit of it in Susanna (table 16, contrast the paucity of narratorial characterization in Bel and the Dragon). TH uses somewhat more explicit description than does the OG.

---

[73] TH contains no imperfect verbs, except forms of εἰμί, between vv. 12 and 33.

[74] Some find it highly significant that in the OG an angel rouses Daniel, while in TH God self does so. My own judgment is that here, as in the Habakkuk scene of Bel and the Dragon, the angel is a transparent stand–in rather than an independent character.

Table 16.—Explicit Characterization in Susanna

Character Speaking	Character Described	OG Characterizations		TH Characterizations	
narrator	elders	passim:	elders and judges	passim:	elders and judges
		5:	criminals	5:	criminals
		10:	bad	28:	criminals
		28:	criminals	32:	lawbreakers
		32:	criminals	61:	false witnesses
		60–62:	false witnesses		
narrator	first elder	54:	godless	—	
narrator	Susanna	7:	good-looking, wife of their brother Joachim, daughter of Hilkiah	2:	wife of Joachim, daughter of Hilkiah, very beautiful, God-fearing
		22:	Jewish	27:	good repute
		31:	extremely pretty	31:	extremely pretty a pleasure to behold
		32:	beautiful	32:	beautiful
		35:	faithful	35:	faithful
		60–62:	innocent	62:	innocent
narrator	parents	—		3:	righteous
narrator	Joachim	—		4:	very rich, most distinguished
narrator	Daniel	passim:	νεώτερος	45:	holy, παιδάριος νεώτερος
		44–45:	insightful	64:	an impressive reputation
narrator	νεώτεροι	62a:	sincere	—	
		62c:	pious, insightful, understanding		
narrator (assembly?)	Lord	—		60:	savior for those who hope in him

Table 16.—*continued*

Character Speaking	Character Described	OG Characterizations	TH Characterizations
elders	Susanna	29: Hilkiah's daughter, Joachim's wife 36–41: adulteress	29: Hilkiah's daughter, Joachim's wife 36–41: adulteress
Susanna	Lord	35a: eternal, all-knowing	42: eternal, knowing secrets, all-knowing
Susanna	elders	35a: evildoers	43: false witnesses, evildoers
Daniel	assembly	48: idiots	48: idiots
Daniel	Susanna	48: daughter of Israel 57: daughter of Judah	48: daughter of Israel 57: daughter of Judah
Daniel	elders	—	49: false witnesses
Daniel	first elder	52: sinner, grown old in evil 53: unjust judge 55: liar	52: sinner, grown old in evil 53: unjust judge 55: liar
Daniel	second elder	56: twisted 57: sick, lawless 59: sinner	56: twisted 57: lawless 59: liar
assembly	Daniel	—	50: holder of eldership

At a few points we do find epithets in the OG which are missing in TH; one case is the OG's fourfold reference to Daniel as νεώτερος (to TH's single παδάριος νεώτερος). The fact that the OG concludes with an exhortation about νεώτεροι suggests that its stress on this feature of Daniel's identity is no accident.

What is a νεώτερος? Stauffer argues, on the basis of Jewish, early Christian, and Hellenistic sources, that the term refers to a man between the ages of twenty and thirty (probably toward the younger end of the range), of age to marry, bear arms, and (not incidentally) begin participating in the community council.[75]   Such an understanding accords well with the attitude toward νεώτεροι in OG 62a-b.

TH, by contrast, describes Daniel as a παδάριος νεώτερος, a young child (according to Stauffer and most other commentators), driven by divine inspiration rather than the idealism of early adulthood.[76] Thus in TH's version the assembly can invite Daniel to "come, sit amidst us . . ." (50) only because they recognize a miracle when they see it (". . . since God has given you eldership").

Another versional difference is that the OG narrator is somewhat more insistent than TH's in explicitly condemning the elders ("the evil," 10; ὁ ἀσεβής, 54). TH's narrator gives more explicit characterization of the "good" characters: Susanna, her family, Daniel, and Lord.

Exploring table 16 further, we see that the characters themselves—especially Daniel—have a great deal to say about one another.   Daniel's reported connections to Lord and the general concordance between his statements and the narrators'[77] lend weight to his evaluations: it does not occur to us to question his statements, even when we have no independent verification of them (as in 52–53 and 56–57). His exuberantly forceful language (e.g. "idiots," "grown old in evil times," "twisted," "sickness," "sinner") seems out of place to modern

---

[75] E[thelbert] Stauffer, "Eine Bemerkung zum griechischen Danieltext," in *Donum Gentilicium*, ed. E. Bammel, C. K. Barrett, and W. D. Davies (Oxford: Clarendon, 1978), 28–37. Stauffer assumes a first century C.E. date for the OG and many of his parallels date from this period; he does not, however, demonstrate a significant change in usage between his sources and those from the late second century B.C.E. (which I have identified as the most likely date for the OG—see chapter 3). Such a positive attitude toward young men is not surprising in a Hellenistic milieu where athletic prowess and youthful energy were much admired—Plato depicts an Egyptian priest telling Solon, "The Greeks are always children; no Greek is an old man" (Plato *Timaeus* 22.b.5.).

[76] Stauffer, 38–39. Such an understanding obviously underlies Baumgartner's interpretation of the story as a "wise child" tale, and Baumgartner notes a number of early sources (including the Syriac and Ignatius) who specify that Daniel is twelve years old at the time of the Susanna story. Walter I. Baumgartner, "Susanna—die Geschichte einer Legende," and "Der Weise Knabe und die des Ehebruchs beschuldigte Frau," chaps. in *Zum alten Testament und seiner Umwelt* (Leiden: E. J. Brill, 1959), 42–66 and 66–67. (These essays originally appeared in *ARW* 24 [1926]: 259–280 and 27 [1929]: 187–88.)

[77] Neither version contains misleading narratorial statements, although deception aplenty occurs in characters' words about one another.

readers—especially when he condemns the first elder before hearing the testimony of the second. It fits nicely, however, with Hellenistic rhetorical conventions (on the OG's assumption that he is young man just taking his place in society), or the tang of prophetic discourse (on TH's assumption that he is a divinely inspired child).[78]

Combining observations made thus far with characterization given through action, we arrive at a fairly stock slate of characters:

The elders are dirty old men, fully deserving of their eventual fate.

Susanna resembles Sweet Polly Purebred: beautiful, virtuous, in dire need of rescue.

Daniel is either an "angry young man" (OG), indignantly protesting the older generation's stupidity, or a classic wise child (TH), prevailing by youthful freedom of vision and speech ("the king has no clothes").

The assembly is gullible, impressed by status and easily led astray—or as easily led to repentance. (Compare characterization of the people in the Torah's wilderness stories.)

Lord and *Lord's angel*, as mentioned above, are helper figures unencumbered by the limitations of knowledge which trouble other figures in the story.

When we examine how the narrators focalize action through various characters' viewpoints (table 17), we find some interesting biases. Neither story gives us much insight into the "virtuous" characters, Susanna and Daniel. We get enough information to establish Susanna's piety and Daniel's inspiration, but in general we do not share their perspectives upon events. Instead, focalization in both versions rests overwhelmingly with the elders.

The two versions do differ in their presentation of the elders' point of view. The OG narrator reports it in a way that ensures their condemnation—for instance, while reporting the elders' initial impressions of Susanna (7) the narrator reminds us that she is not only good-looking, but "wife of *their brother*," "walking around *her husband's* estate"—she is not an "available woman." Thus the OG narrator uses focalization, as well as explicitly evaluative language, to assure our disapproval of the elders. (OG 10 is especially interesting in its combination of these methods.)

---

[78] Matt 7:1–3 ("Do not judge. . .you hypocrites!") offers a comparable sample of inflammatory language.

Table 17.—Focalization Through Characters in Susanna.

	Old Greek			Theodotion	
Vv.	Focalizing Character	Object of Focalization	Vv.	Focalizing Character	Object of Focalization
7	elders	vision			
8	elders	lust	8	elders	vision, lust
9	elders	perversion	9	elders	perversion
10	elders	pain	10	elders	pain
10	Susanna	knowledge			
			11	elders	shame, wish
12	elders	purpose	12	elders	watching
13	elders	arrival			
			14	elders	arrangement
			15	Susanna	wish
			16–18	elders	sight, sound
			18	maids	sight
			26	servants	hearing
			27	servants	shame
28	elders	plans	28	elders	plans
32	elders	purpose	32	elders	purpose
35	Susanna	heart	35	Susanna	heart
35a	Susanna	prayer			
35a	Lord	hearing			
41	assembly	belief	41	assembly	belief
			44	Lord	hearing
44/45	angel	command			
44/45	(Daniel?)	spirit	45	Lord/Daniel	spirit

TH, while preserving the tale's overall condemnation of the elders, allows us more sympathy with their reactions. TH 8 omits the OG's pointed emphasis on Susanna's marital status.[79] TH 11 invites us to enter the elders' feelings by mentioning their shame—it also explicates the desire which the OG referred to simply as "the evil."

We see and hear Susanna's interaction with her maids (15-18) through the elders' awareness ("while they were seeking," "hidden and

---

[79] It also fails to explicate her beauty, but of that we were apprised in TH's opening verses.

spying").[80] The beautiful woman's twice-repeated intention of bathing provokes the reader's imagination as surely as it does the elders', drawing the reader into their lust. Even in the elders' fabricated testimony, TH lingers slightly longer than the OG on the lurid details of what they say they saw. TH treats the elders' lust as investigative commissions often treat pornography—righteously denouncing it, in prurient detail.

Earlier, we observed that the elders' aim controls the Susanna tales: the elders are, in a technical sense, the primary subjects. We have also seen how the narrators repeatedly align our perception with that of the elders. The question arises: who stands at the center of the Susanna tales? Where does their focus lie?

The opening and closing passages suggest different answers for the different versions.[81] The OG begins with a topic verse about crime in Babylon, explicated as a reference to the elders. Attention stays firmly on the elders throughout the first part of the story (5b–28a), although the narrator carefully underscores their villainy.

When the elders are finally upstaged in the trial scene, it is by a "younger" ($\nu\varepsilon\acute{\omega}\tau\varepsilon\rho\circ\varsigma$), who vividly demonstrates how leadership ought to be exercised. The OG closes with an exhortation concerning such young men ($\nu\varepsilon\acute{\omega}\tau\varepsilon\rho\circ\iota$). The OG thus uses the fabula as a case study in the leadership potentials of corrupt old men and sincere, pious young men.

TH's story begins instead with Susanna and her family. Susanna dominates one subscene (her preparations), plays a major role in another (the confrontation), and is center of emotional interest in yet a third (the aftermath). Paradoxically, even TH's sympathetic portrayal of the elders contributes to the positive portrayal of Susanna, leading us to appreciate her bodily charm as well as her virtue.

Susanna's peak moment, in this version, is her (theologically expanded) prayer. Following the prayer, Susanna fades into the background while a new and equally romantic character takes center stage: the divinely inspired child, Daniel. TH accentuates the drama of this scene by introducing dialogue between Daniel and the council. This version's conclusion reports both the rejoicing of the family we first met (63) and the illustrious career Daniel now launches upon (64). It closes as it began, as a story about individuals.[82]

---

[80] Use of the verb ἐπιθυμέω to describe her desire may result from refraction through the elders' consciousness; for another possibility, see note 44.

[81] Recall that this was also the case for Bel and the Dragon.

[82] Quite possibly the story once illustrated the general thesis, "innocent blood will be saved" (cf. 62), but this general theme is now subsumed under the OG's interest in leadership and TH's in the particular characters.

Texts

We have seen that at fabula level, the versions' differing placement of Susanna's prayer results in a two-stranded event pattern for the
OG and a single-stranded one for TH. At the story level, the OG
focuses upon the elders in a consistently disapproving way, contrasting
their corruption with the sincere and effective leadership of the
νεώτερος, Daniel. TH gives more attention to the attractive figures of
Susanna and Daniel, but in so doing, creates an undercurrent of
identification with the lusting elders. Both stories suggest that the fabula
events illustrate behavior typical of the various characters, but TH suggests an iterative nature to some events in the fabula itself, while the OG
presents the affair as a singulative crisis, emerging in a day and resolved
by the end of the next day.

Helmut Engel, at the end of his Susanna study, suggests that in
the OG,

> Erzählend, nicht moralisierend oder theoretisch argumentierend, trägt der Ver-
> fasser seine hoffnungsvolle Überzeugung vor, daß JHWH Israel-Juda, sein
> Volk, retten kann und wird, auch wenn die eigenen gegenwärtigen Macht- und
> Gewalthaber dabei sind, es unter dem Schein der Legalität zu vergewaltigen
> und zu ruinieren. Sus LXX regt dazu an und mahnt, angesichts des Verlaufs
> der dramatischen Erzählung, die Jugend (wieder) so zu formen (und das setzt
> eine Umkehr auch der Erziehenden voraus!), daß sie wieder *ganz* aus der Tora
> legen und so Träger des Geistes werden, der zum rechten Entscheiden und zum
> prophetischen Schuldaufweis ermächtigt.[83]

This agrees well with our observations about the OG emphasis on the
elders, its clear condemnation of their actions, and its contrast between
elders and νεώτεροι.[84] It also accords with my contention that the OG
focuses on issues of leadership for the people, rather than upon Susanna
and Daniel as individuals.

Engel describes TH, by contrast, as "die erbauliche Geschichte
von der schönen gottesfürchtigen Susanna einst in Babylon und den zwei
verbrecherischen Alten."[85] From his source-critically oriented study of

---

[83] Engel, 180-181. Engel's conclusion results partly from the fact that he
has taken, as I have, the OG's opening citation and closing exhortation as important
clues to its agenda.

[84] Engel observes this contrast but rejects Stauffer's interpretation of
νεώτερος, arguing that such a person has not yet reached the age of majority.

[85] Ibid., 181. He goes on to term this the "Entschärfung" of the OG story.

TH's version, he concludes that TH shows the following features as compared to the OG:[86]

(1) "Stilistiche Glättungen" (under which heading Engel includes Semiticisms present in TH but not the OG).

(2) "Erotisierung und Psychologisierung," especially in TH's expansion of the garden confrontation. (We have noted eroticization especially in the narrator's tendency to draw us into the elders' lustful imaginations.)

(3) "Individualisierung und Historisierung," in more precise delineation of the setting and provision of introductory information about the characters. We also have noted TH's tendency to focus on Susanna and Daniel as remarkable individuals rather than representative types. This comes to a head in

(4) "Neugestaltung des Erzählungabschlusses," from the OG's exhortation about νεώτεροι to TH's comments about Susanna's family and Daniel's subsequent success. We have already commented on this feature as it affects story focus. We shall have more to say about it in the section on narratorial style, below.

With these observations in hand, we turn to three striking text-level features of the Susanna narratives: their mix of narrative and non-narrative material, refraction patterns created by interaction of primary and secondary levels of discourse,[87] and narratorial style.

Narrative, Argument and Description

Susanna uses more descriptive material than did Bel and the Dragon, as is indicated already by the number of adjectives used (table 10, chapter 4). For both translators, Susanna's percentage of adjectives is more than twice that of Bel and the Dragon. In Susanna as in Bel and the Dragon, the OG uses a greater density of adjectives than TH.

But a mere adjective count will not suffice to tell us what role description plays in each narrative. In Susanna, as in Bel and the Dragon, most adjectives perform functions other than sensory description. Even statements about Susanna's physical beauty (OG 7 and 31,

---

[86] Engel presents these conclusions, with summary comments and verse citations, on 181–183.

[87] In Bal's terminology, the "primary level" is the narrator's story, while the "secondary level" encompasses material related by characters within the story (134–149). This is a division different from the distinction between the fabula, story, and text (which Bal also terms "levels").

TH 2 and 31) serve less to help us envision the woman than to explain the effect she has on the elders. (The descriptions tell us nothing about her hair color, height, facial features, etc.). Likewise adjectives applied to the elders relate to their story roles ("criminal," "godless," etc.) rather than physical description.

In short, Susanna, like most biblical narrative, subordinates description to plot. Nor do the texts indulge themselves in a great deal of argumentative[88] commentary. The OG's narrator presents general argument only in the concluding exhortation (62a–b, to be examined below). TH's narrator uses no argumentative discourse at all.[89]

Levels of Discourse

The paucity of narratorial description and argument in Susanna is more than compensated for by complex interactions between the narrators' stories and characters' commentary. When we examine characters' general statements (table 18), two points emerge immediately: all these statements come from the story's two most attractive and narratorially endorsed characters, and most of them fall at points of verbatim similarity, as if their content were fundamental to the story.

Another interesting feature of these statements is the difficulty of distinguishing whether they are fabula–specific statements or general ones. For example, Susanna states that it is better to fall into the elders' hands than to sin against Lord. This may be her declaration of decision between the two particular alternatives she faces.[90] But it may also be read as a statement of the general principle on which she then acts by crying out. Daniel's accusation that the first elder "condemned the innocent and freed the guilty" seems even more closely directed to a particular situation. Yet the observation applies also to the *assembly's* just–made decision in Susanna's case, and the problem's generality is underscored by the fact that it is addressed in scripture ("though the Lord says . . .").[91]

---

[88] "Argument" is Bal's umbrella term for "any statement that refers to something of general knowledge outside the fabula," whether opinion or fact (127–129, quote from 128).

[89] TH 60 (". . .and praised the God who saves those who hope in him") might be cited as an exception, but the comment about God here is probably an indirect quotation of the assembly's praise, rather than a narratorial assertion.

[90] The second-person phrasing points in this direction.

[91] Cf. Engel's assertions about the community context of at least the OG story (177–180).

Table 18.—Assertions About Reality by Characters in Susanna.

	Old Greek		Theodotion
Source	Assertion	Source	Assertion
Lord	Lawlessness came from Babylon . . .	Lord	Lawlessness came from Babylon . . .
Susanna	Better fall into your hands than sin before Lord	Susanna	Better fall into your hands than sin before Lord
Susanna	Lord knows all things before they happen	Susanna	Lord knows all things (including hidden ones) before they happen
Daniel	Assembly condemns without having inquired	Daniel	Assembly condemns without having inquired
Daniel	Seeing elders, one says, "they wouldn't lie"		
Daniel	Judges condemn the innocent and free the wicked	Daniel	Judges condemn the innocent and free the wicked
Daniel	Judah's daughters won't endure lawlessness	Daniel	Judah's daughters won't endure lawlessness

This imprecise range of reference makes Daniel's and Susanna's statements effective propaganda. Against the protest, "not all elders are like that!" the storyteller may counter, "I'm only talking about these elders." But there is nothing in the stories (with the possible exception of the OG conclusion) to counter an understanding of the statements as general assertions about the nature of things.

We have noted that the characters in Susanna also make claims about specific events in the fabula. Divergence between the elders' claims and events as reported by the narrator shows the elders to be liars even more certainly than does Daniel's condemnation. This corroboration of Daniel's accusation then prompts us to trust his assertions (52–53, 57) about their wider activities.

However, a comparison of events on the estate grounds as related by the narrator, and the same events as recounted by the elders in their testimony, provides more than proof that the elders are liars. It also provides insight into their psychology, especially in TH's version (which gives more detail both in its depiction of the garden encounter, and in the elders' story about it). Let us compare the two versions of events as related in TH (table 19).

Table 19.—Accounts of the Garden Scene in Theodotion.

Elders' Version	Narrator's Version
	The elders tried to avoid each other
We were walking *alone* when	but met and were plotting when
she came in with two maids	Susanna came in *alone* with two maids
and shut the doors	who shut the doors
and dismissed the maids.	and left as commanded.
A young man came to her,	The elders,
who was *hidden*,	who were *hidden*,
and took his rest with her.	
But we, having seen the lawlessness,	
ran to them	stood and *ran* to her
and having *seen* them being together	and said, "no one *sees* us, be with us,
	or we will testify that a young man was
	with you."
that one we were unable to be in control	
of (ἐγκρατής)	
since he was stronger than we	But she *refused* and cried out
so having *opened the doors*	and an elder *opened the doors*.
he sprang away	The household came running,
but grabbing this one	
we asked her, "who was he?"	
and she *refused* to tell us.	and the elders said their words, such as
	had never been said about Susanna.

Note: Both accounts have been condensed.

The elders' story is a classic mix of "truths that are made to sound sinister, some half truths, and some downright lies."[92] The elders were indeed alone (though not as alone as each had wanted) when Susanna entered and dismissed her maids. The elders indeed ran to her and were refused.

But in many ways, the elders' story betrays their own wishful thinking. As they retell their story, it is not they but the fictional young man who was hidden. He too runs to Susanna, to the reception they wish they had gotten. "No one sees us. . .be with us!" transmutes into their seeing of the longed-for "being with." In their testimony, it is not the elders but the sexually successful young man who opens the doors.[93]

Mieke Bal is doubtless right in hearing a pathetic self-knowledge in the elders' statement, "we were not able to be in control of him, for he was stronger than we."[94] For all their projection, they know their own impotence—they could not do what they claim the young man has done. Furthermore, their term for control, ἐγκρατής, ordinarily refers to *self*-control—which they lack even more than they may lack physical strength.[95] By contrast the young man's "strength" becomes moral strength, a reflection of Susanna's own strength in refusing the elders.

For all the elders' skill in weaving fact with fiction, they make one verifiable error, when they assert that *Susanna* closed the doors of the estate grounds. According to the narrator, Susanna ordered the closing of the doors, but the *maids* performed the act. If, as seems likely, the maids were among those who came running from the house to hear the elders' story in vv. 26–27, then the prestige of the elders overwhelms the maids' own recollection of events.

A similar dynamic underlies the elders' testimony in the OG, but the brevity of its garden scene and its somewhat less detailed testimony weaken the impact. It is TH who most fully explores the psychology of the lechers.

---

[92] Robert R. Gordis, describing Haman's maneuvers in Esther, in "Religion, Wisdom, and History in the book of Esther—A New Solution to an Ancient Crux," *JBL* 100 (1981): 387.

[93] The door imagery invites symbolic interpretation.

[94] Mieke Bal, "Susanna and the Elders in the Apocrypha and in Rembrandt," paper presented at AAR Annual Meeting, Chicago, 1988.

[95] LSJ, s.v.; BAGD, s.v.

Narratorial Style

Who narrates the Susanna stories? TH's narrator appears to stand
outside the tale. We cannot easily identify his or her voice with that of
any fabula character. He or she has free access to the activities and
thoughts of various human characters and even Lord (44). This, then, is
a narrator of the same class that we encountered in Bel and the Dragon.

But TH's narrator exercises his or her powers with less restraint
than shown in the Bel and the Dragon tales. Liberal amounts of explicit
characterization (table 16), access to non-perceptible objects (table 17),
and large amounts of indirect dialogue make the narratorial presence
obvious. We have the impression of hearing a story from a teller, rather
than observing a drama. We find ourselves moving from the carefully
anonymous, seemingly simple style of classical Hebrew narrative to the
much more explicitly controlled style of Hellenistic Greek narrative.

The OG narrator likewise peers into characters' thoughts, uses
explicit characterization freely, and resorts to frequent indirect dialogue,
so that in the OG as in TH, the narrator's presence can be felt
throughout. This presence becomes overt in the conclusion:

> As for us, we must see that young men become men of worth, for when young
> men are pious, an insightful and understanding spirit will always be in them.[96]

Here we clearly encounter a perceptible ("first-person") narrator. Who
is this narrator—and who are "we," thus addressed?

Whatever the difficulties of this text, it clearly points to "us" as
folk concerned with the moral and intellectual qualities of Jacob's
beloved youths, and furthermore, to "us" as folk overseeing the development of those youths into leaders. Thus while the narrators of Bel and
the Dragon and TH's Susanna stand "poised between God and people,"
implicitly claiming "to draw on both sides, to represent both, and to
have the interests of both at heart,"[97] the OG narrative firmly identifies
the narrator (and reader) with real-life elders. In combination with the
god-like or at least inspired powers[98] displayed by the narrator, this
leaves a final impression of elders as benevolently omniscient—in sharp

---

[96] Verse 62b. See the translation notes for further discussion.

[97] Meir Sternberg, *The Poetics of Biblical Narrative: Ideological Literature
and the Drama of Reading*, Indiana Literary Biblical Series (Bloomington: Indiana
University Press, 1985), 118.

[98] On the implications of "omniscience" in ancient narrative, see ibid., 34.

contrast to the relationship of elders and youngers depicted in the story and suggested by this verse itself.

Erich Auerbach, in his famous discussion of Hebrew and Homeric narrative styles, summarizes the opposition as one between two "basic types:"

> On the one hand fully externalized description, uniform illumination, uninterrupted connection, free expression, all events in the foreground, displaying unmistakable meanings, few elements of historical development and of psychological perspective; on the other hand, certain parts brought into high relief, others left obscure, abruptness, suggestive influence of the unexpressed, "background" quality, multiplicity of meanings and the need for interpretation, universal–historical claims, development of the concept of the historically becoming, and preoccupation with the problematic.[99]

Auerbach's characterizations of biblical style have since been developed and supported, especially by the studies of Robert Alter, Adele Berlin, and Meir Sternberg.[100] These scholars, like Auerbach himself, note how biblical narrative's tight, economical style supports a complex picture of human character:

> There is. . .an abiding mystery in character as the biblical writers conceive it, which they embody in their typical methods of presentation. . . .
> . . .This unpredictable and changing nature of character is one reason why biblical personages cannot have fixed Homeric epithets.[101]

The Susanna stories, we have seen, exhibit many characteristic traits of biblical narrative: paucity of physical description, emphasis on dialogue, repetition with variation (the elders' report of the already-narrated garden scene), a concern with the balance between God's control and human freedom. Both versions suggest that although God's intervention may be subtle and mediated through creatures (Daniel), God does keep tabs on the world and will not allow sinners to destroy the faithful.

But unlike classical Hebrew narrative, the Susanna stories do not work toward a portrayal of the complexity of human character. Rather

---

[99] Erich Auerbach, *Mimesis: The Representation of Reality in Western Literature* (Garden City: Doubleday, 1957), 23.

[100] Alter, *The Art of Biblical Narrative* (New York: Basic Books, Inc., 1981); Berlin, *Poetics and Interpretation of Biblical Narrative*, Bible and Literature Series (Sheffield: Almond, 1983); Sternberg. While these writers all focus on Hebrew scripture, the New Testament shows many of the same narrative traits, as observed, for instance, by Robert W. Funk, *The Poetics of Biblical Narrative*, Foundations & Facets: New Testament; Literary Facets (Sonoma, California: Polebridge, 1988).

[101] Alter, 126.

they polarize, making clear and narratorially supported divisions between the virtuous and the perverted.   The iterative emphasis (particularly in TH) on the elders' history of perversion and Susanna's long-standing virtue suggests that such traits are lifelong constants rather than ones that change in response to history.

The Susanna stories share this relatively simplistic, hero/villain division of humanity with many other stories in the Apocrypha and Pseudepigrapha.   Esther—particularly in its expanded form—Tobit, Judith, and *Joseph and Asenath* all come to mind as examples.[102] (These stories also share Susanna's association of chastity with virtue.) But Susanna does not place the division between good and evil along an ethnic line.   Despite the stories' clear consciousness of Jewish identity and expectation that that identity should coincide with moral behavior (56–57), the villains *are* members of the chosen community.

Might we see the stories, then, as expressions of a class conflict within Jewish society—as subversive assertions that power corrupts? Only in a very muted way.   The OG, which as we have seen focuses primarily on the elders themselves, guards in its conclusion against any implication of *generalized* corruption.   The suddenly explicit narratorial voice in v. 62b assures us that while an occasional case of perversion does occur, things in general remain under the control of wise and benevolent elders who are responsibly training a new generation of equally pious and insightful leaders.

TH, in its emphasis on Daniel and Susanna and its insight into the elders' lust, diverts attention away from the social dimensions of the story and toward a study of individual virtue and vice.   It focuses less on the dynamics of power than on those of sexual desire, and while it preaches a message of chastity, it shows a marked fascination with lust.[103]

At various times throughout history—in Israel's expansion to an empire under Solomon, in Judea's misadventures under Hellenistic and Roman overlords, in rural America's observations of cosmopolitan New York and San Francisco—devout religious people trained in the "good old traditions" have suspected their leaders of personal and public perversion, private licentiousness and corruption in office.   They have

---

[102] The New Testament's narratives do not show such a high level of simplification—note especially the complexity of the gospels' characterizations of the apostles.

[103] Compare the writer of *Joseph and Asenath*, who in describing the first meeting of the two holy virgins does not neglect to note the placement of Joseph's hand between Asenath's breasts which are "standing up like apples."

asserted, against those fears, that God will not long tolerate such law-lessness. The Susanna story plays well to such an audience.

But such disaffection is generally not revolutionary. Whether through fear of anarchy or because a basic identification with the rulers remains, suspicion expresses itself in calls for pious government and private restraint, rather than in attempts to overturn the order. So too with our versions of Susanna.

Chapter 6

THE TEXTS IN CONTEXT

We turn now to the interplay between Susanna and Bel and the Dragon and their contexts. We shall explore three major literary intertexts: Habakkuk (alluded to in the title verse of OG Bel and the Dragon, and the Lion's Pit scene of both versions), Jeremiah (explicitly quoted[1] in the first verse of OG Susanna and v. 5 of TH), and the book of Daniel itself. Our Greek stories also contain definite or possible allusions to a number of other Jewish writings. We shall deal first with the citations particular to each story, then with relationships to the book of Daniel.

The fact that most of the intertexts are biblical raises the question, "*Which* Bible?" Our discussion of dates, places, and traditions in chapter 3 suggests that the LXX (or the OG, for Daniel) is the most appropriate intertext for the OG, while the Theodotionic/καίγε recension is "Theodotion's" proper counterpart. Where no καίγε version is available, I shall turn to the MT, since καίγε generally seems closer to the MT than to LXX traditions.[2] Where differences between versions

---

[1] That is, the quotation is explicitly marked as such: Περὶ ὧν ἐλάλησεν ὁ δεσπότης, and seems, as we shall see, to allude to Jeremiah. It is not, however, an exact quotation of any text now known.

[2] Efforts to choose the correct intertext must be tempered by realization that ancient communities sometimes (often?) knew, and accorded authority to, more than one text tradition. For example, the text used by 1QpHab reads "stagger" (cf. the LXX) rather than "show your foreskin" (cf. the MT) in Hab 2:16a. The commentary, however, incorporates *both* meanings. (Geza Vermes, "Interpretation, History of: At Qumran and in the Targums," in *IDBSup*, 441.) Similarly, some early Christian writers—e.g. the author of the Book of Revelation, Justin, and Cyprian—seem to have used either a mixed text or more than one text of Daniel. (Pierre Grelot, "Les versions grecques de Daniel," *Bib* 47 [1966]: 381–402; Robert H. Pfeiffer, *History of New Testament Times With an Introduction to the Apocrypha* [New York: Harper and Brothers, 1949], 443.) If we are correct in identifying TH as a revision prepared for a

remain unmentioned, the reader may assume that the LXX and καίγε/MT traditions are essentially similar and that the intertext is called upon by both the OG and TH versions of our stories. Because intertextual allusions in Susanna shed some light on the situation in Bel, we shall depart from our usual order and discuss Susanna first.

Susanna

The Susanna story displays its intertextuality in a number of explicit citations. Verse 53 (both versions) quotes Exod 23:7 verbatim: "Kill not the innocent and righteous." Later we hear that the assembly, "as the law commands, did to them [the elders] what they had schemed to do to their sister" (OG 60–62). This clearly alludes to Deut 19:19, the Greek wording of which is followed quite closely in TH. Torah (τὸν νόμον Μωυσῆ) is also mentioned in TH 3 and assumed in the death penalty for adultery in both versions.[3]

The most puzzling quotation appears in the heading of OG Susanna:

> περὶ ὧν ἐλάλησεν ὁ δεσπότης ὅτι Ἐξῆλθεν ἀνομία ἐκ Βαβυλῶνος ἐκ πρεσβυτέρων κριτῶν, οἳ ἐδόκουν κυβερνᾶν τὸν λαόν.[4]

The form is clearly that of a quote. But where did The Master say this?

While no known text contains the exact words quoted here, they are reminiscent of a passage in Zech 5.

> Then the angel that was talking with me went out, and said to me, "Raise your eyes, and see this that goes out (τὸ ἐκπορευόμενον)." I said, "What is it?" He said, "This is the measure that goes out"; then he said, "This is their unrighteousness (ἀδικία) in all the earth." And look, a talent of lead lifted up,

---

Greek–speaking community which had previously been using something like the OG, then that translator and community would certainly, at that point, have had access to two traditions.

[3] Deut 22:22, Lev 20:10, cf. Ezek 16:38–40, to which the stripping motif may also have some connection. On fire as a penalty for adultery (Sus LXX 60–62) see p. 149 below.

[4] Repeated in Sus 5b TH. As discussed in chapter 2, Rahlfs and Ziegler both open the OG with v. 6. For retaining 5b see Helmut Engel, *Die Susanna-Erzählung: Einleitung, Übersetzung und Kommentar zum Septuaginta-Text und zur Theodotion-Bearbeitung* (Freiburg: Universitätsverlag, 1985; Göttingen: Vandenhoeck & Ruprecht, 1985), 12–15. The same conclusion was reached by Josef-Tadeusz Milik ("Daniel et Susanne à Qumrân?" in *De la Tôrah au Messie* [Paris: Desclée, 1981], 345–46). Milik extends the quote through OG 6: καὶ ἤρχοντο κρίσεις ἐξ ἄλλων πόλεων πρὸς αὐτούς. The Greek manuscripts, of course, do not mark the end of the citation.

and look, a woman sitting in the middle of the measure. He said, "This is Lawlessness (ἡ ἀνομία)," and cast (ἔρριψεν)[5] her into the middle of the measure, and cast the stone of lead into her mouth. Then I raised my eyes, and look, I saw two women going out, wind in their wings (they had stork wings), and they took the measure up between earth and sky. I said to the angel who was talking with me, "Where are they taking the measure away to?" He said to me, "To build a house for it in the land of Babylon, to prepare, and set it there at its prepared place."[6]

We find here the key ideas of "going out" (but ἐκπορεύομαι, not ἐξέρχομαι), "lawlessness," and "Babylon" (*to* which lawlessness is going, in this scene). Lawlessness is personified as a woman, not as (male) elders, although the immediate context (Zech 5:3–4) suggests that she personifies the misdeeds of men.

The opening line of OG Susanna also has close ties with two passages in Jeremiah. One is Jer 23:15, ἀπὸ τῶν προφητῶν Ἰερουσαλὴμ ἐξῆλθε μολυσμὸς πάσῃ τῇ γῇ.[7] In Susanna the trouble is lawlessness" (ἀνομία) rather than "defilement" (μολυσμὸς), it comes from Babylon, not Jerusalem, and from elders, not prophets. It is possible to make sense of these divergences. But first, let us explore the other Jeremiah passage.

> Because you said, "Lord appointed prophets for us in Babylon"—thus says Lord concerning Ahab and Zedekiah:
>
>> Behold, I am giving them into the hands of the Babylonian king, and he will strike them before your eyes. And they will be taken up as a curse among all the Judean exiles in Babylon—"Lord make you as he did Zedekiah and Ahab, whom the Babylonian king grilled on a fire," because they acted lawlessly (ἐποίησαν ἀνομίαν) in Israel, committed adultery with the wives of their countrymen, and in my name declared a message which I did not order (συνέταξα).
>
> I am witness, says Lord.[8]

An association between this passage and Susanna is explicitly attested by Origen, who says a Jewish acquaintance told him that the names of the elders who accosted Susanna were Ahab and Zedekiah.[9] Nehemiah Brüll cites a number of rabbinic haggadot in which the two perverse prophets prey upon Babylonian women, finally coming to grief

---

[5] This verb appears twice in the denouement of OG Susanna (60–62).

[6] Zech 5:5–10 LXX. The MT reads very similarly, but with a play on the dual meaning of אֵיפָה (measure, basket) that does not come through in Greek.

[7] MT ‏מֵאֵת נְבִיאֵי יְרוּשָׁלַיִם יָצְאָה חֲנֻפָּה לְכָל־הָאָרֶץ‎.

[8] LXX 36:15, 21–23 (a continuous passage in Greek). The MT, if we omit the interpolated verses 16–20, presents the same line of thought.

[9] Origen *Ep. ad Africanum* 7.

when they attempt seduction of Nebuchadnezzar's daughter (or his wife, Semiramis).[10] Interestingly, Nebuchadnezzar then proposes to test them in the furnace to see if they are true, *as Hananiah, Mishael, and Azariah were*, showing a linkage between this set of traditions and those associated with Daniel.

It may also be significant that while 88 and the Syrohexapla say in 44/45 that the angel intervened καθὼς προσετάγη, Papyrus 967 here employs the same verb, συντάσσω, which appears in Jer 36:23 LXX.[11] Also, this verse of Susanna (in both versions) alludes to God by the Greek title δεσπότης rather than the more common κύριος. Milik posits that since both Susanna stories elsewhere use κύριος, δεσπότης must have come from the same source as the citation itself.[12] Amongst Greek versions of books which were later accepted into the Hebrew Bible, Jeremiah and OG Daniel, along with Proverbs, make the most use of this title.[13]

Jeremiah's attack on the two corrupt prophets occurs in the same chapter (LXX 36, MT 29) in which he advises the exiles to settle into Babylon for a long stay. The chapter opens with a heading notifying us that

> These are the words of the book which Jeremiah sent from Jerusalem to the *elders* (πρεσβυτέρους) of the exile, to the priests and to the false prophets, . . .

---

[10] Nehemiah Brüll, "Das apokryphische Susanna Buch," *Jahrbuch für jüdische Geschichte und Literatur* 3 (1877): 1-69. I was unable to consult this work, so I rely upon quotations and discussion in Charles James Ball, "The Additions to Daniel," in *Apocrypha of the Speaker's Commentary*, ed. Henry Wace (London: John Murray, 1888), 2:324-30, 1888. Louis Ginzberg also discusses these traditions (*Legends of the Jews*, 7 vols., indexed by Boaz Cohen [Philadelphia: Jewish Publication Society, 1909-38], 4:336-7, references 5:426 n. 106). The version from *Sanh.* 93a is quoted on p. 153, below.

[11] Angelo Geissen, *Der Septuaginta-Text des Buches, Daniel: Kap. 5-12, zusammen mit Susanna, Bel et Draco, sowie Esther Kap. 1,1a-2,15, nach dem Kölner Teil des Papyrus 967*, Papyrologische Texte und Abhandlungen no. 5 (Bonn: Rudolf Habelt, 1968), 286. Engel, 114, calls attention to the correspondence with Jer 36:23.

[12] Milik, 341 n. 2.

[13] Other books which use the term frequently are Judith, Wisdom, Sirach, and 2 and 3 Maccabees, all deuterocanonical. In Jeremiah, uses of δεσπότης cluster in the first part of the book. However, if Tov is correct in his thesis that all of Jeremiah was originally translated by the same person, after which LXX chs. 29-52 were firmly revised by a second hand, then further occurrences may well have stood in the second part of the book in its original Greek version. Emanuel Tov, *The Septuagint Translation of Jeremiah and Baruch: A Discussion of an Early Revision of the LXX of Jeremiah 29-52 and Baruch 1:1-3:8*, HSM no. 8 (Missoula: Scholars Press, 1976).

by the hand of Elasah son of Shaphan and Gemariah son of Hilkiah (whom Zedekiah, king of Judah, sent to the Babylonian king in Babylon).[14]

Jeremiah then presents an oracle which commands the captives to

build and live in houses, plant gardens (παραδείσους) and eat their produce, take wives, and beget sons and daughters, . . . and seek peace for the land to which I exiled you, and pray to Lord for them, because in their well-being is your well-being.[15]

This positive command is followed by a warning against false prophets (8-9), then the famous promise of restoration after seventy years (10-14). At that time, says God, "you will pray to me, and I will attend (εἰσακούσομαι) to you . . . for you shall seek me with all your heart" (12-13). After this Jeremiah returns to the subject of false prophets, in the section on Ahab and Zedekiah (quoted above, p. 147).[16] The chapter closes with an interchange concerning the exiled priest Shemaiah and his response to Jeremiah's letter. The next chapter begins the "Book of Consolation."

Several ties to Susanna strike the eye. One is the name of the priest "Hilkiah (whom Zedekiah, king of Judah, sent to the Babylonian king in Babylon)." Susanna is described in both versions as Hilkiah's daughter.[17] An identification with Jeremiah's Hilkiah well explains why the man would teach his daughter "according to the law of Moses" (Sus 3 TH) and the relevance of fire as punishment (Sus 60-62 OG, Lev 21:9).

In verse 2 we note a reference to "King Jeconiah and the queen." And while the MT's גְּבִירָה suggests a Queen Mother, the LXX's βασίλισσα means simply "queen," and could well be understood to mean Jehoiachin's wife. Jeconiah is another name for Jehoiachin, some-

---

[14] LXX 36:1, 3. MT 29:1, 3 specifies "the elders *that remain*" and does not specify *false* prophets.

[15] LXX 36:5-7. MT 29:5-7 reads essentially the same.

[16] LXX 15, 21-23. MT interposes an attack on those who have remained in Jerusalem, 16-19 (20 is a transitional verse returning to the subject of the exiles).

[17] Jer 36:3 LXX (29:3 MT); Sus 29 OG; Sus 2, 29, and 63 TH. This Hilkiah is presumably the same one named in 2 Kgs 22. Clement of Alexandria (*Stromata* 1.21) and David Kimḥi identify Hilkiah the priest with Jeremiah's father (Jer 1:1). Hippolytus (*On Susanna* ad loc.) makes the same identification and combines it with Sus 1:2 to conclude that Susanna is Jeremiah's sister. The "Samaritan Susanna" explicitly presents its heroine as daughter of a high priest (Bernhard Heller, "Die Suzannerzählung: Ein Märchen," *ZAW* 54 [1936]: 282-284).

times written Ἰωακιμ in Greek.[18]　　Brüll calls attention to a tale in
Leviticus Rabbah about fears that David's line would die out in captivity.
Nebuchadnezzar's queen, Semiramis, helps arrange a conjugal visit to
the prison by Jehoiachin's wife, but the appointed time falls during the
wife's menses.　　She warns him of her impurity by crying out כשושנה
אדומה ראיתי.[19] Does this explain how Joachim's wife, who maintains
her purity in our story, came to bear the name שושנה?

Jeremiah's instructions to "build houses, plant gardens, take
wives, and beget children" has obviously been carried out by Susanna's
community (note especially the relatively unusual word παράδεισος for
garden in Jeremiah's letter and our story).　　Susanna does not let herself
be persuaded by the unrighteous, but keeps her heart steady in Lord and
prays—and Lord hears (εἰσακούω) her prayer.　　In the OG, the elders die
by fire (vv. 60–62).

Table 20 summarizes similarities and differences between Sus 5b
and the three other passages we have looked at, with respect to the verb
and noun used, the locale named as the source/site of trouble, the persons identified with the trouble, and the specific nature of the problem as
defined by the context.　　Bold print marks concurrence with the Susanna
heading.

Table 20.—Possible Intertexts of Susanna 5b.

Susanna 5b	Zechariah 5:5–10	Jeremiah 23:15	Jeremiah 36:21–23 (LXX)
ἐξῆλθεν	ἐκπορευόμενον	ἐξῆλθε	—
ἀνομία	ἀνομία	μολυσμός	ἀνομία
from Babylon	to Babylon	from Jerusalem	**in Babylon**
elders, judges	woman	prophets	false prophets
adultery, false witness	theft, false oaths	**adultery,** false prophecy	**adultery,** false prophecy

---

[18] E.g. 4 Kgdms 24:6, 8, 12, 15; 1 Esdr 1:43 (1:41 in Rahlfs), and,
signficantly, Jer 52:31. Is this how Joachim came to be "honored above all" (Sus 4
TH)? As long as we are speculating about Joachim, we should also mention that the

We see that while Jeremiah 23 offers the closest grammatical parallel, and Zechariah 5 the most developed parallel image, Jeremiah 36 LXX (29 MT) is closest to having the same content as the Susanna heading, except for the fact that Jeremiah speaks of false prophets rather than elders.[20]

I suggest that we are dealing with what Boyarin refers to as the "(psycho)dynamics of intertextuality."[21]

> Intertextuality is, in a sense, the way that history, understood as cultural and ideological change and conflict, records itself within textuality. As the text is the transformation of a signifying system and of a signifying practice, it embodies the more or less untransformed detritus of the previous system. These fragments of the previous system and the fissures they create on the surface of the text reveal conflictual dynamics which led to the present textual system. Now it is, I would claim, precisely these gaps in the text which the midrash reads.[22]

"Cultural and ideological change and conflict" are, of course, at stake in the book of Jeremiah. Against earlier tradition, Jeremiah makes Jerusalem the source of defilement and Babylon the place of hope (our passages, also the classic vision of good and bad figs in Jeremiah 24). The prophets, who should be the source of religious leadership, instead lead folk astray. Jer 23:15's statement that "defilement goes forth from the prophets of Jerusalem," would become not merely outrageous (as it was already in Jeremiah's day) but virtually incomprehensible to later communities for whom Babylon and Jerusalem were not so much places as symbols of ultimate evil on the one hand and purity and restoration on the other. Our storyteller resolves the stress of 23:15 by combining it with the situation depicted in Jeremiah 29/36, where Babylon is the site

---

book of Judith refers to a high priest Ἰωακιμ. Neither Greek version of Susanna specifies Joachim as either priest or king.

[19] *Lev. Rab.* 19:6. Semiramis, as mentioned above, plays the "Susanna" role in some of the Ahab/Zedekiah midrashim. Carey A. Moore gives references for three such stories in *Daniel, Esther, and Jeremiah: The Additions*, AB (New York: Doubleday, 1977), 85 n. 11.

[20] Walter I. Baumgartner rejects the connection with Jeremiah 29/36 for such reasons. "Susanna—die Geschichte einer Legende," in *Zum alten Testament und seiner Umwelt* (Leiden: E. J. Brill, 1959), 48–49. Carey Moore agrees, calling this a "formidable, if not irrefutable argument against the theory" (85).

[21] Daniel Boyarin, *Intertextuality and the Reading of Midrash*, Indiana Studies in Biblical Literature (Bloomington: Indiana University, 1990), 93.

[22] Ibid., 94.

of false prophetic activity. This yields the more culturally comprehensible statement that trouble "goes forth from Babylon."[23]

The Zechariah passage offers a bridge for this transformation, since it begins with the trouble going out from Judah (as in Jeremiah 23) but ends up with lawlessness residing in Babylon (as in Jeremiah 29/36). One could posit some association between the Susanna stories and Zechariah's calls for justice and truth (7:9-10, 8:16), but the immediate context of the "lawlessness going forth" passage (thieves and those who swear falsely) is of doubtful relevance (the Greek words ὁμνύω/ὁρκίζω and μαρτυρέω are more distant semantically than their English equivalents, "to swear" and "to witness"). A connection between Susanna and Zechariah seems possible but not definite.

Returning to Jeremiah, intertextual tension also suggests how the "false prophets" became "elders, judges." Aside from the inherent discomfort of the idea of false prophecy,[24] Jeremiah's words on prophecy posed two additional problems for the Diaspora communities which produced and read the Greek versions of Susanna. First, they lived their own lives in post-prophetic times; thus tales about elders and judges had more relevance than tales about prophets.

Second, the Ahab/Zedekiah oracle is directed to those who say, "Lord appointed prophets for us in Babylon." This repudiation of the possibility of prophecy in Babylon clashes with the claims of the Daniel tradition (and may explain why the book of Daniel refrains from calling him a prophet, even though he engages in prophetic activity and Greek-speaking communities placed his book among the Prophets).

In Bel and the Dragon, we shall see, Daniel's anomalous career in Babylon is legitimated by involvement of a Judean prophet, Habakkuk. In Susanna, we find two other compensating mechanisms at work. The story clearly *shows* that Daniel has true prophetic inspiration. But all explicit mention of prophecy is suppressed: Daniel himself is not called a prophet, and neither are the villains. The substitution of elders for (false) prophets corresponds to their parallel listing in the introduction to Jeremiah's message (LXX 36:1, MT 29:1).

---

[23] Engel (who also cites these two Jeremiah texts and the one from Zechariah, although he does not discuss their interrelationships) reads Babylon as symbolic of evil and evil-doers: "von Babylon, *das heißt*, von Ältesten-Richtern" (89).

[24] Perhaps this is why 29:8 in the ordinarily expansionistic MT reads simply "prophets" (not "lying prophets") where LXX 36:8 gives us ψευδοπροφῆται. On the other hand, to designate false prophets as such, rather than leaving them lumped in the same category as true prophets, may be LXX's way of handling the pain.

As Boyarin points out, different midrashim on the same text often actualize alternate interpretive possibilities in the text.[25] We see this at work if we compare Susanna to some of the other stories about Ahab and Zedekiah—for instance, the story as related in *Sanh.* 93a:

> Because they have committed villainy in Israel, and have committed adultery with their neighbours' wives, etc. [Jer 29:23]. What did they do? They went to Nebuchadnezzar's daughter: Ahab said to her, "Thus saith God, 'Give thyself unto Zedekiah;'" whilst Zedekiah said to her, "Thus saith God, 'Surrender to Ahab.'" So she went and told her father, who said to her, "The God of these hates unchastity: when they [again] approach thee, send them to me."[26]

Here and in the other rabbinic sources, the two harass *Babylonian* women, while in Susanna their targets are women of Israel/Judah (Sus 57). We appear to be dealing with different interpretations of the phrase עָשׂוּ נְבָלָה בְּיִשְׂרָאֵל וַיְנַאֲפוּ אֶת־נְשֵׁי רֵעֵיהֶם/ἐποίησας ἀνομίαν ἐν Ἰσραήλ, καὶ ἐμοιχῶντο τὰς γυναῖκας τῶν πολιτῶν αὐτῶν. Ordinarily one would take this as a clear reference to adultery with the wives of fellow exiles, but that leaves one wondering why the king of Babylon would involve himself in the punishment. Rabbinic tradition solves the problem by making נְשֵׁי רֵעֵיהֶם refer to women of the pair's *Babylonian* neighbors—one understands why Nebuchadnezzar "fried" the two, if they had been propositioning his daughter.[27] The Susanna stories interpret רֵעֵיהֶם/τῶν πολιτῶν αὐτῶν more straightfowardly as "compatriots from their homeland" (they also motivate the parallel phrase, "folly *in Israel*" [v. 57]), but in the process punishment becomes the action of God and the exilic community, rather than the Babylonian king.

The direction of interpretive motion here needs emphasis: Susanna 5b interprets Jeremiah, not the other way around. Jeremiah is an important text full of tension; Susanna shows one way to play out its implications. We are facing the same phenomenon described by Boyarin for the *meshalim* of the *Mekilta*:

> The mashal accomplishes its work by assigning a deep-structural description to the elliptic narrative of the Torah, which enables the completion of its syntactic structure. . . . That is to say, surely, that the "real" story is *not* by any

---

25 Boyarin, 57-80.

26 Translation by H. Freedman in *Sanhedrin*, The Babylonian Talmud (London: Soncino, 1935), 624.

27 Not only would רֵעֵיהֶם more naturally refer to Judeans, but נָשִׁים to a first approximation designates "wives," not "daughters." These inconsistencies in a midrash quite explicitly attached to the verse should teach us not to expect complete correspondence between a source text and its interpretation.

means to be understood as the solution to the mashal, but almost the opposite. The mashal allows for the structuring of this "real" story in the sense that it prescribes what kinds of characters and narrative functions will be appropriate in filling out the ellipses of the biblical text, and, moreover, it assigns value to these characters and events by assimilating them to a cultural icon which incorporates the culture's values.[28]

Boyarin's description of the mashal as a "cultural icon" deserves a bit more discussion here. Pointing out that the *meshalim* are generally "as conventional and schematic, as fixed, as the morphology of the folk tale described by Propp," he argues that "these basic narrative structures are thus the carriers of values and ideology in the culture."[29] In the same way that historians make events intelligible by telling them as stories with culturally credible plots (be it "poor boy makes good," "greed makes wars," or "God saves by a miracle"), midrash provides a culturally intelligible plot line to organize the problematic biblical text.[30] We have noted that the Susanna stories show close kinship to a host of other stories about virtuous wives and clever interrogators. Precisely this folkloric ordinariness makes Susanna an effective framework for interpretation of the troubling statements in Jeremiah 29/36.

Before moving on to our discussion of intertextuality in Bel and the Dragon, we should note a few other parallels between this story and well-known biblical texts. The gender of the main character suggests an association between Susanna and other biblical heroines, especially Esther and (in the apocrypha) Judith, an association assumed by Carroll in his myth-transformation study.[31] Carroll finds "Israelite" vs. "non-Israelite" the primary category of opposition in this series, with "husband" and "seducer" the possible roles. Carroll's findings reinforce the probability of my interpretation of Susanna as a midrash on Jeremiah 23:15 and 29/36 which is motivated in part by deep unease with the relative roles of Judea and Babylon in Jeremiah's writings.

Susanna's deliverance just as she is being led forth to execution also calls to mind the biblical heroine Tamar. Thus it is of some interest that Milik translates Sus 56 as follows:

---

[28] Boyarin, 85.

[29] Ibid., 88, 92.

[30] Ibid., 80–92. In the parallel with history-writing, Boyarin draws heavily on Hayden White, *Tropics of Discourse* (Baltimore: Johns Hopkins University Press, 1978).

[31] Michael P. Carroll, "Myth, Methodology and Transformation in the Old Testament: The Stories of Esther, Judith, and Susanna," *SR* 12 (1983): 301–312. The Jacobite Syrian Bible groups Susanna, Judith, Ruth, and Esther together in a "Book of the Women." David M. Kay, "Susanna," *APOT* 1:638.

> Pourquoi ta vie sexuelle est-elle désordonneé, tout comme celle des Sidoniens et, en particulier, celle de Juda, lequel se laissait séduire par la beauté qui enflamme le désir?[32]

Milik refers this passage not to the Judah of Genesis 39 but to Judah of the *Testament of the Twelve Patriarchs*, especially *T. Jud.* 10-17.[33] But however correct Milik's remarks about the relationship of Aramaic originals of Susanna and the *Testament of Judah*, the fact remains that both our *Greek* versions of Susanna have Daniel saying καὶ οὐχ (ὡς) Ἰουδα. Thus, if an allusion once existed to Judah as the repentant lecher, our translators have forgotten it.

Milik's argument that Susanna's prayer (OG 35a, TH 42-43, but in their proposed Aramaic original) is "incontestablement" dependent on the Aramaic of *1 Enoch* 9:4-6 is also interesting since the context involves bloodshed and oppression on the earth (9:1) attributable to sexual misconduct by those entrusted with power (9:7).[34] However, the Greek parallels are no more striking than those with many other prayers in Jewish literature of this period.[35]

At the level of verbal similarities, Susanna's cry in TH, "I am in a real bind,"[36] echoes David's statement when confronted with unacceptable choices in 2 Sam/2 Kgdms 24:14. Many interpreters also compare her answer to the elders, especially the phrase "sin before Lord" (v. 23, both versions) with Joseph's response to Potiphar's wife (Gen. 39:9). This comparison seems motivated more by parallels of situation, and connections between Daniel and Joseph, than by actual similarity of statements. An "insightful spirit" (πνεῦμα συνέσεως), given to Daniel in OG 44-45, occurs also in Isa 11:2 and Deut 34:9. The corresponding verses of TH use the term "holy spirit" (τὸ πνεῦμα τὸ ἅγιον) which also occurs in Daniel TH (4:5, 5:14), Ps 51:13, Isa 63:10-11, and Wis 9:17. None of these verbal similarities seems striking or multifaceted enough to assume a deliberate citation; rather, I think, we are dealing with the sorts of coincidences to be expected between writings which share a common world of thought and vocabulary.[37]

32　Milik, 340.

33　Ibid., 344 nn. 49, 51.

34　Ibid., 346-50.

35　For a discussion of parallels, including those discussed by Milik, see Engel, 106-109.

36　Sus 22, Στενά μοι πάντοθεν.

37　To be more precise, some of these writings are contemporary ones which share a common thought-world; others are predecessors which have shaped that thought-world. See Engel, *passim*, for much more extensive exploration of vocabulary overlaps between Susanna and other biblical writings.

Bel and the Dragon

The OG version of Bel and the Dragon begins with the title, Ἐκ προφητείας Αμβακουμ υἱοῦ Ἰησοῦ ἐκ τῆς φυλῆς Λευι. Both versions include a scene (vv. 33–39, which may well have been added fairly late in the story's development),[38] in which an angel ferries Habakkuk from Jerusalem to Babylon to feed Daniel. What are we to make of this association with Habakkuk?

Hoenig, citing a thirteenth–century rabbinical source, suggests a gematria: גור אריה = חבקוק.[39] However, the book of Habakkuk displays several more direct links with the story we are considering. To review briefly, the book of Habakkuk opens with the prophet's complaint that injustice prospers (1:2-4). God responds, "Look! . . . I am rousing the Chaldeans . . . to seize dwellings not their own!" (1:5-11). This raises a second round of questions: "Is he [the enemy] then to keep on emptying his net, and destroying nations without mercy?" God replies, "If it [the end] seems to tarry, wait for it" (2:2-5). This assurance is followed by five woe oracles (2:6-20) against plunder, evil gain, violence, abuse of neighbors, and idolatry. (The idolatry theme appears not only in 2:18-19, the text explored by Roth in his article on idol parodies, but also in 1:16, where it is combined with the motif of offerings and rich food.)[40] Throughout these first two chapters, the indictments may be read as references to *intra*-community violence (thus, as in Isaiah or Jeremiah, Babylon serves as God's instrument of punishment), or as protests against oppression of the people by foreign nations (thus making the book into a promise of community deliverance, as in Jeremiah or Deutero–Isaiah).[41] The book closes with a divine warrior psalm which repeats the themes of punishment and waiting (ch. 3).

If the book of Habakkuk is read as a prediction of Jerusalem's imminent overthrow by Babylon, or even more if it is read as complaint about ongoing Babylonian oppression, then Habakkuk and Daniel would have had overlapping careers, with Habakkuk probably the older of the

---

[38] Carey A. Moore (146–47) summarizes the arguments for viewing this scene as a later addition.

[39] Sidney B. Hoenig, "Bel and the Dragon," *IDB* 1:376.

[40] Wolfgang M. W. Roth, "For Life, He Appeals to Death (Wis 13:18): A Study of Old Testament Idol Parodies," *CBQ* 37 (1975): 33-34.

[41] Carol A. Newsom, "Habakkuk," *HBD* 364.

two.[42] Granted, a Habakkuk who prophesied before Jerusalem's fall would have been *very* old by the time of Cyrus's accession (the OG, which does not name the king in Bel and the Dragon, presents less of a problem than TH on this point), but similar questions arise about Daniel himself. (One gets the impression that Hellenistic vision considerably foreshortened the distance between Assyria's last days and establishment of the Persian empire.) This gives the joint appearance of Habakkuk and Daniel a *prima facie* reasonableness—but are there further reasons why Habakkuk might be associated with Daniel?

One can begin by citing general theological congruences. Habakkuk's question, "How long?", expresses a central concern of the apocalyptic section of Daniel. God's reported answer to Habakkuk performs the same sort of hope–giving function as do Daniel's visions—note especially how strongly the language of a "vision" for the "appointed time" in Habakkuk 2:3 resonates with the apocalyptic part of Daniel. By contrast, Habakkuk's question about the welfare of the righteous vis-à-vis the wicked rings not only through the apocalyptic section of Daniel but in its court stories as well.

The climax toward which Bel and the Dragon tends, the king's acclamation of κύριε ὁ θεός, realizes Habakkuk's promise that "earth will be filled with knowledge of the Lord's glory" (Hab 2:14) and "you will be recognized when the years draw near" (3:2).[43] This notion of acclaim from the foreign sovereign might also bear some connection with the LXX reading of Habakkuk 1:11 (τότε μεταβαλεῖ τὸ πνεῦμα, καὶ διελεύσεται, καὶ ἐξιλάσεται· αὕτη ἡ ἰσχὺς τῷ θεῷ μου—"then he will turn his spirit, and review,[44] and make propitiation: 'this strength is my God's'"), which can easily be read as a prediction of conversion.[45]

---

[42] I refer to the situation as represented in the Bible, not as historically reconstructed. Both traditional and critical opinion generally put Habakkuk's career toward the end of the Judean monarchy, although critical scholarship also sees the work of later sources in the book. A few Jewish traditions put Habakkuk at some other time, such as during the reign of Manasseh. See Louis Ginzberg, *The Legends of the Jews*, 7 vols. (Philadelphia: Jewish Publication Society, 1909-38), 4:278 and 6:314, 373, and 387.

[43] LXX: ἐν τῷ ἐγγίζειν τὰ ἔτη ἐπιγνωσθήσῃ. The MT reads more like a request, thus NRSV "in our own time make it known."

[44] BAGD, s.v., no. 4.

[45] MT אָז חָלַף רוּחַ וַיַּעֲבֹר וְאָשֵׁם זוּ כֹחוֹ לֵאלֹהוֹ, "then like a wind he swept by, transgressed and was guilty, this one whose strength was his god."

Both the Bel and Lions' Pit stories also eventuate in punishment of evildoers (Bel 22, 42). This theme appears in a general way in Habakkuk and quite specifically in the LXX's statement that "destruction will come upon the ungodly."[46] In both versions of Bel and the Dragon, however, the courtly connivers are indicted for deceit and attempting to destroy Daniel, not for impiety. This gives the Daniel story a somewhat different slant than Habakkuk.

From the standpoint of Hellenistic Diaspora communities who produced our Greek legends, there is a conflict between the depiction of Babylon (or, typologically read, any foreign land/empire) as a place of opportunity, the very king of which will finally recognize God's sovereignty, and Babylon as a place of violence and deceit, not to mention idol-worship. Bel and the Dragon shows how Babylon can be both at once, with God's sovereignty the common theme uniting the two.

We saw the same tension in Susanna's relationship with Jeremiah 29/36, and noted there the particular problem involved with Daniel as a *prophet* in Babylon. The meal delivered to Daniel by Habakkuk, a Judean prophet,[47] colorfully validates Daniel's own status as a religious leader while preserving Judah's position as the authoritative source of nurture for the Diaspora community.[48]

One final, rather odd set of connections may link the Habakkuk scene of Bel and the Dragon to the book of Habakkuk proper. The psalm in Habakkuk concludes,

> διότι . . . τὰ πεδία οὐ ποιήσει βρῶσιν·
> . . . .
> κύριος ὁ θεὸς δύναμίς μου
> καὶ τάξει τοὺς πόδας μου εἰς συντέλειαν·
> ἐπὶ τὰ ὑψηλὰ ἐπιβιβᾷ με
> τοῦ νικῆσαι ἐν τῇ ᾠδῇ αὐτοῦ.

> Though . . . the fields should produce no food,
> . . . .
> The Lord God is my strength,
> And he will place my feet firmly;
> He will set me on high places.
> to triumph in his song.[49]

---

[46] συντέλεια εἰς ἀσεβεῖς ἥξει, Hab 1:9. MT כָּלֹה לְחָמָס יָבוֹא might possibly be read as "they all come to violence" but "they all come *for* violence" is a more natural reading. (The antecedent of כֻּלֹּה in the preceding verse is plural.)

[47] *Lives of the Prophets* 12 expands on this.

[48] The OG does not specify Habakkuk's point of departure. Is it simply assumed? Or (contrary to the hypothesis just suggested) is it unimportant?

[49] Hab 3:17-19.

Now, this passage speaks of *fields* (πεδία) which produce *no food* (βρῶσιν), while in Bel and the Dragon, Habakkuk carries *food* (ἄρτους and ἕψημα) to the field (πεδίον) for the reapers. Since the kinds of food are different and one set of fields is barren while the other keeps reapers busy, this hardly constitutes a certain allusion. On the other hand, the scene envisioned in Bel and the Dragon may be in deliberate *contrast* to that in the book: the psalm presents a time of difficulty and mourning, while the story alludes to a later time of restoration.[50] In this connection Scholz's identification of the meal as a figure for the messianic banquet deserves mention.[51]

Yet another possible connection with Bel and the Dragon in this short passage lies with the obscure statement that "he will place my feet εἰς συντέλειαν, and set me upon τὰ ὑψηλά."[52] On the one hand, this verse has been cited as grounds for the tradition that Habakkuk has priestly ancestry (Bel 1 OG, see 1 Esdr 5:58 for mention of a Levite named Jesus). On the other, this may have provided a kernel for traditions about Habakkuk's aerial travel. (The specific means of travel is, of course, reminiscent of Ezekiel; Elijah traditions may also be involved. See discussion beginning on p. 163 below.)

---

[50] The Habakkuk section of the pseudepigraphal *Lives of the Prophets*, which probably dates to early in the first century C.E., makes direct reference to Habakkuk's succor of Daniel but focuses on the harvest: "When the Chaldeans turned back, and the remnant that was in Jerusalem (went) to Egypt, he was living in his own district and ministering to those who were harvesting his field. When he took the food, he prophesied to his own family, saying, 'I am going to a far country, and I will come quickly. But if I delay, take (food) to the harvesters.' And when he had gone to Babylon and given the meal to Daniel, he approached the harvesters as they were eating and told no one what had happened" (*Lives of the Prophets* 12:4-7). D. R. E. Hare, "*The Lives of the Prophets*: A New Translation and Introduction," in *OTP* 2:380-81 (date) and 393 (trans.). For Greek text see Charles Cutler Torrey, *The Lives of the Prophets: Greek Text and Translation*, JBL Monograph Series, vol. 1 (Philadelphia: Society of Biblical Literature and Exegesis, 1946), 28; or Eberhard Nestle, *Marginalien und Materialien* (Tübingen: J. J. Heckenhauer'sche Buchhandlung, 1893), 26-27. Torrey gives only the shorter (and probably older) Q text, Nestle gives Q and the longer of the Epiphanius versions.

[51] Anton Scholz, *Commentar über das Buch "Judith" und über "Bel und Drache"* (Würzburg: Leo Woerl, 1896), 228. This is not an isolated contention but part of Scholz's entire allegorical program which he develops in great detail. For instance, he argues on the basis of v. 27 that ἕψημα here indicates not just an ordinary stew but an offering; ἐνθρύπτειν he connects with the breaking of bread at Passover (again a backward glance at v. 27, this time to μάζαι); the reapers he associates with the final harvest as described in Matt 9:37-38.

[52] MT "like the deer" (כְּאַיָּלוֹת) and "*my* heights" (בָּמוֹתָי).

In summary, the figure of the prophet Habakkuk appears in both versions of Bel and the Dragon. This is (more or less) chronologically appropriate.   Habakkuk's polemic against idolatry suits the Daniel story's theme of unmasking false gods. His concern that the righteous be vindicated and his promise that God will finally show Babylon who is sovereign make him a fitting agent for God's miraculous salvation of Daniel (which finally prompts the king's confession). It is especially significant that a *Judean* prophet thus supports the prophet of the Diaspora. Specific phrases in Habakkuk may explain the association of eating with idols (Hab 1:16), Habakkuk and the fields (3:17), and perhaps the idea of Habakkuk being transported through the air (3:19).

Connections between Bel and the Dragon and Habakkuk are, however, tighter in the OG than for TH. First and foremost this results from the title which links the OG to a "prophecy of Habakkuk." But furthermore, if I am correct in assuming that the LXX provides the correct intertext for the OG, while we must turn to the καίγε recension (or, lacking that, the MT) to find TH's partner, we find that several of the connections we have discussed pertain only to the OG: "the earth will be filled with the glory of the Lord" (3:2), "he [the foreign conqueror] will turn...and make propitiation" (1:11), and "destruction will come upon the ungodly" (1:9). It seems that as TH tightened Bel and the Dragon's ties to Daniel, associations with Habakkuk were loosened— understandable enough, if the book of Habakkuk in question no longer fit those ties.

Before leaving Habakkuk, we have one more matter to consider. Some manuscripts of Susanna (in various languages) associate *Susanna* with "the prophecy of Habakkuk";   Eusebius and Apollonarius also understand this title to apply to Susanna.[53] This may be due simply to the placement of Susanna after Bel and the Dragon (the same title would then be understood to apply to both). Yet consider the statements

> Why do you show me trouble,
> and problems to look upon?
> Judgment is before me,
> And the judge receives [a bribe].
> Thus law is frustrated,
> because an impious one prevails over the righteous;
> because of this, perverted judgment goes out.
>
> (Hab. 1:3-4, LXX)

---

[53] Theodor von Wiederholt, "Die Geschichte der Susanna," *TQ* 51 (1869): 380-381.

This could serve as heading for Susanna as surely as Habakkuk's idol-parody passages could for Bel and the Dragon.   If the ascription of Susanna to a Habakkuk collection were correct, then Susanna and Bel and the Dragon would actualize the two readings of Habakkuk mentioned above (p. 156), with Susanna reading Habakkuk as a complaint about the miscarriage of justice *within* the people, and Bel and the Dragon reading it as a protest against the atrocities and idolatries of a foreign empire.[54]

We have seen that Susanna, like the book of Daniel proper, shows close links to Jeremiah.   Brüll argued that as Susanna explicates Jeremiah 29/36, Bel and the Dragon expands upon Jeremiah 51:34-35, 44 (MT).[55]   Let us take a look at this chapter of Jeremiah:

> "King Nebuchadrezzar of Babylon has devoured me,
>> he has crushed me;
> He has made me an empty vessel,
>> he has swallowed me like a monster (כַּתַּנִּין);
> He has filled his belly with my delicacies,
>> he has spewed me out.
> May my torn flesh be avenged on Babylon,"
>> the inhabitants of Zion shall say.
> "May my blood be avenged on the inhabitants of Chaldea,"
>> Jerusalem shall say.
> . . . .
> Like lions they shall roar together;
>> they shall growl like lions' whelps.
> When they are inflamed, I will set out their drink
>> and make them drunk, until they become merry
> and then sleep a perpetual sleep
>> and never wake, says the LORD.
> . . . .
> I will punish Bel in Babylon,
>> and make him disgorge what he has swallowed.[56]

The LXX version of this chapter (Jeremiah 28 LXX) omits Bel's name in verse 44, but in 34 it does translate תַּנִּין as δράκων.   The preceding chapter (Jeremiah 50 MT, 27 LXX) also mentions Bel (v. 2,

---

[54] See Boyarin's discussion of a similar phenomenon in the *Mekilta's* various readings of Exodus; especially his chapter on "Dual Signs, Ambiguity, and the Dialectic of Intertextual Readings," 57-79.

[55] Nehemiah Brüll, "Die Geschichte von Bel und dem Drachen," *Jahrbuch für jüdische Geschichte und Literatur* 8 (1887): 28-29, cited with endorsement by Ball, 344-349.   Moore considers this theory "still by far the most probable explanation" of the stories' origin (122).

[56] Jer 51:34-35, 38-39, 44, NRSV.

although with a variant spelling in the Greek), snakes (δράκοντες, LXX 27:8, but MT 50:8 has goats), and lions (v. 17).

The two chapters in question (LXX 27-28, MT 50-51) comprise Jeremiah's oracle of destruction for Babylon. Twice we hear that God will stir up the king(s) of the Medes to destroy Babylon.[57] Within the oracle are sprinkled promises of restoration for the lost sheep of Israel/Judah (27/50:4-5, 19-20; 28/51:5-6) and a brief idol parody which begins with celebration of LORD as creator (28/51:15-19).

These oracles, read historically, raise a problem: a king from the north did conquer Babylon, but not in the bloodbath predicted by Jeremiah. Read typologically from the standpoint of communities which prospered in following Jeremiah's advice to the exiles (29/36), the oracles against Babylon are even more problematic: does one want this to happen to the land in which one is prospering?

Both history and hope then drive the transformation from deliverance for Judah to deliverance of the Jew, and from utter destruction of Babylon to destruction of its false gods and their priests (quite in keeping with Jeremiah's tone). We see something of the same transformation in the Epistle of Jeremiah, which accepts the Diaspora as a fact of life and now focuses on polemic against idols. It promises angelic protection (v. 7), mocks the impotence of foreign gods in general and Bel in particular (v. 40), and even satirizes the activities of the priests (vv. 18,29,33).[58]

What other textual connections does Bel and the Dragon display? Verse 2 of the OG assigns priestly status to Daniel, as it did to Habakkuk. 2 Esdr 8:2 and 20:7[59] each mention a priestly Δανιηλ, which is interesting since this book also names Hananiah, Azariah, and Mishael. The Ezra/Nehemiah stories share with Bel and the Dragon a fundamentally positive view of Persian kings and the possibility of a religiously and politically successful career in their courts. However, the connection provides no real illumination of Bel and the Dragon and is probably more in the nature of a traditional "source" or "influence."

The Lions' Pit story offers several possible allusions in addition to its Habakkuk connection. The theme of a pit with lions in it appears in Ps 56 LXX (57 MT), but specific vocabulary links are lacking. (Note

---

[57] LXX 28:11, 28 (singular), MT 51:11, 28 (plural).

[58] Bel's name and the genre of idol parody also link our story to Isa 46:1 ("Bel fell, Nebo was smashed"). Bel and the Dragon shares Deutero-Isaiah's positive attitude toward Cyrus (named in Bel TH only), conviction that the foreign imperial power will be brought to recognize God's sovereignty, and emphasis on God as creator.

[59] In MT, Ezra 8:2, Neh 10:7.

especially that the story and psalm use different words for both "lion" and "pit.") Ps 90 LXX (91 MT) speaks of "the lion and the snake" (λεόντα καὶ δράκοντα) and also of angels given charge and bearing one up, but other motifs fail to correspond.[60] A connection to the psalm, if it exists, would seem to lie fairly far from the surface of the present text.

Habakkuk's mode of transport is reminiscent of Ezek 8:3 (καὶ ἀνέλαβέ με τῆς κορυφῆς μου, καὶ ἀνέλαβέ με πνεῦμα ἀναμέσον τῆς γῆς καὶ ἀναμέσον τοῦ οὐρανοῦ) although the verbs and prepositions are different, and only TH of Bel and the Dragon uses the term κορυφῆς. Another difference, of course, is that Ezekiel is transported from Babylon to Jerusalem, in a vision, while Habakkuk goes from Jerusalem to Babylon, where he hands over a quite concretely transported lunch.

To a lesser extent, the exotic transport reminds one of Elijah's departure in the whirlwind (2 Kgs/4 Kgdms 2:11).[61] The Elijah stories likewise present us with the motif of the prophet fed by divine intervention (1 Kgs/3 Kgdms 17:4-6,16; 19:5-8). It may well be that the transport and feeding motifs have been derived from the Ezekiel and Elijah stories via a general tradition about signs of prophetic power.[62]

The Greek Books of Daniel

Susanna and Bel and the Dragon are bound to the book of Daniel explicitly, by the figure of Daniel, and implicitly, by genre and motifs. Such connections are not different in kind from those which bind the Greek stories to books such as Habakkuk and Jeremiah.

In addition, to the extent that our stories actually constitute part of the book of Daniel, we must reckon with diachronic effects resulting from the position of tales within the book. But differences between diachronic and synchronic intertextuality should not be overemphasized. The Book of Daniel probably belonged to the class of literary compositions that would be read/heard repeatedly (like a popular song today) rather than a single time (like most magazine stories). On the second and subsequent readings/hearings, the latter parts of such a story are

---

[60] The psalm appears to be a royal one. If Scholz is correct in seeing messianic overtones in the figure of Daniel (197-233 passim), the connections make more sense.

[61] Note also Obadiah's comment in 1 Kgs/3 Kgdms 18:12.

[62] They may even represent interculturally valid symbols of shamanic power. See Susan Niditch's comments on aerial transport in "The Visionary," in *Ideal Figures in Ancient Judaism*, ed. John J. Collins and George W. E. Nickelsburg, Septuagint and Cognate Studies vol. 12 (Chico, California: Scholars Press, 1980), 153-179.

already known as the earlier parts are encountered (a gospel reader knows about the resurrection while reading about the transfiguration). This diminishes sequential effects, which are, however, somewhat preserved by the readers' "suspension of knowledge" (we catch our breath when the wicked witch confronts Dorothy, however many times we have seen the witch melt away). One special effect of ordering, the privileged role of beginnings and endings in shaping interpretation, is if anything strengthened by repeated reading.

Were the Susanna and Bel and the Dragon stories indeed considered part of the book of Daniel? Evidence is mixed. The oldest OG manuscript, Papyrus 967, places Bel and the Dragon after Daniel 12 (for convenience we shall use the MT chapter numbers for Daniel) and Susanna after Bel and the Dragon. No headings or footings (other than page numbers) intervene between the stories. At the end of Susanna a brief postscript appears: "Daniel. Peace to the writer and the readers. Amen."[63] Here, the additions appear simply as part of the book of Daniel.

In the Chigi manuscript and the Syrohexapla, by contrast, OG Susanna appears *between* Daniel 12 and Bel.[64] (The Vulgate also uses this order.) Both manuscripts head OG Daniel with a notice that this is "Daniel according to the Seventy," append a corresponding note after Daniel 12, then continue with a heading for Susanna. Thus far the additions seem to be treated as independent. But the postscript "Daniel according to the seventy" appears again *after* Bel and the Dragon, as if the additions were part of Daniel proper. In short, Susanna and Bel and the Dragon appear to have the status of appendices in these manuscripts: attached to Daniel, but separate from the main flow of the narrative.

Since the distinction between Daniel and the additional chapters in these post–hexaplar manuscripts may well be attributable to the nature of the Hexapla (the lack of a Semitic counterpart would have marked out the additions as different), I shall follow the witness of Papyrus 967 and assume that the OG presented the stories as part of Daniel, in the order Daniel, Bel and the Dragon, Susanna.

Most TH manuscripts and ancient versions (including Old Latin and Hippolytus's commentary) place Susanna before Daniel 1 and Bel after Daniel 12. More often than not, they number Susanna and Bel

---

[63] Geissen, 15, 33, 290. I have no idea where Carey Moore came up with his statement that "in the oldest extant Greek text of Daniel, Papyrus 967, . . . the story of Susanna comes *before* Daniel 1" (90 n. 28, his emphasis).

[64] Geissen, 33; Ziegler, 8–9.

among the visions of Daniel.[65] I shall take an inclusion of both books in Daniel, with Susanna at the beginning and Bel and the Dragon at the end, as characteristic of TH.

Admittedly, this runs counter to the witness of 88 and SyrH, which arrange TH as they do the OG: Daniel, Susanna, Bel and the Dragon. However, 88's TH version prefaces Susanna with the first two verses of Bel.[66] This probably indicates that Bel and the Dragon once followed Daniel 12 directly and Susanna was only later inserted into the intermediate position. It seems possible that Origen displaced TH Susanna to the "appendix" position (as in the OG) because it lacked a Semitic original, but kept the appendices in TH's order (Susanna before Bel and the Dragon) since TH was the accepted Christian text and closer (in Daniel proper) to the Semitic as well.

At this point it should be mentioned that TH (like MT) gives genre priority over chronology in ordering the chapters. (If arranged chronologically, the chapter sequence would be Susanna [?], 1-4, 7-8, 5-6, 9, 11-12, 10, Bel and the Dragon.[67]) Papyrus 967, by contrast, places the OG chapters in chronological order (1-4, 7-8, 5-6, 9-12; dates are not given for Bel and the Dragon and Susanna).[68]

What difference does it make for the additions and the book of Daniel itself when all fourteen chapters are read together?[69] We shall begin with effects common to both versions and then consider nuances particular to the OG and TH, respectively.

---

[65] See the apparatus in Ziegler.

[66] Geissen, 33.

[67] Where relative dating of chapters is ambiguous, I retain their canonical sequence. The ordering of chapters 1 and 2 presents a problem since it is hard to see how Daniel could be a full-fledged courtier in the *second* year of Nebuchadnezzar (ch. 2) if he had first undergone *three* years of training in Nebuchadnezzar's court (ch. 1). However, ch. 1 clearly intends to portray the beginning of Daniel's career. Although Susanna is undated, I place it first because this version of the story describes Daniel as a very young man (παιδάριον νεώτερος, v. 45).

[68] This is different than the chronological order given for TH because TH dates Daniel 10 to the *third* year of Cyrus, OG to the *first*. (Again, where sequence is ambiguous, I retain canonical order.) Susanna's position in this apparently chronological sequence reinforces internal indications that OG Susanna sees Daniel as a young *man*, not a child. SyrH and 88 follow the usual (MT/TH) chapter order within Daniel proper. Did 967 rearrange to improve the chronology, or did Origen rearrange to align the chapters with MT/TH? A case could be made for either. For consistency I shall follow 967 in this matter as I do in its arrangement of Bel and the Dragon and Susanna, but the case remains open.

[69] The OG and TH vary not only in their treatment of Susanna and Bel and the Dragon, but in their renderings of Daniel 1-12. We shall consider these variations only as they enter into the book's pattern of interaction with our additional stories.

Common Effects

The book of Daniel presents us with two major literary genres and two corresponding characterizations of Daniel.[70] The court legends, chapters 1-6, present Daniel and his friends as wise and successful courtiers who are also faithful Jews. The apocalyptic visions, chapters 7-12, present Daniel as a divinely inspired seer. In 1-6 Babylon is a dangerous but ultimately benevolent place in which even foreign emperors finally recognize the sovereignty of God Most High.[71] Chapters 7-12 present a much higher-contrast picture of God's people caught in a maelstrom of violence and oppression until, in a world-changing advent, God intervenes to punish the wicked powers and restore the faithful and their land to peace and prosperity.

The parts are unified by the theme of God's sovereignty and the question of how it relates to the highly visible power of foreign empires. The conflicts of courtiers under an (ultimately benign) foreign king in the legends correspond to the conflicts of nations as yet unrestrained by the divine ruler in the apocalyptic portion. Adherence to the true God brings salvation in both parts of the book, and Daniel's receipt of special revelation figures throughout.

The two-part structure of Daniel presents the reader with a choice of worldviews. Will God's sovereignty and good life for God's people be realized within the structures of heathen imperial power in foreign lands, as in the stories, or will oppression end only when God destroys the empires and reinstates the faithful in their homeland?

---

[70] For form-critical distinctions in Daniel, see especially John J. Collins, *Daniel, with an Introduction to Apocalyptic Literature*, Forms of the Old Testament Literature (Grand Rapids: Eerdmans, 1984); and Lawrence M. Wills, *The Jew in the Court of a Foreign King: Ancient Jewish Court Legends*, HDR (Minneapolis: Fortress, 1990), 79-144. As the titles indicate, Collins is especially strong on genre distinctions relating to apocalyptic, while Wills focuses only on the legends. This basic legend/apocalyptic division is common to virtually all Daniel scholarship. André LaCocque is one of the few who departs from it, with a structural proposal aligned to the language divisions of the book and focusing on past, present, and future as key structural determinants (*Daniel in His Time*, Studies on Personalities of the Old Testament [Columbia, South Carolina: University of South Carolina Press, 1988], 8-12).

[71] For an interesting literary reading of this portion and the strange interdependence it generates between Lord and the foreign kings, see Danna Nolan Fewell, *Circle of Sovereignty: A Story of Stories in Daniel 1-6*, Bible and Literature Series (Sheffield: Almond, 1988).

"There are times when the hand of God can be detected in the processes of history and times when it has to be looked for at the End."[72]

For the reader whose worldview is more aligned to that of the legends, the apocalyptic section becomes a relatively distant, figural assurance of the discipline God will invoke on kings who fail to realize their positive possibilities.   (Such reading is common in mainline Protestant churches.)   For the reader who resonates more with the apocalyptic portion, the legends come to be read less as statements about the empires' positive possibilities and more as demonstrations that God will protect the faithful persecuted by those empires.

The additions found in the Greek books of Daniel (Susanna, Bel and the Dragon, and also the sixty-eight verses added to Daniel 3) all fall on the legendary side of the balance, portraying a world in which life goes on and justice, despite temporary setbacks, can be realized. The Greek chapter arrangements also reinforce the legendary side since all the Greek books begin *and* end with legends, diminishing the dramatic "last word" impact of Daniel 12's promises.[73]

In chapter 2 we discussed a distinction within the Daniel legends between *court contests* (Daniel 2, 4, and 5) and *court conflicts* (Daniel 3 and 6).[74]   To review, contest stories tell about a hero who succeeds at a task all others fail (interpreting the king's dreams or the handwriting on the wall).   In conflicts, by contrast, action flows from court rivals' attempts to ruin each other.

While neither Susanna nor Bel and the Dragon fits neatly into these categories, both show more conflict than contest features.   They portray situations in which "life goes on" in patterns familiar from history, but they emphasize its danger rather than the opportunities it

---

[72] John E. Goldingay, *Daniel*, WBC (Dallas, Texas: Word Books, 1989), 322. Goldingay presents an excellent summary of these and other issues in his concluding chapter (320-34).

[73] One might argue that we get instead a chiastic effect which *underlines* the apocalyptic; but I think the specific, immediate-future orientation of Daniel 12 blunts this argument: one loses more by appending stories of life-as-usual than one gains by the framing effect.

[74] W. Lee Humphreys, "A Life-style for Diaspora: A Study of the Tales of Esther and Daniel," *JBL* 92 (1973): 211-223; S. Niditch and R. Doran, "The Success Story of the Wise Courtier: A Formal Approach," *JBL* 96 (1977): 179-193.   Daniel 1 is bracketed as a hybrid specially composed for its introductory position.

poses for advancement through (more or less) friendly competition.[75] Wills suggests the following differences in tone between these stories and Daniel 1–6:

1) Daniel 1–6 emphasize an interventionist theology while the additions do not to the same extent;

2) Daniel 1–6 are in general more negative toward the king than the additions, . . .

3) the crisis in Daniel 1–6 is not intentionally initiated by the heroes, as it is in Bel and the Dragon;

4) in Daniel 1–6 the heroes maintain their observances, while in Bel and the Dragon they destroy others'; and

5) there is no reductionistic explanation of idols in Daniel 1–6, as there is in Bel and the Dragon.[76]

This list, while interesting, is highly colored by Wills's focus on Bel and the Dragon (he deals with Susanna only in passing, and not at all with the additions to Daniel 3) and his view of it as an earlier form of Daniel 6. For instance, his source–critical dismissal of the Habakkuk scene as a late addition to Bel and the Dragon (which it probably is) surely influences his contention that the additions show a "less interventionist theology," for the Habakkuk airlift which appears in both our present versions constitutes a supernatural intervention as dramatic as anything found in Daniel 1–6.

In the Habakkuk scene, attention shifts from the contested claim of sovereignty (who is sovereign, the foreign king or Daniel's God?) to God's protection of one caught between the contestants. The miraculous catering calls our attention directly to God's care for Daniel. Only indirectly does it promote the king's ultimate recognition of God, although that theme still figures in the story.

The lengthy additions to Daniel 3 fall at precisely the same point in their story and have the same effect. Without the additions, preservation of the three Jews serves primarily as a means to show Nebuchadnezzar his limits. With the additions, in the Greek versions of the story, our attention is directed more to the three who are saved.

---

[75] Wills, 77, agrees that "the main plot elements of the court conflict are all here," but in an "adaptation of the standard court legend genre to a Jewish middle–class audience, which in this case is not particularly concerned with the issues of the position of Jews *qua* Jews in the pagan empire." Under the influence of Roth, Wills treats Bel and the Dragon (especially in its OG form) more as an idol parody than a court legend (Wills, 131–34), but I think his desire to show an evolution from OG Bel through TH Bel and OG Daniel 6 to MT Daniel 6 has influenced him in this. A struggle-to-the-death between factions figures prominently in both versions of Bel and the Dragon.

[76] Wills, 133–34.

In Susanna also the story's interest lies with the one delivered and the means of her deliverance, illustrating the summary verse, "so innocent blood was saved that day" (Sus 62, both versions). Here and in Daniel 3, the difference is not so much a more positive portrayal of the king, as a shift of interest away from the king toward the Jewish hero(in)es.

Given this shift of interest away from the foreigners, Wills's final three observations about the greater assertiveness of Jews and Judaism vis-à-vis paganism in the additions come as no surprise.

Emphasis on the faithful in Susanna, Bel and the Dragon, and the Greek versions of Daniel 3 slants one's reading of Daniel 1-2 and 4-6 as well. The reader now tends to interpret these stories, also, more as stories about God's protection of the faithful and less as stories about God's education of emperors. This coincides with the effect of the apocalyptic section on the stories (see above). The very active portrayal of Daniel in Susanna and Bel and the Dragon also lends authority (by making Daniel a more vivid and powerful figure) to his apocalyptic visions. Susanna, finally, reinforces the apocalyptic section's distinction between faithful and impious Jews. Thus the additions reinforce themes in both parts of Daniel, not just the legendary section.

When we move the other way, to ask about the impact of Daniel on our reading of the additions, three main effects may be distinguished. First, we are prompted to seek the guiding theme of God's sovereignty in the stories, especially in Susanna which, by itself, gives more emphasis to the contrast of the pious and the wicked. Second, again in Susanna, Daniel moves toward center stage since his is the figure which links the story to the rest of the book. Third, the prominence of Jeremiah in Daniel 9 reinforces Jeremiah's intertextual presence in the additions, especially for Susanna, which connects to the same chapter of Jeremiah. Bel and the Dragon, which resembles other Daniel stories more closely to start with, shows fewer juxtaposition effects, although parallelism with Daniel 6 may prompt the reader to note more of its court legend components and give less weight to the idol parody aspects.

Differences Between Versions

We noted in chapter 2 that the greatest differences between the Greek versions of Daniel occur in the legendary material (especially Daniel 4-6 and Susanna), not in the apocalyptic sections. We have also seen that the court legends involve two different subgenres, the contest and the conflict. Wills argues that these two types of legends show different types of development between the OG and MT/TH versions of Daniel. The contests increasingly stress mantic wisdom (rather than ordinary courtly savvy), while the conflicts, which move more in the world of everyday reality, shift from distinguishing competing parties on the basis of ethnic identity toward a greater stress on piety.[77] Overall,

> The direction of development . . . is toward a focusing on the issue of righteousness and obedience to the laws of God, and not Jewish ethnic identity. . . . In this way the Danielic corpus leaves behind the normal application of the court legend genre, and becomes an instrument of a scribal group of devout Jews. . . . Several tendencies can be observed in the redaction of Daniel 1–6 which are already moving in the direction of a strict Jewish personal piety. It is in Daniel 1–6 that we can best see the radicalization of wisdom genres that might have been a parallel development to the renaissance of apocalypticism in the third and second centuries.[78]

These trends (derived mostly from observations on Bel and the Dragon and Daniel 1–6) coincide with those observable in the Susanna story's development. In the OG, Lord's angel *gives* Daniel an insightful spirit (mantic wisdom) while in TH God stirs up Daniel's own saintly spirit (piety). OG Susanna dramatizes issues of Jewish self-government (ethnic awareness) and concludes with an exhortation on the nurture of "Jacob's beloved." TH elaborates the drama of a lovely, virtuous, pious woman (educated in the Law of Moses!) and concludes with family celebration of Susanna's purity.[79]

These differences between the Greek versions are reinforced by sequence effects. Susanna, standing at the head of TH Daniel, sets the tone for the rest of the book, inclining us to read it as a lesson-book in virtue. The fact that here we meet Daniel as a young boy gives the entire book something of a biographical flavor, with unity provided more by Daniel's story than by the theme of God's sovereignty vs. the foreign kings'. The book closes with Habakkuk's succor of Daniel and Cyrus's acclaim of *Daniel's* (again the individualizing note) God.[80]

---

[77] Ibid., 148–52. Wills's analysis involves many levels of reconstructed sources and redactional stages, but the OG and MT/TH are his most important points of reference. In the summary list of trends on pages 145–6, items 1c,d,f; 2a,c,d; 3a,b,c; 4a,b,c; 5b; 6a,b; and 7a,b,c specifically compare the OG and TH of the additions or the OG and MT (=TH) of Daniel proper.

[78] Ibid., 151.

[79] Plus, of course, a notice of her rescuer's subsequent reknown.

[80] Cyrus's acclaim provides a formal rounding-off but is not a major story scene, in and of itself. It is interesting, however, to see how Cyrus's acclaim of Daniel's God in the final lines parallels the closing of the Chronicler's history (2 Chronicles 36, which eventually became the closing chapter of the entire Hebrew canon).

The OG, which places Susanna at the very end of the book, produces a very different effect. Here the book of Daniel opens (as it does in MT) with a note about the reign and fate of King Jehoiakim, followed by a series of court legends illustrating the adventures of Jews in the pagan court. We then come to the apocalyptic interlude.[81] But the book does not end with Daniel 12's promises of exaltation for "the whole people"[82] and resurrection of the insightful to shine like stars. The Greek versions, unlike the MT, return us to the (relatively) humdrum life of the foreign court in Bel and the Dragon, which psychologically distances the reader from the crisis tone of the apocalypse and suggests that the End might not be so very close, after all.[83] Then, at the very end of the book, the OG gives us Susanna's story. As we began with Jehoiakim (Greek Ἰωακιμ) and a self-ruled Jewish community, we end with a Joachim in a self-ruled Jewish community. (Engel argues that we may even be back in Judah, "Babylon" in the OG serving as a metaphorical term for evil, rather than a geographical designation.)[84]

Coming *after* the apocalyptic section's promises of sovereignty restored to the Jewish people (Dan 7:27, 12:1-3), and especially its dark allusions to division within the people (11:35, 12:2,10), the Susanna story rings a sobering note. "Take hope," its message seems to be, "but remember what self-rule can be. The pious can prevail—but life on earth goes on." OG Daniel ends with an exhortation to educate young men properly (Sus 62). It thus acquires, like TH Daniel, the flavor of a hortatory tract, but whereas TH promoted individual virtue, the OG rings a more social note.

---

81 Interludes, if we follow 967's chapter arrangement, which interweaves apocalyptic and legendary chapters.

82 πᾶς ὁ λαός, Dan 12:1 OG. TH reads simply "your people." This would seem to support Wills's thesis that the OG displays greater ethnic consciousness.

83 In the fabula, the events of the visions occur hundreds of years after those of Bel and the Dragon, so by strict linear logic the story's placement should not matter. But narratively, it makes a great deal of difference whether the book ends with the "one thousand three hundred thirty-five days" message or goes on to tell another tale of Daniel's life in court.

84 Engel, 89.

Chapter 7

STORY AND LIFE

What have we learned about the faith worldviews embedded in the Greek Daniel legends? We have seen that the plots follow fairly conventional folk patterns and tend toward a genre, the court legend, which is typically used by ruled ethnic groups to assert their identity and worth. In the Bel and the Dragon stories, the driving aim of the plot is God's, although God does not (technically speaking) appear as an actor in the story. In the first two acts, Bel and The Serpent, Daniel's own human cleverness suffices for success. In the Lion Pit story, however, Daniel plays a passive role, and supernatural intervention brings about the happy ending.[1]

In Susanna's plot, the villains' desire to control Susanna drives the story. Their desire is frustrated when Susanna's determination, Daniel's skill, and the assembly's power ally against them. Lord intervenes at only one point in the fabula[2] and may be described as a helper, whose aid is necessary but not sufficient to bring about a happy ending. The OG plot branches into two event–chains which interact with each other, while TH smooths the two series into a single sequence.[3] In both stories, steadfastness finally defeats deception.

Both plots (Bel and the Dragon and Susanna) center on singulative, crisis–type events, suggesting a view of life controlled by sudden

---

[1] In a very broad sense, this sequence recapitulates the wisdom tradition's shift from early emphasis on human possibility and responsibility (albeit in tension with acknowledgment of divine power) to later emphasis on human limitations and need for divine assistance.

[2] Lord's key intervention comes in the granting/awakening of Daniel's spirit as Susanna is led to execution. Lord's angel appears again to hurl fire at the villains in the final scene of the OG, but this does not affect the plot since punishment is already being carried out by the assembly.

[3] TH also smooths chronological sequence in Bel and the Dragon.

twists and turns. Susanna, especially in TH, balances this with a suggestion that actions in crisis exemplify long–standing character traits.
However, all the characters (in both versions of both stories) are traditional one–dimensional types. Only the king in Bel and the Dragon
shows any change (from idol–worshiper to acclaimer of Lord), and that
change is a stock element of the genre.

Different versions of the stories center on different characters.
Daniel is "hero" of OG Bel and the Dragon; TH (for all its improved
assimilation to the book of Daniel) takes the king as its center of
reference. OG Susanna centers on judges and judicial responsibility; its
Daniel is a righteous young man just entering the world of legal process.
TH shows more interest in the pious, attractive characters Susanna and
Daniel; its Daniel is a divinely inspired child.

When we attend to narrative tone, we find that both Bel and the
Dragon tales employ anonymous omniscient narration which aligns our
sympathies with the divine viewpoint.[4] In these strongly scenic narratives, characters and their actions speak for themselves.[5] Susanna's narrators shape the story more visibly with variable pacing, indirect
dialogue and, most of all, explicit characterization. In both stories, but
especially in Susanna, TH displays more interest in the minds of the villains. Idol worship is ludicrous, the narratives show, and chastity the
road to success, but we get at least a glimpse of lust's allure.

The stories' atmospheres, particularly their interactions with
other texts, resonate strongly with the Judah/Babylon tensions found in
the books of Jeremiah and Habakkuk. These tensions similarly drive the
twelve chapters of MT Daniel. The legends of Daniel 1–6 suggest that
pagan empires and emperors can function in sympathy with God's purposes, and that God's people can build successful lives in foreign lands.
The apocalyptic visions of Daniel 7–12 take a darker view, suggesting
that not only pagan empires but even some Jews are wrongly inclined—
so much so, that God's sovereignty can be realized only in cataclysmic
destruction of the empires and reinstatement of the faithful. The Greek
versions reinforce the legendary side of the book—but pick up themes
from the apocalyptic portion as well.

---

[4] This is an easier task in the Daniel legends than in the ethically murky
stories of the Yahwist.

[5] The narrators still control what happens, but they give the *impression* of
conveying uninterpreted facts.

We turn now to the intersections between these Greek Daniel legends, the Hellenistic world, and its Jewish Diaspora—but with several cautions in mind. The first, so obvious it hardly needs mentioning, is that our information about Jewish life in Hellenistic times is sharply limited.[6]

Second, our conclusions about the time and place of each translation are tentative. While a few decades—or even a century—may not look like much from our temporal distance, the Hellenistic world experienced the same sort of rapid social upheavals that characterize our own day. As the American context changed between the 1950s and the 1960s, the situation in Alexandria changed rapidly during the succession struggles of the 140s B.C.E. Situations might also vary significantly from city to city.

Third, our stories have histories. Not every idea in "Theodotion's" version derives *de novo* from the translator; much comes from the OG story that the translator/reviser adapted. The OG, in its turn, probably translates a Semitic original which in its turn almost certainly drew on a non-Danielic tale. We must always reckon with the possibility that a given aspect of a story (e.g., "tallow, pitch, and hair") derives from its lineage and does not reflect the contemporary community's concerns at all.

On the other hand, the very act of translation indicates a resonance between story and community, an interest which justifies the effort and expense of translation.[7] Not everything may jive—but *something* must, or the tale would be ignored. Changes introduced in a new version presumably reflect the new community's interests and tastes—thus the divergences between TH and the OG tell us something about TH's community.[8]

---

[6] I use "Hellenistic" in the broad sense, to denote the cosmopolitan, *koine*-speaking culture that dominated the eastern Mediterranean area well into Roman times.

[7] Writing materials were reasonably expensive, and presumably "time was money" in the Hellenistic world as in our own—whether or not the translator was paid for this specific effort.

[8] Comparison between the versions tells less about the OG than it does about TH—the OG shows less interest in private piety than TH does, yet the OG may have had dramatically *more* interest than its antecedent did—we cannot be sure. A biological analogy may be helpful here. Evolutionary theory does not suggest that every feature of a species represents optimal adaptation to its current environment. It does suggest that (a) occupation of a given environmental niche occurs when the species in question

Finally, we must remember that my reading of the stories is not final or comprehensive. I have aimed at as complete an analysis as possible, but my questions and observations have been limited by my own experience, historical position, and available parallels. The possibility always remains that a different reading may uncover elements even more relevant to the historical situation than those I have seen.

Despite these uncertainties, the question of the narratives' relationships to the concerns of their communities deserves a look. I shall begin by discussing the general realities of life in the Hellenistic Diaspora, in relation to the versions' common literary features. I shall then turn to version-specific features and discuss them in relation to the Alexandrian community of the late second century B.C.E. (OG) and northern Syria and Asia Minor in the mid-first century (30-50) C.E. (TH).[9] Finally, I shall present summary reflections on both the historical issues and their contemporary implications.

Common Features and the Diaspora World

During the centuries following Alexander's conquests, Greek language and education penetrated urban and upper-class life throughout the Near East. Trade expanded and mercenary soldiers of many nationalities settled in military/agricultural communities far from their original homes. These factors increased intercultural exchange in a region which already had a rich tradition of population movement and mixings. The Greeks (who seldom bothered to learn local languages) were less influenced by the contact than their subject peoples (who generally learned Greek language and ways without entirely abandoning

---

is, *overall*, better adapted to that niche than its competitors are (although some particular features might actually be counter-adaptive), and (b) the *direction* of development will be toward better adaptation (remembering that in the process, the niche itself may change, requiring a change in the adaptive direction).

[9] Since the precise locale of TH remains uncertain, I shall discuss two representative cities, Ephesus and Antioch: Ephesus because it was a fairly typical Asia Minor city and the traditional site for TH, and Antioch because it was the major Jewish center of Syria and is the sort of location to which Koch's Daniel-specific location analysis points. Klaus Koch, "Die Herkunft der Proto-Theodotion-Übersetzung des Danielbuches," *VT* 23 (1973): 362-365.

their own languages and traditions).[10] Yet even on the Greek side, Hellenistic culture was a new development, distinct from the culture of classical Greece.

Some of the difference arose from the influx of new concepts, religions, and customs. Part derived from the fact that the key political unit was now the monarchic state (unified by military might and power politics) rather than the classical *polis* (bound by citizens' shared history, customs, and practical interests). In the huge transnational kingdoms of the Antigonids, Ptolemies, and Seleucids, social disruption and intercultural contact worked to weaken local ethnic identities in favor of "world citizenship" on the one hand and increased individualism on the other. Social rifts within subject peoples (caused by rapid Hellenization of urban and elite groups, while rural and low-class folk often held to older traditions) complicated the issue of ethnic loyalty.[11]

In this cultural maelstrom, several religious questions and responses seemed especially important. One question was, "how do different religions and their truth claims relate to one another?" The dominant response was syncretism—identification of deities with one another and superimposition of rituals from different sources. Another response, especially among the educated elite, was to question the very existence of "gods." Others rallied to protect their old ways, a response readily understandable in terms of both class conflict and cognitive dissonance.[12]

Another important question, especially given the era's political and cultural volatility and breakdown of old support structures, was "how can I quell anxiety?" A great many people turned to esoteric salvation cults which provided emotional release and ritual assurance of deliverance. Others turned to the philosophical schools which urged

---

[10] Clearly, many individuals (especially in the ruling classes) became extremely Hellenized, while others (especially in the rural areas and lower classes) maintained the old ways practically unchanged. The overall effect, however, seems to have been in the middle range suggested here. For a fascinating discussion of accomodation and resistance to Hellenization in non-Greek cultures, see Arnaldo Momigliano, *Alien Wisdom: The Limits of Hellenization* (Cambridge: University Press, 1975; paperback edition 1990).

[11] This was true even for the Greeks (and Romans) themselves. The "folk back home" often disapproved of Hellenistic innovations such as the ruler cults discussed below.

[12] Again the Jews are usually given as a parade example, but the rioters in Ephesus (Acts 19:23-34), although cast as crass commercialists by Luke (25, 27), were also mustering in favor of ancestral traditions.

attainment of *ataraxia* by variously nuanced combinations of right attitude and appropriate (usually sedate) lifestyle.[13]

One interesting outcome of the period's political and religious ferment was that many of the powerful, highly visible, often idiosyncratic kings and queens of the Hellenistic states became foci of ruler cults.

> Other gods are either far away or have not ears, or do not exist, or pay no heed to us at all: but you we can see in very presence, not in wood and not in stone, but in truth. And so we pray to you.[14]

These cults appealed well to the politically ambitious and to those who desperately hungered for effective leadership, but less well to those with more egalitarian political traditions or whose religion—Judaism being the case in point—precluded any god but One.

When Alexander died, Judea found itself pinned, as it had been through most of its history, between powerful Mesopotamian (now Seleucid) and Egyptian (now Ptolemaic) states. Coping with foreign rulers was not a new problem, and the transition from Persian to Ptolemaic rule seems to have gone fairly smoothly. But, especially after the Seleucids took over in 198 B.C.E., the "cultural imperialism" of the Hellenists (as opposed to the more *laissez faire* stance of the Persian empire) created problems for a people whose religion contained two central tenets—monotheism and aniconism—incompatible with the general trends of Hellenistic paganism and the specific demands of ruler cults.[15] The general tensions of Hellenistic life and the special problems of its interaction with Judaism intertwined with existing internal conflicts to create an extremely tense situation.[16] Outwardly, this tension exploded into conflict with foreign rulers, the most famous confrontations being the Maccabean rebellion and the war with Rome in 66–70 C.E. Inwardly, a number of sects and factions developed, making

---

[13] The Stoics and Epicureans (who do not deserve their lurid reputation) were the most important of these schools; both urged sober living although the supportive reasoning varied.

[14] Processional song for Demetrius I Poliorcetes, quoted by Michael Grant, *From Alexander to Cleopatra: The Hellenistic World* (New York: Scribner, 1982; MacMillan, Collier Books, 1990), 96. Page references are to the paperback edition.

[15] Not all rulers demanded public worship—some merely allowed it, some eschewed it—so the severity of the problem varied from ruler to ruler and place to place.

[16] On the development of these tensions prior to the Hellenistic period see Paul D. Hanson, *The Dawn of Apocalyptic: The Historical and Sociological Roots of Jewish Apocalpytic Eschatology*, revised ed. (Philadelphia: Fortress, 1979).

Palestinian Judaism of the Hellenistic period an extraordinarily complex phenomenon.[17]

Meanwhile, not all Jews lived in Judah. Well before Alexander's time, Jewish deportees, refugees, and mercenary soldiers had settled in other lands. Even more moved abroad during the Hellenistic period. Jewish slaves, mercenaries, out-party priests and civil servants moved to Egypt, Syria, Asia Minor, and beyond. Alexandria and Antioch supported especially large and influential Jewish populations. Many Diaspora Jews spoke Greek but not Hebrew, so by the third century B.C.E., Jewish writings were being translated into Greek for their use.[18]

These Diaspora Jews seem to have maintained fairly close contact with the homeland. Those who could afford it made pilgrimages to Jerusalem, and a number of Diaspora communities established synagogues there.[19] Jews abroad tended to distance themselves from the factional quarreling in Judea; they were far more concerned with how to get along with their Gentile neighbors and rulers.

In terms of social position, an individual Jew living abroad might be anything from a slave to a highly placed merchant or civil official with full citizenship. Military colonies (cleruchies) typically had their own governments—operating within the confines of royal policy, of course. In the large urban centers Jewish communities, like other ethnic enclaves, were typically organized into *politeumata* with substantial rights of self-government. A *politeuma* was governed by an ethnarch or a council of elders and had its own court system. A well-disposed monarch or city government often granted other specific privileges such as the right to collect the half-shekel Temple tax and send it to Jerusalem.

---

[17] An extensive literature has arisen around this complexity. For a suggestive overview, see Michael Edward Stone, *Scriptures, Sects and Visions: A Profile of Judaism from Ezra to the Jewish Revolts* (Philadelphia: Fortress, 1980). Scholars increasingly tend to view even the Maccabean revolt as a primarily internal struggle. See e.g. Martin Hengel, *Judaism and Hellenism: Studies in Their Encounter in Palestine During the Early Hellenistic Period*, 2 vols. (London: SCM, 1974), 1:267-309.

[18] Language varied by region, of course. A substantial part of the Diaspora spoke Aramaic (as did the common folk in Palestine) and a religious literature appeared in that language, as in Greek (much of MT Daniel is written in Aramaic).

[19] S. Safrai, "Relations Between the Diaspora and the Land of Israel," in *The Jewish People in the First Century: Historical Geography, Political History, Social, Cultural and Religious Life and Institutions*, ed. S. Safrai and M. Stern; in collaboration with D. Flusser and W. C. van Unnik, *CRINT*, Section One in two vols. (Philadelphia: Fortress, 1974-6), 1:184-215.

While most peculiarly Jewish observances could be accommodated in such a system, refusal to worship city or state deities could hardly be officially endorsed. In good times it was handled by looking the other way; in bad times it became an occasion for persecution. Such disturbances often arose from ill-feeling between ethnic *politeumata*:

> The basic source of conflict in most of the big Graeco-Jewish urban centres was the potential equality between two parallel organizations, the tension being reinforced both by the cultural abilities and ethnic religious consciousness of the Jewish associations and by the consequent ambiguity of their civic status.[20]

The synagogue, which was to become so important for Judaism after the Temple's fall, has a complex history with multiple roots in our period. In early Palestinian usage, the word "synagogue" is most often associated with study, although rabbinic legislation assumes a judicial function for it. Diaspora Jews tended to call their meeting-places prayer-houses (προσευχαί). Prayer groups would have functioned at a different level from the *politeuma* (which was part of the city's civic structure), being more parallel to pagan religious societies and burial clubs.[21]

Many pagans seem to have been interested in Judaism, especially in Asia Minor. Its monotheism and stress on ethics fit well with some of the popular philosophies (especially Stoicism). Writers like Philo and Josephus do not hesitate to stress this. Particular customs like Sabbath observance attracted other God-fearers.

Among Jews, responses to religious confrontation seem to have run the gamut from a full-blown syncretism that quickly lost its Jewish character (famous examples are Dositheus, an Egyptian official of the third century B.C.E., and Philo's nephew Tiberius Alexander, a high Roman official)[22] through apologetic and missionary literature that stresses the antiquity of Jewish belief (often presenting Abraham as culture-giver for the entire ancient Mediterranean world) and its affinity

---

[20] S. Applebaum, "The Legal Status of the Jewish Communities in the Diaspora," in Safrai and Stern, 1:420–463.

[21] Shaye J. Cohen, *From the Maccabees to the Mishnah* (Philadelphia: Westminster, 1987), 111–114; Harald Hegermann, "The Diaspora in the Hellenistic Age," in *The Hellenistic Age*, ed. W. D. Davies and Louis Finkelstein, *The Cambridge History of Judaism* vol. 2 (Cambridge, University Press, 1989), 151–154; for more detail see S. Safrai, "The Synagogue," in Safrai and Stern, 908–944. In a city with only one prayer group/synagogue, *politeuma* and synagogue might be essentially the same organization.

[22] D. Flusser, "Paganism in Palestine," in Safrai and Stern, 1091–92.

to Hellenistic philosophy, to a Torah piety much like that of later rabbinic Judaism.

Where do our Greek Daniel legends fit in this complex religious and cultural matrix? In chapter 6, we saw that the opposition "Judah/Babylon" dominates the intertextual dynamics of our stories. The terms of this opposition are fluid. Traditionally, Judah represents the fullness and goodness of life in the presence of God; Babylon represents wickedness and danger. These traditional values assert themselves in Jeremiah, Habakkuk, and the book of Daniel itself.

Yet in Jeremiah, Habakkuk, and Daniel, Judah also appears as a place of corruption, perversion, and/or famine, while the Babylonian king serves God, and Babylon offers hope (in Jeremiah and Daniel) of success and prosperity for Jewish folk.

For Diaspora Jews, the ambiguities of the Judah/Babylon opposition reflected reality. "Babylon" (be it Alexandria, Ephesus, Antioch, or Rome) *was* a pagan land, and dangerous—it also offered remarkable opportunity in the free-wheeling Hellenistic period. Judah (whether under the Seleucids, the Hasmoneans, or Rome) remained the homeland, site of the Temple (at the time of our translations), the direction in which one prayed. It was also economically straitened and suffering from factional strife and corruption in high places.

Alongside this spatial opposition, the book of Daniel offers two worldviews: one (in the legends) ultimately optimistic about human possibilities within the structures of pagan empire; one (in the visions) seeing deliverance only in divine destruction of the powers of this corrupt age. Scholarly attention has focused mostly on the latter (because of its novelty, its importance in Christianity, and also because it gets the final word in the MT, with which most scholars work). But the textual history of Daniel suggests that in post-Antiochan times it was the book's *legendary* side, not the apocalyptic, which captured editorial interest. This is true for the Palestinian tradition (culminating in MT), which edited chapters 4–6 into a much more developed form than we see in the OG, but it is even more evident in the Diaspora texts (the OG and TH) with their legendary additions.

We have seen that Bel and the Dragon and Susanna, like Daniel 3 and 6, display features of the court conflict genre—one which stresses rivalry (not merely friendly competition) between competitive ethnic groups, and typically functions to reinforce the identity of the group which tells it. It is quite easy to see the appeal of this genre to Jewish residents of cities such as Alexandria, Ephesus, and Antioch, all of which experienced, at one time or another, rivalry between ethnic *politeumata*. Daniel's problem in the Bel and Serpent stories—pressure to worship the gods of a pagan state—would have been particularly real to highly placed Jews with citizen status, since their *de facto* exemption from this requirement was never legally secure. The Bel and the Dragon's peculiar focus on eating (Bel who does not eat, the serpent who does, the lions who refrain and Habakkuk who helps Daniel to eat) may express some of the anxiety provoked in worshipers of an aniconic God by the fleshy presence of the "divine" rulers (see the hymn to Demetrius, page 178, above).[23]

Susanna modulates the generic formula to portray an intra–Jewish conflict rather than an interethnic one. I am somewhat dubious about the argument that this originated as polemic against the Hasmonean kings.[24] One could just as well argue that it represents a polemic against Pharisaic leadership, with the two elders representing leaders of the two schools.[25] Abuse of power by influential persons appears to be a problem in every human civilization, and the Jewish tradition's warnings against prejudice in judgment are as old as Exodus (23:6-8, quoted in Sus 53). The problem becomes especially acute in rapidly changing, unsettled urban situations with high stakes and few traditional restraints.[26] We need not look to Judean politics to find corruption—the courts of the *politeuma* certainly offered scope for such abuse. Yet we must not forget that the Susanna story, like the other court legends, is ultimately optimistic about the possibility of God's will being done on earth.

What about connections between our stories and *Hellenistic* (rather than specifically Jewish) interests? I find it significant that the two additional stories of Greek Daniel deal with the two aspects of Jewish identity which the Hellenistic world found most attractive: monotheism (Bel and the Dragon) and ethics (Susanna),[27] so that the tales at once mock the more vulnerable aspects of paganism and show

---

[23] It might also reflect anxiety about the role of temple-meals in pagan society—note the recurrence of this theme in Paul's letters.

[24] E.g. Helmut Engel, *Die Susanna-Erzählung: Einleitung, Übersetzung und Kommentar zum Septuaginta-Text und zur Theodotion-Bearbeitung* (Freiburg: Universitätsverlag, 1985; Göttingen: Vandenhoeck & Ruprecht, 1985), 177. Even if this explanation is valid for the OG's origin, we must look elsewhere to explain the story's continuing popularity.

[25] The antiquity of the two-school tradition is debated; Louis Finkelstein argues that it extends back into the Persian period ("The Men of the Great Synagogue [*circa* 400-170 B.C.E.]," in Davies and Finkelstein, 229-244, and "The Pharisaic Leadership After the Great Synagogue," ibid., 245-277).

[26] Compare Qohelet's remarks.

[27] Contrast Daniel 1, which features the dietary laws.

Judaism's compatibility with paganism at its best.[28]   This does not necessarily mean that the stories were intended for missionary use. (Their assumption that the reader is familiar with Jewish figures and concepts suggests otherwise.) Rather, "those elements which make Judaism attractive to outsiders are precisely those which also strengthen its hold on insiders."[29]

The stories also display a quite Hellenistic tendency to focus on the adventures of individuals. The individuals in question are not "fraught with background,"[30] in the characteristic style of classical Hebrew narrative. Rather they are the stock characters of romance: the clever courtier, the lovely virtuous young woman, scheming enemies. Epithets can capture these characters with ease. Their stories are not full-blown Hellenistic romance, but they do show characteristic features—attractive protagonists, exotic settings, dramatic crises.[31]

The Old Greek and Theodotion
in their Individual Settings

It seems clear that, in a general way, the Greek books of Daniel and their added legends do reflect the circumstances and concerns of communities in the Hellenistic Diaspora. Let us now probe further and ask whether the *differences* between the Greek versions noticeably reflect the varying circumstances of the communities which produced them, looking first at the OG, then at TH.

Alexandria and the Old Greek

The OG, we saw in chapter 3, was probably translated in Alexandria in the late second century B.C.E. Alexandria, established by and named for Alexander the Great, sat on the western angle of the Nile delta where it became a major conduit for east/west trade. (It picked up

---

[28] John J. Collins identifies these complementary strategies in *Between Athens and Jerusalem: Jewish Identity in the Hellenistic Period* (New York: Crossroads, 1983), 8–9.

[29] Cohen, 57; for a virtually identical argument see Collins, 9.

[30] Erich Auerbach, *Mimesis: The Representation of Reality in Western Literature* (Garden City: Doubleday, 1957), 12.

[31] For concurring opinions see Lawrence M. Wills (*The Jew in the Court of a Foreign King: Ancient Jewish Court Legends*, HDR [Minneapolis: Fortress, 1990], 199) and Cohen's description of the "typical Greek novella or romance, complete with a heroine in distress, narrow escapes, and a happy ending," 43.

the slack from Tyre, which Alexander had recently destroyed.) It served as administrative center for the Ptolemaic empire, and its Museum and Library attracted the period's greatest scientists, scholars, and writers. Among their other duties, these experts were put to work enhancing the temples erected by Ptolemaic rulers:

> In this temple of Sarapis, strange wonders could be seen. They included the sight of an iron statue of Ares propelled into the embrace of a lodestone Aphrodite by the combined action of magnets and invisible wires. . . . It was likewise in Alexandrian shrines that the principle of the siphon was applied to making water into wine; and when the congregation arrived in the temple, hidden hydraulic bellows ingeniously caused fanfares of trumpets to blare out, or the altar-fire to burst into a seemingly miraculous blaze. Moreover, the expansive force of hot air created by burnt offerings was utilized to throw open the temple doors and propel the image of its god forward, so that he came to meet and greet his devotees; and a variety of novel lighting effects included the internal illumination of statues so that light shone out of their eyes.[32]

Josephus alleges that Alexandrian Jews were granted full citizenship by Alexander himself at the city's founding.[33] This is probably an overstatement; however, it does seem that the Jews held a good civic position in Alexandria from early times.[34] In fact, they fared better than native Egyptians, who retained significant power only in the temples. Egyptian resentment of the Jews found expression during the reign of Ptolemy II Philadelphus (283–246 B.C.E.) in the accusations of the priest Manetho, which were still being cited centuries later.[35]

Jewish influence in Alexandria peaked during the reign of Ptolemy VI Philometor (181–145 B.C.E.). Egyptian hostility against the Greeks and Macedonians was rising, depriving the king of native support, and many of the Greeks allied with Philometor's brother and rival Ptolemy VII Neos Philopater,[36] so that the Jewish community comprised the king's most reliable group of supporters.

Meanwhile, the homeland was making its turbulent transition from Seleucid to Hasmonean rule. In 175–174 B.C.E., the Zadokite High Priest Onias III was deposed by Antiochus IV Epiphanes and took refuge in Egypt. Around 160, his son Onias IV built a temple in

---

[32] Grant, 230.

[33] *Ag. Ap.* 2 § 35; *J. W.* 2 § 487.

[34] Hegermann, 121–122.

[35] Grant, 45; Hegermann, 136–137. For a more detailed discussion of Manetho, raising the possibility that the anti-Judaic identifications are later insertions, see Emilio Gaba, "The Growth of Anti-Judaism or the Greek Attitude Towards Jews," in Davies and Finkelstein, 630–33.

[36] Hegermann, 141–42.

Leontopolis (a Jewish military colony in the vicinity of Alexandria) which continued to operate, according to Josephus, until after the destruction of the Jerusalem Temple in 70 C.E.[37]

When Philometor died, the Alexandrian Jews rallied in support of his widow Cleopatra II, but she lost her succession bid to Ptolemy VIII Physcon (145-116 B.C.E., to which period our translation probably dates). Ptolemy VIII apparently retaliated with a "savage persecution of the Jews in Alexandria and the rest of Egypt" at the beginning of his reign.[38] (He also drove out many of the scholars from the Library and Museum, which never again drew staff of comparable prestige.)[39]

In fairly short order the succession question was resolved by marriage between Physcon and Cleopatra. Of the subsequent era Hegermann says,

> Apart from its tension-filled beginnings, the reign of the seventh [*sic*] Ptolemy (145-116 B.C.E.) was again a favourable period for the Jews. It was among the Greek citizens of Alexandria that the king's opponents were to be found, and these were dealt with harshly. In addition he had to quell numerous rebellions among the Egyptian population. But it appears that the antagonism which is found in the early Roman period between the Greek citizens of Alexandria and the Jewish inhabitants had its origins in these decades, at a time when the Jews remained loyal to the king, while the Greeks were being treated harshly and without mercy. There must have been many Jews among the large numbers of foreigners who were accorded Alexandrian citizenship during these years.[40]

Thus we see a pattern of positive relations between the Jews and the monarch, accompanied by bitterness between the Jewish population and the Egyptians and Greeks, whom Grant describes as "addicted to over-excitement and rioting."[41] This pattern seems to have continued into the

---

[37] Stone, 79–80; Josephus *Ant.* 13 § 62–73, *J. W.* 7 § 420–436.

[38] Hegermann, 142, although he inexplicably refers to Euergetes II as Ptolemy VII rather than Ptolemy VIII. (Cf. Helmut Koester, *History, Culture, and Religion of the Hellenistic Age, Introduction to the New Testament*, vol. 1, Hermeneia: Foundations and Facets [Philadelphia: Fortress, 1982], 222, or any other authoritative source on the period—regnal dates are listed slightly differently in various sources, but they agree in identifying Euergetes II Physcon as Ptolemy VIII, not Ptolemy VII.) This seems to be the persecution so colorfully described in 3 Maccabees 5 (wrongly attributed there to Ptolemy IV, cf. Josephus *Ag. Ap.* 2 § 53–55).

[39] Grant, 259.

[40] Hegermann, 143. The *Epistle of Aristeas* was probably written during this period; see Collins, 81–86.

[41] Grant, 48.

reigns of Ptolemy IX and X, whose generals included two of Onias IV's sons.[42]

The relevance of Bel and the Dragon to such a setting is easily seen. We have noted that the OG version of this story alleges priestly connections for Daniel; given Ptolemaic interactions with the Oniad family, the idea of a Jewish priest as high court official becomes quite plausible. The power position of Daniel vis-à-vis the priests in the OG, and his close alignment with the king, ring credibly against the deployment of factions in Ptolemaic Alexandria. The theme of crude deception by Bel's priests, so unconvincing to modern eyes, makes sense in the context of the extravaganza the Museum's scientists devised for the Sarapis temple. (Note that the OG slips in an explicit reference to the priests' "deceit" in v. 19.) We have also mentioned that Egypt is one location where veneration of live snakes was practiced in the Hellenistic period.[43]

We noted in chapter 4 that the OG's introduction to the Lion Pit story (vv. 28–32) repeatedly stresses the role of the rabble (v. 28 "everyone from the countryside," v. 30 "the crowd from the countryside," vv. 31–32 "the crowds") although the king gives his response not to the crowds directly but to his courtiers (τοὺς συμβιωτὰς αὐτοῦ, v. 31).[44] This language acquires considerable strength when we read it in the context of native Egyptian resentment against influential urban Jews, and the role of the temples as the last stronghold of the Egyptians' own traditional leaders.

OG Susanna's concern to cultivate faithfulness in the community's own leaders makes sense in the contexts of both the very strong, essentially self-governed Alexandrian *politeuma* and the struggles for leadership in Palestine throughout the second century B.C.E.[45] Daniel's accusation that the second elder's seed is corrupt "like Sidon's, not Judah's" might possibly reflect the rancor of the final break between the Samaritans and the Jerusalem-centered Jews, which took place during this period. (The Samaritans called themselves "Sidonians.")[46]

---

[42] Hegermann, 143; Koester, 222.

[43] See Wis 15:18-19 and especially *Ep. Arist.* 138, coming from roughly the same time and place as our OG translation.

[44] After mentioning "the Babylonians" in v. 28, TH fades off into pronouns.

[45] The Alexandrian *politeuma* seems to have been governed sometimes by an ethnarch, sometimes by a council of elders. See S. Applebaum, "The Organization of the Jewish Communities in the Diaspora," in Safrai and Stern, 473-477.

[46] The Samaritans attempted to placate Antiochus IV Epiphanes by agreeing to name their temple for Zeus; John Hyrcanus retaliated by destroying the Gerizim temple in 128 B.C.E. Cohen, 169-170; Momigliano, 108-9.

In chapter 6 we saw that OG Daniel as a whole begins and ends in self-ruled Jewish communities. The opening chapter (Daniel 1) moves quickly from Jerusalem to Babylon, where we learn through a series of stories (Daniel 1–6) that although exile is indeed dangerous, it is not at all impossible for a faithful Jew to prosper there (as Jeremiah had promised). In the next section (Daniel 7–12), hopes for return and an end to oppression burn hot, raising expectations that Jeremiah's "seventy years" will soon be fulfilled. But the final two stories (Bel and the Dragon and Susanna) return to the soberer hopes of the early chapters—hopes for survival and success in a world where wickedness remains very much alive. The closing story, Susanna, suggests that even when the Jewish community has opportunity to rule itself, God's intervention is needed to keep things going straight.

The foregoing summary sounds almost like a diary of the Egyptian (and Judean) Jewish communities' experiences in the two centuries following Alexander. Under the new rulers many Jews had moved to new homes in foreign lands and found they could prosper there. Events of the Antiochan persecution in the homeland—and the succession struggle of the 140's in Egypt—prompted reassessment and development of a more dualistic outlook.[47] But in both Judah and Egypt, life continued after the crises, with all its struggles for position and power, and opponents who were not always pagan. The arrangement of OG Daniel superbly reflects this historical movement.

Ephesus, Antioch, and Theodotion

The TH version of the Greek Daniel legends, we have seen, has a generally more "popular" (folkloric/romantic) and less politically conscious character than the OG. In Susanna, its Daniel is an inspired child, rather than an angry young man, and placement of this story at the head of the book gives an overall organization that emphasizes biography rather than politics.[48] Chronological order within the individual additions is also simplified.[49]

---

[47] This clearly happened in Judah; I hypothesize that the Egyptian persecutions two decades later may have had a similar effect, especially since the ideas were now in the air.

[48] This is true if we go by the suggested age of Daniel in the various stories. With respect to absolute dating, however, 967 (OG) shows the greatest chronological concern.

[49] In Susanna, we saw that displacement of the prayer from v. 35a to 42–43 results in a linear rather than branched-chain fabula. In Bel and the Dragon, TH places

TH's presentation of the Susanna story plays up the personal features of various characters—Susanna's beauty and piety, the elder's lasciviousness, Daniel's saintliness—and suggests that these are long-standing features of character, not quirks suddenly evidenced in this moment of crisis. Susanna and Daniel take center stage, for this has become a story about their virtue and deliverance, rather than about the responsibilities of eldership. But the narrator also allows us glimpses into the thoughts of the villains, who in this story are dirty old men rather than corrupt judges. This feature and the highly expanded garden scene suggest that sheer narrative interest is edging aside theological and hermeneutical agendas.

TH's version of Bel and the Dragon also pays somewhat more attention than does the OG to the thoughts and intentions of Daniel's opponents, and it certainly lays greater stress on the Babylonian locale. In this story, the foreign king rather than Daniel holds center stage. However, TH shows less awareness than the OG of court etiquette and tends to play up extravagant and miraculous elements of the story.

Both TH stories use more explicit theological language than their OG counterparts and show more signs of assimilation to the rest of the book of Daniel.[50]

We saw in chapter 3 that this translation probably originated in northern Syria or Asia Minor in the mid–first century C.E. Our information on this part of the Diaspora is much scantier than our information on Egypt. We shall take Ephesus and Antioch as representative locales—Ephesus because of its traditional association with Theodotion's work, Antioch because of its northern Syrian location, its status (alongside Alexandria) as one of the most important Diaspora locations of the early Roman world, and finally, the fact that the titles used in Daniel 3 TH seem to point to a location such as Antioch.[51]

---

vv. 13 and 15 so that we know the events of the night *before* Daniel and the king arrive at the gate the following morning.

[50] The most obvious points of assimilation are the conclusion of Susanna and the introduction to Bel and the Dragon.

[51] Attribution of Theodotion to Ephesus is supported, as we saw in chapter 3, by some linguistic evidence. H. St. John Thackeray, *The Septuagint and Jewish Worship: A Study in Origins*, 2nd ed., The Schweich Lectures, 1920 (London: Oxford University Press, 1923), 25–28; Sidney Jellicoe, "Some Reflections on the καιγε Recension," *VT* 23 (1973): 15–24; see also Dominique Barthélemy, *Les devanciers d'Aquila*, VTSup 10 (Leiden: E. J. Brill, 1963), 154–55. These arguments do not relate specifically to Daniel. The case for a north Syrian location based on Daniel 3 TH comes from Koch (362–365).

The major port city of Ephesus sits near the Ionian coast of Asia Minor. The Ptolemies controlled it in the third century B.C.E. It next passed into Seleucid hands, finally falling under Roman control when Pompey marched through in 63 B.C.E.[52] Its economic situation deteriorated as these rulers bled away profits. Wills argues from his study of court legends in Herodotus and the Greek sources that the Ionians used this genre precisely as the Jews did, to affirm their ethnic identity and value in a time of political subservience.[53]

Religiously, the city's most famous cult centered on Artemis (see Acts 19:23–41), but the Ephesians had wide-ranging interests. Divine claims of the Roman emperors were taken more seriously here than in Rome.[54] A number of gentiles attended synagogue on sabbath and syncretistic cults of "God Most High" and "God of Sabbath" were popular in Asia Minor, especially at the turn of the era.[55] Ephesus eventually became an important center for early Christianity; it was visited several times by Paul and may have had connections with the Johannine community as well.[56]

The Ephesian Jews had considerable status (many were Roman citizens) and confirmed privileges, including the right to collect Temple tax and freedom from court appearances on Sabbath.[57] In spite of, or perhaps because of this, they experienced friction with other ethnic groups. Josephus tells us that in 13 B.C.E., the Ionian cities complained to Marcus Agrippa that Jews who wanted to participate in public life should worship the public gods.[58] The Roman authorities, however, generally upheld traditional arrangements in favor of the Jews; even exempting those who were Roman citizens from military service.[59] Jewish tablets found east of Ephesus on Rheneia (the cemetery island of Delos) suggest that angels were very popular in this region.[60]

---

[52] Koester, 21–22, 45.

[53] Wills, 59–61.

[54] The precedent had been set as early as Alexander's time. Koester, 33–35, 369.

[55] Cohen, 55; Martin Hengel, "The Interpenetration of Judaism and Hellenism in the Pre-Maccabean Period," in Davies and Finkelstein, 210.

[56] John E. Stambaugh and David L. Balch, *The New Testament in its Social Environment*, Library of Early Christianity (Philadelphia: Westminster, 1986), 147.

[57] M. Stern, "The Jewish Diaspora," in Safrai and Stern, 152; Josephus *Ant.* 14 § 262-64, 16 § 167.

[58] Hengel, "Interpenetration," 207; Josephus *Ant.* 12 § 125-26.

[59] Stern, "The Jewish Diaspora," 143, 152.

[60] Hengel, "Interpenetration," 208.

Antioch was founded by Seleucus I as capital of his new empire; and according to Josephus, the special privileges of its Jewish *politeuma* were established at the very outset and maintained undiminished by the Romans.[61]   Although a tradition developed that the martyrdoms of Eleazar and Hannah and her sons had taken place in Antioch, even the Maccabean rebellion does not seem to have wrought great changes in the lives of Antioch's Jews.[62] So far as we know, ethnic violence involving the Jews did not erupt in Antioch until about 40 C.E., during Caligula's reign (a time of rioting in Alexandria as well).[63] Claudius, taking office in 41 after Caligula's death, confirmed traditional Jewish rights throughout the empire and sent a copy of his edict to Antioch.[64] Things seem to have settled down fairly rapidly.

> The Antiochene Jewish community . . . continued to flourish. Pro-Jewish sentiments and proselytization remained fairly common. The atmosphere was also conducive to the spread of Christianity and Antioch soon became one of its major missionary bases.[65]

Evidence of this essentially cordial atmosphere can be seen in the fact that Antioch was one of the few towns in Syria which left its Jewish minority alone during the upheavals in 66 C.E.[66]

What meaningful connections exist between these situations and narrative features of TH's Greek Daniel legends? We can understand the attraction of court legends in environments where they were cross-culturally understood media for ethnic self-assertion, and we might posit that the relatively less assertive role of Daniel in TH's Bel and the Dragon and his weaker alignment with the king reflect the shift from second century Alexandria (where the Jews played a key role in supporting the king) to times and cities in which the Jews were simply one of several subject peoples.

We may also note that in this period, the Jewish *nation* was involved in escalating conflict with Rome. At the same time, in cosmopolitan cities like Ephesus and Antioch, Judaism's theological and ethical features were attracting Gentile converts. ("The king has become a Jew" was a live possibility in Syria and Asia Minor in this period.)[67]

---

[61] Josephus *Ag. Ap.* 2 § 39; *Ant.* 12 § 119.

[62] 2 Macc 6:18-7:42; Stern, 138-40; Hengel, "Interpenetration," 211.

[63] Stern, 139-140; Stambaugh and Balch, 147.

[64] Applebaum, "Organization," 478.

[65] Stern, 140.

[66] Ibid.

[67] Stern, 174. The best-known example is probably the conversion of the Adiabene queen Helena and her son (Josephus *Ant.* 20 § 17-53).

Against this background, our stories' emphasis on theology and individual piety, rather than national identity, makes good sense.

These arguments, however, seem more related to the general Hellenistic context than to the specific situations in Antioch and Ephesus in 30–50 C.E. In particular, our stories give no hint of the anti–Jewish violence which broke out in Antioch during Caligula's reign (although the book of Daniel might increase in popularity at such a time). When we try to relate the stories to what we know of spirituality in Ephesus and Asia Minor in this period, we note that angels play less of a role, not more, in TH's retelling of Susanna,[68] and Sabbath is not mentioned at all.

Reflections:
The Greek Daniel Legends in Context

Students in my Biblical Narrative class and members of the local biblical storytelling group have both observed that the Daniel additions seem different from the other biblical stories we study. The Greek Daniel legends lack the complex, problematic quality of classic biblical narrative; instead they show virtuous heroes and heroines triumphing, as they should, over clearly evil villains. They seem "nice" stories, in a not entirely complimentary sense.[69]

Narratological analysis and close reading confirm these impressions of straightforwardness in plot, characterization, and tone (the major complication being TH's mixed attitude toward the elders' lust). But when we take intertexts and historical horizons into account, the stories begin to look less naive. Beneath their surface churns the turbulent sea of Hellenistic life and the complex, sometimes self–contradictory array of options offered by Judaism's authoritative writings.[70] Do foreign lands support faithful living, or do they not? Can gardens planted in Babylon bear righteous fruit?

---

[68] In Sus 44 TH, God awakens Daniel's spirit directly, not through an angel, and no angel participates in the executions.

[69] Scholars often seem to assume that the stories' "charm" (another adjective suggesting pleasant inconsequentiality) derives from their folklore connections, but folktales are seldom so Morally Correct.

[70] It seems evident, from the way prophetic writings are handled in the New Testament, at Qumran, and indeed in the book of Daniel, that not only Torah but the Prophets (including Jeremiah and Habakkuk) were "authoritative writings." Daniel itself sits astride the line between source text and interpretation.

Diaspora Jews needed intelligible, credible, and effective ways of relating their scriptures to their lives. Intelligibility required prioritization and coordination of competing meanings; credibility required semblance between the world portrayed in interpretation and the one experienced by the community; effectiveness required that interpretations indicate appropriate behavior and provide motivation for it.

Bel and the Dragon and Susanna work toward these interpretive ends. They balance conflicting attitudes toward "Babylon"; address the ethnic and religious problems faced by Diaspora Jews; and assure them that while religious and moral virtue (specifically, chastity and avoidance of idolatry) require courage, God will sustain the righteous. Added to the book of Daniel, they de-emphasize its apocalyptic and nationalistic tendencies and accent the aspects most relevant to ongoing Diaspora life.

Just how situation–specific was this process? We have seen a solid connection between general aspects of the stories and general concerns of Diaspora Judaism in the Hellenistic period. We also found significant connections between the OG (especially Bel and the Dragon) and Alexandria of the late second century B.C.E. But while TH fits its first-century C.E. setting in a general kind of way, it lacks particular correlations. This might be because our historical information is too scant to illuminate particular connections. Or perhaps we looked at the wrong time or place (evidence about TH's provenance is fairly thin). Or it might be that interpretive stories like these respond to broad cultural currents, rather than local tides and eddies.

Viewed in terms of such broad currents, the Masoretic book of Daniel expresses a religious community's expectation of imminent deliverance from corruption and oppression.[71] The OG tones down the expectation of final deliverance but retains a concern for communal ethics. TH's Daniel moves farthest in the direction of Hellenistic interest in the individual, stressing personal ethics as the key to survival in an ongoing world. It has also, we recall, progressed farthest in terms of literary integration with the rest of Daniel.

This adaptation to the Hellenistic milieu[72] and integration with the rest of Daniel surely stand alongside its agreement with the proto-Masoretic tradition as reasons for TH's displacement of the OG in

---

[71] We noted in chapter 6 that communities which do not experience the world as terminally corrupt find other ways to read the book—or ignore it altogether.

[72] As noted above, Hellenism in the broad sense continued well into Roman times, especially along the Mediterranean's eastern rim.

Christian usage.[73] What our literary/theological study does not explain is why Christians adopted the additions and Jews did not. Logically, believers in the Christian message of the kingdom's imminence should have preferred the apocalyptically flavored MT of Daniel, while early rabbinic Judaism, with its sober assessment of possibilities and practical behavioral emphasis, should have cherished the additions.

Instead, Judaism kept the short version of the book, while Christianity adopted an expanded text. This supports the prevailing opinion that "canonization decisions" were a crystallization of existing custom rather than deliberately weighed theological judgments. The fact that the additions in TH seem to come from a different hand than the main body of Daniel suggests that the additions were not present in the Semitic text used by the primary translator—and that Semitic text became the Masoretic standard. Christians, by contrast, inherited the Greek Bible of Diaspora Judaism, which had contained the additions from the time of the first Alexandrian edition. Thus Christians ended up with the additions and Jews without—contrary to theological logic.

This study of Bel and the Dragon and Susanna in their ancient settings raises questions about contemporary scriptural interpretation, questions applicable to religious communities which reject the additions as well as to those which still revere them. It is with three of these questions that I close this study.

The first question springs from the progressively more individual accent of post-Antiochan Daniel editions, an individualistic emphasis which seems similar to trends of our own time. Sexual misconduct by political candidates enrages the electorate; misappropriation of funds generates far less interest. Current conversations about ecology provide another example: Earth Day '90 generated a great deal of interest in recycling household garbage, while problems such as regulation of the global carbon budget dropped nearly out of sight.

One then asks *why* interest shifted to the individual in Hellenistic times. Are the same dynamics at work today, or do we observe the

---

[73] Agreement with the proto-Masoretic tradition as a factor in Christian adoption of TH is suggested by Jerome's comment, "They use Theodotion's version, but how this came to pass I cannot tell . . . This one thing I can affirm—that it [the LXX Daniel] differs widely from the original, and is rightly rejected." Jerome "Preface to Daniel", NPNF second series (Grand Rapids: Wm. B. Eerdmans, 1952), 6:492.

same effects from different causes?[74] Or is individualization of ethics a universal tendency? How do we counter it? Or should we? In Antiochan and again in Roman times, individuals' refusal to worship public gods led to major social shifts (with seemingly positive results for Christianity, more dubious ones for Judaism). Do private morals bear more public fruit than the current rage for political theology can see?

The second question involves the hermeneutic process at work in the Daniel additions. The problem of relating religious texts (which are often self-contradictory and sometimes downright offensive) to a complicated world has not disappeared. Modern folk frequently respond as those ancient Jews did, by telling stories—stories in sermons, stories in Sunday School booklets, stories in the family room over coffee after the service. It might be highly instructive to take the questions I have posed to Bel and the Dragon and Susanna and apply them to the illustrations used in religious curricula.   How do the writers respond to the (inter-)text's tensions? Which themes do they develop, and how do they subtly alter their source texts? What "textual psycho-dynamics" do our own midrashim reveal?

The evident importance of reinterpretation in ancient and modern times forces a third question: what relevance does historical-critical biblical study have for modern faith communities? If the key religious meanings of scripture emerge through interpretive appropriation, why bother figuring out what "original audiences" thought?

I offer two tentative answers to this question. First, recurrent problems often elicit similar responses—e.g., rapidly changing multi-cultural environments may consistently evoke an individualistic focus. Biblical study, like other kinds of historical study, points up such general human tendencies and suggests options for responding to similar situations today. (It may also alert us to the problems of various responses.)

Second, interpretations often influence us so deeply that we take them for the "plain meaning" of a text—witness seminarians' conviction that Genesis 2-3 "obviously" shows Satan introducing Original Sin into the world. Some find it reassuring that the Bible says precisely what

---

[74] With respect to the Jewish community, one might postulate that the shift of interest from public to private ethics reflected the community's decreasing political power. However, an individualistic emphasis characterized most Hellenistic cultures. Might it be attributed instead to the vastly expanded size or cultural diversity of king-doms? If so, we might find a parallel case in the shift to "personal religion" which Jacobsen oberves in Mesopotamia during the second millennium B.C.E.   Thorkild Jacobsen, *The Treasures of Darkness: A History of Mesopotamian Religion* (New Haven: Yale University Press, 1976), esp. pp. 147-164.

their churches have taught. To such students, historical–critical scholarship seems purely deconstructive, especially when the "original meanings" it reveals are too diverse and strange to take the place of traditional ones.

But for those who find traditional theological formulations problematic (as do many folk in my own mainline church, and even more who have left it), scholarly approaches offer at least the possibility of reading the Bible "honestly" (without obligation to discern predetermined doctrines, and with the option of rejecting particular biblical or traditional teachings). To date, the process has often stopped at this point, because of the feeling that only "original" meanings are legitimate—one must accept them, or none at all.

Yet my examination of the Daniel legends shows how, even in biblical times,[75] scriptural texts functioned less as a "plain sense" authority than as occasions for context–sensitive interpretation through continued storytelling.[76] Modern religious communities might do well to embrace this as precedent for a new and lively round of *derash* (inquiry, interpretation). Can the gardeners of twentieth–century Babylons, encountering the rich and troublesome Bible revealed by historical–critical scholarship, produce midrashim as elegant and functional as the Greek legends of Daniel?

---

[75] "Biblical" at least for Christians, whose Bible–writing did not end with Daniel 1–12.

[76] W. Lee Humphreys follows a similar line in a very nice introductory textbook, *Crisis and Story: Introduction to the Old Testament*, 2nd ed. (Mountain View, California: Mayfield Publishing Company, 1990).

BIBLIOGRAPHY

Aarne, Antti. *The Types of the Folktale: A Classification and Bibliography*. Second Revision. Translated by Stith Thompson. Folklore Fellows Communications, no. 184. Helsinki: Academia Scientarum Fennice, 1961.

Adams, Hazard, ed. *Critical Theory Since Plato*. San Diego: Harcourt Brace Jovanovich, 1971.

Alter, Robert. *The Art of Biblical Narrative*. New York: Basic Books, 1981.

Applebaum, S. "The Legal Status of the Jewish Communities in the Diaspora." In *The Jewish People in the First Century: Historical Geography, Political History, Social, Cultural and Religious Life and Institutions*, 2 vols., ed. S. Safrai and M. Stern, in collaboration with D. Flusser and W. C. van Unnik, 1:420–63. CRINT. Philadelphia: Fortress, 1974.

————. "The Organization of the Jewish Communities in the Diaspora." In *The Jewish People in the First Century*, ed. S. Safrai and M. Stern, 1:464–503. CRINT. Philadelphia: Fortress, 1974.

Auerbach, Erich. *Mimesis: The Representation of Reality in Western Literature*. Garden City: Doubleday, 1957.

Bal, Mieke. *Narratology: Introduction to the Theory of Narrative*. Toronto: University of Toronto Press, 1985.

————. "Susanna and the Elders in the Apocrypha and in Rembrandt." Paper Presented at AAR Annual Meeting. Chicago, 1988.

Ball, Charles James. "The Additions to Daniel." In *Apocrypha of the Speaker's Commentary*, 2:323–60. London: John Murray, 1888.

Barthélemy, D. "Notes critiques sur quelques points d'histoire du texte." In *Übersetzung und Deutung*, Festschrift for Alexander Reinard Hulst, 9–23. Nijkerk: Callenbach, 1977. Also published as chap. in *Études d'histoire du texte de l'Ancien Testament*. OBO 21. Fribourg: Editions Universitaires, 1978; Göttingen: Vandenhoeck and Ruprecht, 1978.

_____. *Les devanciers d'Aquila*. VTSup 10. Leiden: E. J. Brill, 1963.

Bascom, William. "The Forms of Folklore: Prose Narratives." *Journal of American Folklore* 78 (1965): 3–20.

Bauer, Walter. *A Greek–English Lexicon of the New Testament and Other Early Christian Literature*. English Edition No. 2. Translated and ed. William F. Arndt and F. Wilbur Gingrich. Chicago: University Press, 1979.

Baumgartner, Walter I. "Susanna—die Geschichte einer Legende." *ARW* 24 (1926): 259–280. Reprinted as chap. in *Zum Alten Testament und seiner Umwelt*. Leiden: E. J. Brill, 1959.

_____. "Der weise Knabe und die des Ehebruchs beschuldigte Frau." *ARW* 27 (1929): 187–188. Reprinted as chap. in *Zum Alten Testament und seiner Umwelt*, 66–67. Leiden: E. J. Brill, 1959.

Berlin, Adele. *Poetics and Interpretation of Biblical Narrative*. Bible and Literature Series. Sheffield: Almond, 1983.

Bissell, Edwin Cone. *The Apocrypha of the Old Testament: With Historical Introductions, a Revised Translation, and Notes Critical and Explanatory*. New York: Charles Scribner's Sons, 1903.

Boyarin, Daniel. *Intertextuality and the Reading of Midrash*. Indiana Studies in Biblical Literature. Bloomington: Indiana University, 1990.

Bradley, Marion Zimmer. *Mists of Avalon*. New York: Alfred A. Knopf, 1983.

Brüll, Nehemiah. "Das apokryphische Susanna Buch." *Jahrbuch für jüdische Geschichte und Literatur* 3 (1877): 1–69.

_____. "Die Geschichte von Bel und dem Drachen." *Jahrbuch für jüdische Geschichte und Literatur* 8 (1887): 28–29.

Bultmann, Rudolf. *History of the Synoptic Tradition*. New York: Harper and Row, 1963.

Burkitt, F. C. *The Old Latin and the Itala*. Cambridge: University Press, 1896.

Busto Saiz, J. R. "El texto Teodociónico de Daniel y la traducción de Símaco." *Sef* 40 (1980): 41–55.

Carroll, Michael P. "Myth, Methodology and Transformation in the Old Testament: The Stories of Esther, Judith, and Susanna." *SR* 12 (1983): 301–12.

Carson, D. A. "The Purpose of the Fourth Gospel: John 20:3 Reconsidered." *JBL* 106 (1987): 639–51.

Chatman, Seymour. *Story and Discourse: Narrative Structure in Fiction and Film*. Ithaca: Cornell University Press, 1978.

Cohen, Shaye J. *From the Maccabees to the Mishnah*. Philadelphia: Westminster, 1987.

Collins, John J. *Between Athens and Jerusalem: Jewish Identity in the Hellenistic Period*. New York: Crossroads Books, 1983.

_____. *Daniel, with an Introduction to Apocalyptic Literature*. Forms of the Old Testament Literature, vol. 20. Grand Rapids: Eerdmans, 1984.

Coughenour, Robert A. "Iron." In *Harper's Bible Dictionary*, ed. Paul J. Achtemeier. San Francisco: Harper & Row, 1985.

Crenshaw, James L. *Samson: A Secret Betrayed, a Vow Ignored*. Atlanta: John Knox, 1978.

Cross, Frank Moore. "Fragments of the Prayer of Nabonidus." *IEJ* 34 (1984): 260–64.

Dan, Ilana. "The Innocent Persecuted Heroine: An Attempt at a Model for the Surface Level of the Narrative Structure of the Female Fairy Tale." In *Patterns in Oral Literature*, ed. Heda Jason and Dimitri Segal, 13–30. The Hague: Mouton, 1977.

Daubney, William H. *The Three Additions to Daniel*. Cambridge: Deighton and Bell, 1906.

Davies, Witton. "Bel and the Dragon." *APOT*, ed. Robert Henry Charles, 1:652–64. Oxford: Clarendon, 1913.

Delcor, Matthias. *Le livre de Daniel*. Paris: J. Gabalda, 1971.

Dundes, Alan, ed. *Sacred Narrative*. Berkeley: University of California Press, 1984.

Dunn, Robert P. "Discriminations in the Comic Spirit in the Story of Susanna." *Christianity and Literature* 31 (Summer 1982): 19–31.

Engel, Helmut. *Die Susanna-Erzählung: Einleitung, Übersetzung und Kommentar zum Septuaginta-Text und zur Theodotion-Bearbeitung.* Freiburg: Universitätsverlag, 1985; Göttingen: Vandenhoeck & Ruprecht, 1985.

Fewell, Danna Nolan. *Circle of Sovereignty: A Story of Stories in Daniel 1-6.* Bible and Literature Series. Sheffield: Almond, 1988.

Finkelstein, J. J. "The Bible, Archeology, and History." *Commentary* 27 (April 1959): 341-49.

Finkelstein, Louis. "The Men of the Great Synagogue (*circa* 400-170 B.C.E.)." In *The Cambridge History of Judaism.* Vol. 2, *The Hellenistic Age,* ed. W. D. Davies and Louis Finkelstein, 229-44. Cambridge: University Press, 1989.

_____. "The Pharisaic Leadership After the Great Synagogue." In *The Cambridge History of Judaism.* Vol. 2, *The Hellenistic Age,* ed. W. D. Davies and Louis Finkelstein, 245-77. Cambridge: University Press, 1989.

Flusser, D. "Paganism in Palestine." In *The Jewish People in the First Century,* ed. S. Safrai and M. Stern, 2:1065-1100. CRINT. Philadelphia: Fortress, 1974.

Fokkelman, J. P. *Narrative Art and Poetry in the Books of Samuel.* Vol. 1, *King David (II Samuel 9-20 and I Kings 1-2).* Assen: Van Gorcum, 1981.

Fritzsche, Otto Fridolin. "Zusätze zu dem Buche Daniel." In *Kurzgefasstes exegetisches Handbuch zu den Apokryphen des Alten Testaments,* ed. O. Fritzsche and C. Grim. Leipzig: Weidmann'sche Buchandlung, 1851.

Funk, Robert W. *The Poetics of Biblical Narrative.* FFNT. Sonoma, CA: Polebridge, 1988.

Gaba, Emilio. "The Growth of Anti-Judaism or the Greek Attitude Towards Jews." In *The Cambridge History of Judaism.* Vol. 2, *The Hellenistic Age,* ed. W. D. Davies and Louis Finkelstein, 614-56. Cambridge: University Press, 1989.

Geissen, Angelo. *Der Septuaginta-Text des Buches Daniel: Kap. 5-12, zusammen mit Susanna, Bel et Draco, sowie Esther Kap. 1,1a-2,15, nach dem Kölner Teil des Papyrus 967.* Papyrologische Texte und Abhandlungen, no. 5. Bonn: Rudolf Habelt, 1968.

Gibson, J. C. L. *Canaanite Myths and Legends*. Original editor G. R. Driver. 2d ed. Edinburgh: T. & T. Clark Ltd., 1978.

Ginsberg, H. Louis. *Studies in Daniel*. Texts and Studies of the Jewish Theological Seminary of America. New York: Jewish Theological Seminary of America, 1948.

Ginzberg, Louis. *The Legends of the Jews*. Index by Boaz Cohen. Philadelphia: Jewish Publication Society, 1909–38.

Goldingay, John E. *Daniel*. Word Biblical Commentary. Dallas, TX: Word Books, 1989.

Goleman, Daniel. *Vital Lies, Simple Truths: The Psychology of Self-Deception*. New York: Simon & Schuster, 1986.

Gordis, Robert. "Religion, Wisdom, and History in the Book of Esther—A New Solution to an Ancient Crux." *JBL* 100 (1981): 359–88.

Grant, Michael. *From Alexander to Cleopatra: The Hellenistic World*. New York: Scribner, 1982; New York: MacMillan, Collier Books, 1990.

Grelot, Pierre. "Les versions grecques de Daniel." *Bib* 47 (1966): 381–402.

Gunkel, Hermann. *Das Märchen im Alten Testament*. Religionsgeschichtliche Volksbücher. Tübingen: J. B. Mohr, 1921. Reprinted in English translation as *The Folktale in the Old Testament*. Sheffield: Almond, 1987.

Gunn, David M. *The Story of King David: Genre and Interpretation*. JSOTSup. Sheffield: University of Sheffield, 1978.

Häag, Thomas. *The Novel in Antiquity*. Berkeley and Los Angeles: University of California Press, 1983.

Hamm, Winfried. *Der Septuaginta-Text des Buches Daniel: Kap. 1–2, nach dem Kölner Teil des Papyrus 967*. Papyrologische Texte und Abhandlungen, no. 10. Bonn: Rudolf Habelt, 1969.

————. *Der Septuaginta-Text des Buches Daniel: Kap. 3–4, nach dem Kölner Teil des Papyrus 967*. Papyrologische Texte und Abhandlungen, no. 21. Bonn: Rudolf Habelt, 1977.

Hanson, Paul D. *The Dawn of Apocalyptic: The Historical and Sociological Roots of Jewish Apocalpytic Eschatology*. Philadelphia: Fortress, 1979.

Hare, D. R. E. "The Lives of the Prophets: A New Translation and Introduction." In *OTP*, ed. James H. Charlesworth, 2:379–99. Garden City, New York: Doubleday, 1985.

Hartman, Louis F., and Alexander A. Di Lella. *The Book of Daniel.* AB. Garden City: Doubleday, 1978.

Hegermann, Harald. "The Diaspora in the Hellenistic Age." In *The Cambridge History of Judaism.* Vol. 2, *The Hellenistic Age*, ed. W. D. Davies and Louis Finkelstein, 115–66. Cambridge: University Press, 1989.

Heller, Bernhard. "Die Suzannerzählung: Ein Märchen." *ZAW* 54 (1936): 281–87.

Heltzer, Michael. "The Story of Susanna and the Self-Government of the Jewish Community in Achaemenid Babylonia." *AION* 41 (1981): 35–39.

Hengel, Martin. "The Interpenetration of Judaism and Hellenism in the Pre-Maccabean Period." In *The Cambridge History of Judaism.* Vol. 2, *The Hellenistic Age*, ed. W. D. Davies and Louis Finkelstein, 167–228. Cambridge: University Press, 1989.

_____. *Judaism and Hellenism: Studies in Their Encounter in Palestine During the Early Hellenistic Period*, 2 vols. London: SCM, 1974.

Hippolytus. "Commentary on Susanna." ANF 5:177–194. Grand Rapids, MI: Eerdmans, 1881.

Hoenig, Sidney B. "Bel and the Dragon." *IDB* 1:376–77.

Huet, Gedeon. "Daniel et Susanne: note de littérature comparée." *RHR* 65 (1912): 277–84.

Humphreys, W. Lee. *Crisis and Story: Introduction to the Old Testament.* 2d ed. Mountain View, CA: Mayfield, 1990.

_____. "A Life-Style for Diaspora: A Study of the Tales of Esther and Daniel." *JBL* 92 (1973): 211–23.

Jacobsen, Thorkild. *The Treasures of Darkness: A History of Mesopotamian Religion.* New Haven: Yale University Press, 1976.

Jakobson, Roman. "The Metaphoric and Metonymic Poles." In *Critical Theory Since Plato*, ed. Hazard Adams, 1113–16. San Diego: Harcourt Brace Jovanovich, 1971.

Jason, Heda. "The Fairy Tale of the Active Heroine: An Outline for Discussion." In *Le Conte, Pourquoi? Comment?*, ed. G. Galame-Griaule, V. Görög-Karady, and M. Chiche, 79–97. Paris: CNRS, 1984.

_____. "Literary Documents of the Past and Their Relation to Folk Literature." In *Folklore and Oral Communication*, 167–78. Zagreb: Zavod Za Istrazivanje Folklora Instituta Za Filologiju I Folkloristiku, 1981.

Jellicoe, Sidney. "Some Reflections on the καιγε Recension." *VT* 23 (1973): 15–24.

Jerome, St. "Preface to Daniel." NPNF Second Series, 6:492–93. Grand Rapids: Eerdmans, 1952.

Kay, David M. "Susanna." *APOT*, ed. Robert Henry Charles, 1:638–51. Oxford: Clarendon, 1913.

Koch, Klaus. "Die Herkunft der Proto-Theodotion-Übersetzung des Danielbuches." *VT* 23 (1973): 362–65.

Koester, Helmut. *Introduction to the New Testament*. Vol. 1. *History, Culture, and Religion of the Hellenistic Age*. Hermeneia: Foundations and Facets. Philadelphia: Fortress, 1982.

Kort, Wesley. *Story, Text and Scripture: Literary Interests in Biblical Narrative*. University Park: Pennsylvania State University Press, 1988.

Kraft, Robert, with the Computer Assisted Tools for Septuagint Studies Project (CATSS). *Morphologically Analyzed Greek Jewish Scriptures*. On *PHI/CCAT CD-ROM 1*. Center for Computer Analysis of Texts (CCAT), University of Pennsylvania, CD–ROM version published by the Packard Humanities Institute, Los Altos, CA, 1987.

Kristeva, Julia. *Desire in Language: A Semiotic Approach to Literature and Art*. ed. Leon S. Roudiez. New York: Columbia University Press, 1980.

LaCocque, André. *Daniel in His Time*. Studies on Personalities of the Old Testament. Columbia, SC: University of South Carolina Press, 1988.

Landersdorfer, Simon. "Der Drache von Babylon." *BZ* 11 (1913): 1-4.

Lanser, Susan S. *The Narrative Act: Point of View in Prose Fiction*. Princeton: Princeton University Press, 1981.

Lbase for CD-ROM. Version 5.0. Silver Mountain Software, Dallas, TX, 1990.

Levenson, Jon D. *Creation and the Persistence of Evil.* San Francisco: Harper & Row, 1988.

Lévi–Strauss, Claude. "The Structural Study of Myth." In *Contemporary Literary Criticism: Modernism Through Post-Structuralism*, ed. Robert Con Davis, 307–22. New York: Longman, 1986.

Liddell, Henry George, and Robert Scott. *A Greek–English Lexicon.* Revised and augmented by Henry Stuart Jones and Roderick McKenzie. Oxford: Clarendon, 1968.

MacKenzie, Roderick A. F. "The Meaning of the Susanna Story." *CJT* 3 (1957): 211–18.

McKnight, Edgar V. *The Bible and the Reader: An Introduction to Literary Criticism.* Philadelphia: Fortress, 1985.

Malory, Sir Thomas. *Le Morte Darthur.* Published in English as *The Acts of King Arthur and His Noble Knights*, by John Steinbeck, ed. Chase Horton. New York: Farrar, Straus and Giroux, 1976.

Marshall, John T. "Bel and the Dragon." In *Hastings Dictionary of the Bible*, 1:267-68. New York: Scribner, 1901.

Milik, J. T. "'Prière de Nabonide' et autres écrits d'un cycle de Daniel: fragments Araméens de Qumrân 4." *RB* 63 (1956): 407–15.

———. "Daniel et Susanne à Qumrân?" Chap. in *De la Tôrah au Messie.* Paris: Desclée, 1981.

Milne, Pamela J. *Vladimir Propp and the Study of Structure in Hebrew Biblical Narrative.* Bible and Literature Series. Sheffield: Almond, 1988.

Momigliano, Arnaldo. *Alien Wisdom: The Limits of Hellenization.* Cambridge: Cambridge University Press, 1975; paperback edition 1990.

Montgomery, James A. *A Critical and Exegetical Commentary on the Book of Daniel.* ICC. New York: Scribner, 1927.

Moore, Carey A. *Daniel, Esther, and Jeremiah: The Additions.* AB. New York: Doubleday, 1977.

Nestle, Eberhard. *Marginalien und Materialien.* Tübingen: J. J. Heckenhauer'sche Buchhandlung, 1893.

Newsom, Carol A. "Habakkuk, the Book Of." In *Harper's Bible Dictionary*, ed. Paul J. Achtemeier, 364. San Francisco: Harper & Row, 1985.

Niditch, S., and R. Doran. "The Success Story of the Wise Courtier: A Formal Approach." *JBL* 96 (1977): 179–93.

Niditch, Susan. *Underdogs and Tricksters: A Prelude to Biblical Folklore.* New Voices in Biblical Studies. San Francisco: Harper & Row, 1987.

_____. "The Visionary." In *Ideal Figures in Ancient Judaism*, ed. John J. Collins and George W. E. Nickelsburg, 153–79. Septuagint and Cognate Studies, vol. 12. Chico, CA: Scholars Press, 1980.

Nota Bene Multilingual Word Processor. Version 3.1, with Special Language Supplements and N.B.Ibid, copyright 1989 by Equal Access Systems, Inc. and XyQuest, Inc., and Version 4.0 with Lingua, copyright 1992 by N. B. Informatics, Inc. Published by Dragonfly Software, 285 W. Broadway, Suite 600, New York, NY 10013.

Oesterley, W. O. E. *An Introduction to the Books of the Apocrypha.* New York: MacMillan, 1935.

Ong, Walter J. "The Writer's Audience is Always a Fiction." *Proceedings of the Modern Language Association* 90 (1975): 9–21. Reprinted in *Contemporary Literary Criticism: Literary and Cultural Studies*, ed. Robert Con Davis and Ronald Schleifer. 2d ed., 83–99. New York: Longman, 1989.

Origen. *The Writings of Origen.* ANF vol. 10. Edinburgh: T. & T. Clark, 1871.

Pezard, Andres. "Betrice et les soupes d'Habacuc." In *Melanges d'histoire des religions*, ed. A. Bareau, 557–68. Paris: Presses Universitaires de France, 1974.

Pfeiffer, Robert H. *History of New Testament Times with an Introduction to the Apocrypha.* New York: Harper and Brothers, 1949.

Propp, V[ladimir]. *Morphology of the Folktale.* Ed. by Louis A. Wagner. 2d ed. Austin: University of Texas Press, 1968.

Rahlfs, Alfred. *Septuaginta*, 2 vols. Stuttgart: Deutsche Bibelgesellschaft, 1935; single-volume edition 1979.

Riffaterre, Michael. "Intertextual Representation: Mimesis as Interpretive Discourse." *Critical Inquiry* 11 (1984): 141–62.

_____. "Intertextual Scrambling." *Romanic Review* 68 (1977): 197–206.

_____. "The Intertextual Unconscious." *Critical Inquiry* 13 (1987): 371–85.

_____. "The Poetic Functions of Intertextual Humor." *Romanic Review* 65 (1974): 278–93.

Roth, Wolfgang M. W. "For Life, He Appeals to Death (Wis 13:18): A Study of Old Testament Idol Parodies." *CBQ* 37 (1975): 21–47.

Rowley, Harold H. "The Unity of the Book of Daniel." *HUCA* 23 (1950–51): 233–73. Reprinted as a chapter in *The Servant of the Lord and Other Essays on the Old Testament*, 237–68. London: Lutterworth, 1952.

Safrai, S. "Relations Between the Diaspora and the Land of Israel." In *The Jewish People in the First Century*, ed. S. Safrai and M. Stern, 1:184–215. CRINT. Philadelphia: Fortress, 1974.

_____. "The Synagogue." In *The Jewish People in the First Century*, ed. S. Safrai and M. Stern, 2:908–44. CRINT. Philadelphia: Fortress, 1974.

Safrai, S., and M. Stern, eds. in collaboration with D. Flusser and W. C. van Unnik. *The Jewish People in the First Century: Historical Geography, Political History, Social, Cultural and Religious Life and Institutions*, 2 vols. CRINT. Philadelphia: Fortress, 1974.

Saussure, Ferdinand de. "The Object of Linguistics." Chap. in *Course in General Linguistics* (The Philosophical Library, 1959). Reprinted in *Contemporary Literary Criticism: Literary and Cultural Studiesu*, ed. Robert Con Davis and Ronald Schleifer. 2d ed., 152–58. New York: Longman, 1989.

Schmitt, Armin. *Stammt der sogenannte "Θ"-Text bei Daniel wirklich von Theodotion?* Mitteilungen des Septuaginta-Unternehmens. Göttingen: Vandenhoeck und Ruprecht, 1966.

Scholz, Anton. *Commentar über das Buch "Esther" mit seinen Zusätzen und über "Susanna"*. Würzburg: Leo Woerl, 1892.

_____. *Commentar über das Buch "Judith" und über "Bel und Drache"*. Würzburg: Leo Woerl, 1896.

Schüpphaus, Joakim. "Der Verhältnis von LXX- und Theodotion-Text in den apokryphen Zusätzen zum Danielbuch." *ZAW* 83 (1971): 49-72.

Schürer, Emil. *The History of the Jewish People in the Time of Jesus Christ: A New English Version.* 3 Vols. Rev. and ed. Geza Vermes, Fergus Millar, and Martin Goodman. Edinburgh: T. & T. Clark, 1973.

Spiegel, Shalom. "Noah, Daniel and Job." In *Louis Ginsberg Jubilee Volume*, 305-35. New York: American Academy for Jewish Research, 1945.

Stambaugh, John E., and David L. Balch. *The New Testament in Its Social Environment.* Library of Early Christianity. Philadelphia: Westminster, 1986.

Stauffer, E. "Eine Bemerkung zum griechischen Danieltext." In *Donum Gentilicium*, ed. E. Bammel, C. K. Barrett, and W. D. Davies, 27-39. Oxford: Clarendon, 1978.

Stern, M. "The Jewish Diaspora." In *The Jewish People in the First Century*, ed. S. Safrai and M. Stern, 1:117-83. CRINT. Philadelphia: Fortress, 1974.

Sternberg, Meir. *The Poetics of Biblical Narrative: Ideological Literature and the Drama of Reading.* Indiana Literary Biblical Series. Bloomington: Indiana University Press, 1985.

Stone, Michael Edward. *Scriptures, Sects and Visions: A Profile of Judaism from Ezra to the Jewish Revolts.* Philadelphia: Fortress, 1980.

Suleiman, Susan R., and Inge Crosman, eds. *The Reader in the Text: Essays on Audience and Interpretation.* Princeton: Princeton University Press, 1980.

Swete, Henry Barclay. *An Introduction to the Old Testament in Greek.* Revised by Richard Rusden Ottley. Cambridge: Cambridge University Press, 1914; reprinted Peabody, MA: Hendrickson, 1989.

Thackeray, H. St. John. *The Septuagint and Jewish Worship: A Study in Origins.* 2d ed. The Schweich Lectures, 1920. London: Oxford University Press, 1923.

Thesaurus Linguae Grecae, published on *Pilot CD ROM #C*. Copyright, Regents of the University of California.   University of California, Irvine, CA, 1987.

Toelken, Barre. *The Dynamics of Folklore*. Boston: Houghton Mifflin, 1979.

Tompkins, Jane P., ed. *Reader–Response Criticism: From Formalism to Post–Structuralism*. Baltimore: Johns Hopkins University Press, 1980.

Torrey, Charles C. *The Apocryphal Literature*. New Haven: Yale University Press, 1945.

————. *The Lives of the Prophets: Greek Text and Translation*. JBL Monograph Series. Philadelphia: Society of Biblical Literature and Exegesis, 1946.

Tov, Emanuel. *The Septuagint Translation of Jeremiah and Baruch: A Discussion of an Early Revision of the LXX of Jeremiah 29–52 and Baruch 1:1–3:8*. HSM no. 8. Missoula: Scholar's Press, 1976.

Toy, Crawford H. "Bel and the Dragon." In *The Jewish Encyclopedia*, 2:650–51. New York: Funk and Wagnalls, 1905.

Trible, Phyllis. *God and the Rhetoric of Sexuality*. OBT. Philadelphia: Fortress, 1978.

————. *Texts of Terror*. OBT. Philadelphia: Fortress, 1984.

Uspensky, Boris. *A Poetics of Composition: The Structure of the Artistic Text and Typology of a Compositional Form*. Berkeley: University of California Press, 1973.

Vermes, Geza. "Interpretation, History Of: At Qumran and in the Targums." In *IDBSup*, 438–43. Nashville: Abingdon, 1976.

Webster's New Collegiate Dictionary. Springfield, MA: G. &. C. Merriam, 1974.

White, Hayden. *Tropics of Discourse*. Baltimore: Johns Hopkins University Press, 1978.

White, T. H. *The Sword in the Stone*. New York: Putnam, 1939.

Wiederholt, Theodor von. "Die Geschichte der Susanna." *TQ* 51 (1869): 287–321; 337–99.

Williams, Ronald J. *Hebrew Syntax: An Outline*. 2d ed. Toronto: University Press, 1976.

Wills, Lawrence M. *The Jew in the Court of a Foreign King: Ancient Jewish Court Legends*. HDR. Minneapolis: Fortress, 1990.

Ziegler, Joseph, ed. *Susanna, Daniel, Bel et Draco*. Septuaginta; Vetus Testamentum Graecum auctoritate Societatis Gottingensis editum. Göttingen: Vandenhoeck & Ruprecht, 1954.

Zimmermann, Frank. "Bel and the Dragon." *VT* 8 (1958): 438–40.

_____. "The Story of Susanna and Its Original Language." *JQR* 48 (1957-8): 236–41.

Zöckler, Otto. "Die erzählenden Zusätze zu Daniel." In *Die Apokryphen des Alten Testamentes*. Kurzgefasstes Kommentar zu den Heiligen Schriften des alten und neuen Testamentes sowie zu den Apokryphen. München: Oskar Beck, 1892.

AUTHOR INDEX

211

SUBJECT INDEX

SCRIPTURE INDEX

Note: passages appearing in both the MT and the LXX are indexed by their MT location (e.g. for Jer 36:23 LXX see Jer 29:23). The two versions (OG and TH) of the Daniel legends are indexed jointly. For references to pseudepigraphal works see the subject index.